Ransoming Prisoners in Precolonial Muslim Western Africa

Rochester Studies in African History and the Diaspora

Toyin Falola, Series Editor
The Jacob and Frances Sanger Mossiker Chair in the Humanities
and University Distinguished Teaching Professor
University of Texas at Austin

Recent Titles

Coming of Age in the Afro-Latin American Novel: Blackness, Religion, Immigration
Bonnie S. Wasserman

Masquerade and Money in Urban Nigeria: The Case of Calabar
Jordan A. Fenton

West African Soldiers in Britain's Colonial Army, 1860–1960
Timothy Stapleton

Decolonizing African Studies: Knowledge Production, Agency, and Voice
Toyin Falola

Youth and Popular Culture in Africa: Media, Music, and Politics
Edited by Paul Ugor

Disability in Africa: Inclusion, Care, and the Ethics of Humanity
Edited by Toyin Falola and Nic Hamel

Opposing Apartheid on Stage: King Kong the Musical
Tyler Fleming

West African Masking Traditions: History, Memory, and Transnationalism
Raphael Chijioke Njoku

Cultivating Their Own: Agriculture in Western Kenya during the "Development" Era
Muey C. Saeteurn

A complete list of titles in the Rochester Studies in African History and the Diaspora series may be found on our website, www.urpress.com.

Ransoming Prisoners in Precolonial Muslim Western Africa

Jennifer Lofkrantz

University of Rochester Press

First published 2023
Paperback edition 2026

University of Rochester Press
www.urpress.com
and Boydell & Brewer Limited
www.boydellandbrewer.com

Our Authorised Representative for product safety in the EU is Easy Access System Europe – Mustamäe tee 50, 10621 Tallinn, Estonia, gpsr.requests@easproject.com

ISBN-13: 978-1-64825-064-4 hardback
ISBN-13: 978-1-64825-146-7 paperback
ISSN: 1092-5228

Cataloging-in-publication data available from the Library of Congress

A catalogue record for this title is available from the British Library

For my parents, Eric and Dawne Lofkrantz,
who gave me the foundation to build the life I wanted

Contents

List of Tables viii

Acknowledgments ix

Introduction 1

1. Islamic Discourse on Slavery and Ransoming before 1800 23
2. The Policy and Practice of Ransoming in the Maghrib 53
3. Jihad, the Sokoto Caliphate, and Ransoming 80
4. The Jihad of 'Umar Taal and its Ransoming Nonpolicies 113
5. The Negotiation and Practice of Ransoming Prisoners 143

Conclusion 173

Bibliography 179

Index 211

Tables

Acknowledgments

I first began thinking about and researching the ransoming of prisoners in West Africa—and changing my PhD dissertation topic to the subject—as a doctoral student at York University. I am forever grateful for the intellectual environment, training, and opportunities provided to me by my professors and my graduate school colleagues in the Department of History and at the Harriet Tubman Institute for Research on Africa and Its Diasporas. My grad school years provided the base; however, this book reflects a maturation of my thinking on ransoming and new interests in both intellectual history and in making more explicit connections between past and present. While based on some of the same research I conducted for my dissertation in Mali, Niger, and Nigeria, this book is quite different. Several sections are based on additional research I conducted in France and Nigeria in 2012, thanks to the funding I received from St. Thomas University through the Global and International Initiative Grant and the Major Research Grant, and in 2017–2020 while I was a faculty member at American University of Nigeria. This project has also been partially supported by Gulf University for Science and Technology under project code: ISG 279503.

Throughout my career, I have been fortunate to be a part of several university communities and participated in numerous workshops and conferences that have helped shape my thinking and approach. In hindsight, the time I spent at St. Thomas University, at St. Mary's College of California, and at American University of Nigeria was especially important in terms of the evolution of my approach to this book. Also influential were the papers presented and the conversations I had with participants at the workshop on historical and contemporary ransoming in Africa and the Mediterranean world organized by Olatunji Ojo, Paul Lovejoy, and myself at York University, in 2014, and the workshop on Sahelian Identities in Times of Crisis organized by Amy Niang, Baz Lecocq and Isaie Dougnon held at Point Sud: Centre for Research on Local Knowledge, Bamako in 2016. I am also thankful for the numerous conversations I have had over the years on the topic of ransoming, intellectual history, jihad movements, enslavement, and identity with the many colleagues who are too numerous to name. For the direct feedback and advice I received on this manuscript, I want to especially thank Mariana Candido and Ismael Montana; both read all or parts of the manuscript at different stages and Olatunji Ojo, who challenged my ideas on ransoming through our collaboration on the study of failed ransom negotiations in West Africa. I also want to thank Brad Cross, Karen Robert, Julia Torrie, Myrna Santiago, and Elena Songster for listening to my ideas and giving me useful advice on the writing process. Even though I only joined Gulf University for Science and Technology, Kuwait in Fall 2022, I want to thank my colleagues in the Department of Humanities and Social Sciences, the College of Arts and Sciences and the Research and Development Office for their support in completing this book. I save my final thank you not only to the anonymous reviewers of my manuscript who gave me useful feedback and whose advice I have taken into account but also to the series editor, Toyin Falola, who not only supported this book project but has also been a mentor to me and to many historians of Africa since we were in graduate school or earlier.

Introduction

On April 14, 2014, a Salafi Jihadist group operating in northern Nigeria, Niger, Chad, and Cameroon, commonly known as Boko Haram, kidnapped 276 girls from Government Secondary School in Chibok, Borno State, Nigeria.[1] Although this was not the first time that Boko Haram had kidnapped civilians (nor was it the last), the sheer audaciousness of kidnapping this many people—and in particular this many teenaged girls—at once, garnered international attention in the weeks that followed. The motivation for the mass kidnapping was to ransom them for either money or for Boko Haram prisoners held in Nigerian jails. In a video released on May 5, 2014, the undisputed leader of Boko Haram at the time, Abubakar Shekau, threatened to sell the girls into slavery, claiming that it was allowed by "his religion." This video was followed by another video on May 12, 2014, where he stated that he was willing to negotiate a prisoner exchange—the girls for his followers imprisoned in Nigeria.[2]

Boko Haram has arisen out of what has been labeled a "modernization shock" in northern Nigerian Muslim society, as the inhabitants of the region dealt with colonial rule, the introduction of British law and education, integration into the postcolonial Nigerian state, and the economic changes that

1 "Nigeria: Police Revise Number of Kidnapped Students," *The Associated Press*, May 2, 2014. Under the leadership of Abubakar Shekau, Boko Haram calls itself "the community of the people of the Sunna who fight for the cause by means of jihad according to the method of the Salaf" (jama'at ahl al-sunna li-l-da'wa wa l-jihād 'ala minhāj al-salaf). Its original name under its founder Muhammad Yusuf was "the people of the Sunna and the community as well as [those who accept the obligation] to emigrate" (ahl al-sunna wa-l- jama'a wa-l-hijra). For more on the history of Boko Haram, see Loimeier, "Boko Haram," 137–155, and Anonymous, "The Popular Discourses," 118–44.

2 Nossiter, "Nigerian Islamist Leader Threatens to Sell Kidnapped Girls," *New York Times*, May 5, 2014; "Boko Haram Offers to Swap Kidnapped Nigerian Girls for Prisoners," *Reuters*, May 12, 2014.

these adjustments wrought.[3] Colonial rule and the integration of northern Nigeria into modern Nigeria divided northern Nigerian Muslims into three broad groups. The first group was composed of the leaders and followers of the established Qādiriyya and Tijāniyya ṭurūq (Sufi brotherhoods) who dominated during the Sokoto Caliphate period (1804–1903). The second group comprised the Islamic modernists who sought to Islamicize modernity such as Ahmadu Bello, the premier of Northern Nigeria since the 1950s and 1960s, and Aminu Kano, the leader of the Northern Elements Progressive Union, which was the main opposition party in the 1950s to the 1970s. The third group comprised those who argued that Islamic modernism as implemented by the political elite in northern Nigeria was either not radical enough in terms of implementing political change or was basically un-Islamic.[4] It is from the third strain of modern northern Nigerian political opinion that Boko Haram is derived from, as an offshoot of the mainstream Nigerian Salafī organization Jamā'at 'izālat al- bid'a wa iqamat al- sunna (the group for removing religious innovation and establishing Sunna), known by its acronym JIBWIS or "Izala" for short. Perhaps the only commonality shared by the extreme range of Muslim political thought in modern northern Nigeria is the belief that government policy and action must be grounded in interpretation of Islamic law. This has been a commonly held belief in Muslim regions of West Africa since at least the eighteenth century.

Intellectually, Boko Haram is radically different from the movement that established the Sokoto Caliphate in 1804–10, centered on what is now northern Nigeria, and the jihad movements that preceded and followed the Sokoto movement in the western and central Sudan region of West Africa. Boko Haram is theologically influenced by the Salafī and Wahhābi movements, whereas the Sokoto movement was based on the Mālikī madh'hab (school of law) and the Qādiriyya ṭarīqa (Sufi brotherhood). However, what this twenty-first-century movement shares with the eighteenth- and nineteenth-century movements is the belief that policy must be grounded in interpretation of Islamic law, the idea that jihad is a legitimate method of political reform, and that the ransoming of both military and civilian prisoners is acceptable.

3 On the interplay between colonial rule and Muslim politics in Northern Nigeria see Reynolds, "Good and Bad Muslims," 601–18.

4 Loimeier, *Islamic Reform and Political Change in Northern Nigeria*, 325–30.

Starting with Nāṣir al-Dīn's movement on the Senegal River in the 1670s, a series of jihads swept across West Africa. These include the movements that established Fuuta Jalon and Fuuta Toro in the mid-eighteenth century and the movements that established the Sokoto Caliphate and the Caliphate of Ḥamdallāhi at the beginning of the nineteenth century. The jihad movements culminated with the 'Umarian movements of the 1850s and 1860s in the western Sudan region. There are a variety of interpretations as to the causes and motivations of the jihads that focus on religious, social, political, ethnic, and economic factors.[5] More recently, Paul Lovejoy argues that the West African jihads, in particular the Sokoto jihad, should be understood as part of the Atlantic revolutions.[6] The West African jihads did take place at roughly the same time as the American, French, Haitian, and Spanish American revolutions. The successful West African jihads did result in profound social and political change. The events of the West African interior did have a great impact on the Atlantic world and the relationship between Africans and Europeans. However, the Atlantic revolutions shared common intellectual roots as ideas of liberty and freedom ping-ponged between Europe and the Americas, reverberating differently depending on time, place, and class. The West African jihads, on the other hand, had different intellectual roots, entrenched in the Muslim West African discursive tradition. Through the medium of enslaved Africans, African intellectual thought, including Muslim thought, contributed to the ideas circulating in the revolutionary Atlantic. However, the revolutionaries in Europe and the Americas did not have a similar influence on Muslim West African revolutionary thought.

Each West African jihad movement was unique and arose out of a particular set of circumstances. As Roman Loimeier states, the jihads are "best understood as resulting from a long historical evolution of Muslim societies in that region and their interaction with specific local, social and political

5 On the jihad movements in West Africa, see Ware, *The Walking Qu'ran*; Hiskett, *The Sword of Truth*; Last, "Reform in West Africa"; Klein, "Social and Economic Factors in the Muslim Revolution"; Gomez, *Pragmatism in the Age of Jihad*; Robinson, *The Holy War of Umar Tal;* Hanson, *Migration, Jihad, and Muslim Authority in West Africa*; Zehnle, *A Geography of Jihad*; Hiribarren, *A History of Borno*; Naylor, *From Rebels to Rulers*, Nobili, *Sultan, Caliph and the Renewer of the Faith*; Humphrey Fisher, "A Muslim William Wilberforce?"; Lovejoy, *Jihād in West Africa.*

6 Lovejoy, *Jihād in West Africa*, 2–3.

contexts."[7] In this regard, he is in agreement with Mervyn Hiskett, who, while focusing on the Sokoto jihad, contextualizes the jihads as a step in the spread of Islam across West Africa as individuals in previously remote regions were attracted to Islamic culture.[8] Yet, a shared complaint of the jihadists was that the governments that they were overthrowing were not governing according to what they considered to be accepted interpretations of Islamic law and were not adequately protecting the rights of freeborn Muslims. Considering their shared complaint, unsurprisingly, a goal shared by the seventeenth-, eighteenth-, and nineteenth-century jihad movements was the desire to root governance within their preferred interpretation of Islamic law and to protect people whom they considered to be Muslims. By looking at examples from the past, it is possible to understand the historical, cultural, and Islamic legalistic framework in which Boko Haram is operating, such as the interpretation and use of the concept of takfīr (declaring a self-professed Muslim to be an infidel), and its unique interpretation of the Muslim West African canon in general, when it holds individuals for ransom and threatens their enslavement if no ransom is forthcoming.[9]

This book focuses on the ransoming of prisoners in the nineteenth century at this time of intellectual-led immense political change in the Muslim societies of precolonial West Africa. During the jihad era, members of society were grappling with the questions of who was and who was not a Muslim, how Islamic law could and should be implemented in their societies, what rights and protections recognized freeborn Muslims should have and what role governments should play in ensuring those rights, especially during a time when slavery was legal. The discussion and implementation of ransoming procedures exposes their answers to these questions as well as broader issues and ideas on slavery, freedom, and religious and ethnic identity. This

7 Loimeier, *Muslim Societies in Africa*, 111.

8 Hiskett, *The Sword of Truth.*

9 For the use of takfīr by Muhammad Yusuf, the founder of Boko Haram, see for example Kassim trans., "Clearing the Doubts of the Scholars," 35–40. 'Uthmān b. Fodiye and 'Umar Taal's use of takfīr will be discussed in chapters 3 and 4. It is important to note that even though Boko Haram consistently tries to situate themselves as the fulfillers of 'Uthmān b. Fodiye's jihad in order to get support in northern Nigeria, they want to replace the Sokoto tradition with their own interpretation of Islam based in Salafi Jihadist thought. See Lofkrantz, "Intellectual Traditions, Education and Jihad"; Kassim, "Defining and Understanding the Religious Philosophy of jihādī-Salafism and the Ideology of Boko Haram."

book is therefore not just about the ransoming of prisoners but is also about the changing religious and political landscape of the region and the transmission of ideas during the jihad era. West African ideas, interpretation, and reinterpretation of the intellectual and legal canon provided the structure within which ransoming took place. This book therefore contributes to the resurgent field of West African intellectual history as exemplified by Bruce Hall's work on the changing ideas of race in the Sahara, Rudolph Ware's and Ousmane Kane's work on Islamic education and transmission of learning, and James Sweet's work on the intellectual thought of African *vodunon* (priests) in the Atlantic world.[10] As Nancy Rose Hunt notes, contemporary intellectual historians of West Africa "labor with ways of knowing and kinds of thought, vocabularies, and the like."[11] One of the foci of this book is to contextualize ransoming policies and practices within jihad-era scholars' interpretation of law and previous intellectual thought.

Ironically, although all the jihads shared a commonality in that they were led by scholars who wanted to enforce a greater compliance with the Mālikī madh'hab and to protect the rights of freeborn Muslims from state institutions that they perceived as harmful—the most harmful among which, according to them, was illegal enslavement—captivity and enslavement continued throughout the nineteenth century, including the captivity and enslavement of freeborn Muslims. The jihads, in their bid to overthrow governments and establish new states, caused the condition, warfare, that led to individuals being enslaved and sold within West Africa or into either the transatlantic or trans-Saharan slave trades if they were not ransomed.

Ransoming and enslavement were therefore intimately linked since they were both viewed as legitimate options for dealing with war captives; in addition, ransoming was viewed as a remedy for potential illegal enslavement. According to the Mālikī madh'hab, the school of law practiced in the region both prior and after the jihads, there are six legitimate options for dealing with a war captive—free release, taxation, execution, exchange, ransoming, and enslavement. A captive who failed to be ransomed in an era of legal enslavement would most likely be enslaved. Therefore, of particular interest to the discourse on ransoming is the discourse on slavery. As research has shown, since at least the late fifteenth century, West African Muslims have

10 Hall, *A History of Race in Muslim West Africa;* Ware, *The Walking Qu'ran*, Kane, *Beyond Timbuktu*, Sweet *Domingos Álvares*.

11 Hunt, "The Affective, the Intellectual and Gender History," 339.

been debating slavery within their societies.[12] Moreover, as Sandra Greene has demonstrated, both Muslim and non-Muslim West African nineteenth-century public opinion on slavery and the transatlantic slave trade ran the gamut from horror to wholehearted approval.[13] In Muslim West Africa, the intellectual discourse on slavery was focused on religious status as the basis for enslavement, the onus to prove freeborn Muslim status, and legal and illegal enslavement. The debate on and the prevalence of ransoming as a remedy for illegal enslavement demonstrates that West Africans were also proactive at government and individual levels in implementing measures to rescue individuals from captivity who were at risk for enslavement.

Muslim West African societies, however, were not the only African societies debating the ethics of slavery nor the only ones advocating the ransoming of their kin and society "insiders." Indeed, Muslims would not have been able to ransom their coreligionists if their non-Muslim neighbors had not also practiced ransoming. During the era of legal enslavement and slave-trading, non-Muslim Africans also had clear ideas about who could be enslaved and who could not. African states, especially those involved in the transatlantic slave trade in West Africa and West Central Africa, sought to regulate the slave trade and facilitate what they considered to be legal enslavement and slave-trading while preventing what they determined to be illegal enslavement.[14] Kin often resorted to ransoming to free captives who they considered ought not to have been at risk of enslavement.[15]

---

12 See, for example, Hunwick, *Shari'a in Songhay;* Hunwick "Al- Maghīlī and the Jews of Tuwāt"; Hunwick and Harrack, *Mi'rāj al-Ṣu'ūd;* Hunwick, "Secular Power and Religious Authority in Muslim Society"; Cleaveland, "Ahmad Baba al-Tinbukti and his Islamic Critique of Racial Slavery in the Maghrib"; Lovejoy, "The Bello-Clapperton Exchange"; Humphrey Fisher, "A Muslim William Wilberforce?"

13 Greene, "Minority Voices."

14 Ojo, "The Atlantic Slave Trade and Local Ethics of Slavery in Yorubaland"; Law, "Legal and Illegal Enslavement in West Africa"; Lovejoy and Richardson, "Anglo-Efik Relations"; Thornton, "African Political Ethics and the Slave Trade."

15 Lofkrantz and Ojo, "Slavery, Freedom and Failed Ransom Negotiations"; Ojo, "[I]n Search of their Relations"; Diouf, "The Last Resort." For a discussion of the same phenomenon in West-Central Africa see Candido, *An African Slaving Port*, 191–93; and Ferreira, *Cross-Cultural Exchange in the Atlantic World*, 55, 98.

Fundamentally, the discourse on ransoming is a discussion of law. Most recent work on legal history in West Africa and Islamic Africa focuses on questions of abolition, emancipation, marriage, and divorce in the early colonial period and how Africans negotiated these new colonial legal landscapes.[16] By contrast, this book explores precolonial legal responses to the question of enslavement and, specifically, remedies for illegal enslavement in Muslim West African societies. A clearer understanding of slavery in Muslim societies in Africa and also of African ideas on abolition becomes possible when the policies based on the debate on slavery and actual practices of ransoming in Muslim West Africa are examined. These earlier ideas and practices affected how Africans would view colonial law regarding slavery, freedom, and dependency.

Research on ransoming in West Africa is still in its infancy but growing rapidly. Ransoming had been mentioned as an alternative to enslavement in studies of slavery in Africa.[17] However, it has only been since the mid-2000s that ransoming in West Africa has been studied directly—although in a limited geographic and temporal scope. One of the major contributions of this nascent literature has been to clarify the conflation of slaves with captives and the redemption of slaves with ransoming, both common to works on the Mediterranean basin and Eastern Europe. These studies on ransoming in West Africa highlight the fact that people valued their freedom and the freedom of their family members and were willing to pay for it, while emphasizing African agency in preventing what people considered to be illegal or unethical captivity and enslavement.[18] This book contributes to this

16 See, for example, McMahon, *Slavery and Emancipation in Islamic East Africa*; Jean-Baptiste, *Conjugal Rights*; Burrill, *States of Marriage;* Rodet, "Islam, pluralisme juridique et relations de genre," 173–83; Roberts and Lawrence, *Trafficking in Slavery's Wake*; Burrill et al., *Domestic Violence and the Law.*

17 See, for example, Meillassoux, *The Anthropology of Slavery.* See also Linares, "Deferring to Trade in Slaves," 113–39; Hubbell, "A View of the Slave Trade from the Margin," 25–47.

18 Diouf, "The Last Resort"; Lofkrantz, "Ransoming Policies and Practices"; Lofkrantz, "Protecting Freeborn Muslims"; Lofkrantz, "Intellectual Discourse in the Sokoto Caliphate"; Lofkrantz and Ojo, "Slavery, Freedom and Failed Ransom Negotiations"; Lofkrantz, "Ransoming Captives in the Sokoto Caliphate"; Ojo, "'[I]n Search of their Relations"; Niang, "The Political Economy of Ransoming in the Sahel"; Carpenter, "Ransom as Political Strategy."

emerging field by being a transnational study set within the context of the nineteenth-century jihads that explores the connections and disconnections between intellectual thought, government policy, and the actions of captors and potential payers of ransom across the wide geographic region of the western and central Sudan region of West Africa and the Maghrib and across multiple political jurisdictions.

This study approaches the question of ransoming through an examination, first, of intellectual debates on enslavement and ransoming from the fifteenth through eighteenth centuries; second, of nineteenth-century policies based on understandings of those intellectual debates in the context of the jihads; and, finally, of West African practices of ransoming in the nineteenth century. It does so in large part by using biography. Just as the use of biography in the work on abolition in the early colonial period by Sandra Greene and Eve Troutt Powell, among others, demonstrates how owners and slaves navigated systems of law, ethics, and culture, so too does the use of biography illustrate how captors and captives traversed legal, ethical, and cultural structures to advance their interests in terms of ransoming and preventing enslavement.[19] The use of biography also highlights that ransoming was a gendered practice, as the majority of people ransomed were men, and the voices we hear from the legal treatises and reports of ransoms are largely male. In examining the intellectual foundations of ransoming, how the policies were based on understandings of intellectual thought and how policies translated into actual practices in Muslim West Africa—this book moves away from a historiography on slavery that has focused more on the collective experience and on demography than on how individuals were enslaved.[20] It engages the broader questions of conceptions of legal and illegal enslavement, processes of enslavement and prevention of enslavement in Africa, and how these affected individuals during an era when slavery expanded in West Africa.

This book also expands upon our understanding of ransoming in the Mediterranean basin. It demonstrates how the Maghrib and West African discourses on ransoming were connected and how governments in these two regions interpreted and used their common foundation in the Mālikī madh'hab differently to address their particular socioeconomic circumstances of captivity and ransoming. Until recently, most of the literature

---

19 Greene, *Slave Owners of West Africa;* Troutt Powell, *Tell This in My Memory.*

20 See, for example, the chapters on slavery in Gomez, *African Dominion*; and Domingues da Silva, *The Atlantic Slave Trade from West Central Africa.*

on ransoming in the Mediterranean basin has focused on the holding of European captives in the Maghrib even though both Muslims in North Africa and Christians in Europe participated in captive taking and ransoming. This is reflected in both the early discussions of European captives, as demonstrated by the publication of captivity narratives throughout the period, and in the scholarship up to the mid-1990s. These studies concentrated on the conditions under which European captives were kept in the Maghrib and the negotiations for their release, the role of Christian brotherhoods in the organization of ransoms, the business aspect of ransom negotiations, and the division of ransom costs.[21] More recently, historians such as Natalie Rothman and Gillian Weiss have included both sides of the Mediterranean and have focused on ransoming as an important means of interaction across political and religious boundaries and as a lens through which to explore ideas of patronage, social discipline, and spiritual salvation in early modern Christian and Muslim societies. They have demonstrated how the connections across the Mediterranean shaped the social, economic, and political ramifications of holding captives for ransom and how the issue of ransoming subjects/citizens affected the formation of identity in southern Europe and the Maghrib.[22] This book expands on this literature by contextualizing Maghribi Mediterranean ransoming practices against the background

21 See Clissold, *The Barbary Slaves*; Friedman, *Spanish Captives in North Africa and the Early Modern Age*; Fontenay, "Le maghreb barbaresque et l'esclavage méditerranéen au XVIe– XVIIe siècles"; Bachrouch, "Rachat et libération des esclaves chrétiens à Tunis au XVIIe siècle"; Davis, *Christian Slaves, Muslim Masters*; Colley, *Captives, Britain, Empire and the World*; Dursteler, "On Bazaars & Battlefields."

22 Rothman, "Becoming Venetian"; Weiss, *Captives and Corsairs;* Weiss, "Ransoming 'Turks' from France's Royal Galleys." See also Coleman, "Of Corsairs, Converts and Renegades"; Matar, *Britain and Barbary*; Matar, "Piracy and Captivity in the Early Modern Mediterranean"; Belhamissi, *Les captifs algériens et l'Europe chrétienne.* See Kaiser, "Zones de transit" and Hershenzon, "'[P]ara que me saque cabesea por cabasa" for recent analyses of how European and Maghribi intermediaries transferred and transported freed captives. Also see Brooks, *Captives and Cousins.* While the book is focused on captivity, raiding and enslavement between Spanish and Indigenous communities in what is now the American Southwest, Brooks argues that Spanish conceptions of enslaveability and ransoming in the region were based on the preexisting conceptions of captivity and slavery of their Iberian homeland (23–24).

of Morocco's relations with its southern neighbors and the greater Muslim western African world.

This book, therefore, bridges social, intellectual, and legal history to highlight the ramifications of the debate among religious leaders, legal authorities, and policymakers on the actual practice of ransoming in Muslim western Africa. The intellectual debate among scholars on the legality of ransoming to free captives in danger of sale into slavery resulted in policies that affected how ransoming was actually practiced in West Africa during the jihad era. In its operation, ransoming was a means to allow for the liberation of certain individuals who had been captured but not yet sold into slavery and thereby secure their release from captivity, while generally not benefiting the people already enslaved. Ransoming provided an outlet for release from captivity for those who, according to local Islamic legal interpretations and customary rights, should not be enslaved, particularly freeborn Muslims, and also provided the opportunity for those individuals whose social and economic status permitted their family and friends the means to obtain the release of captive individuals to do so. The practice of ransoming thus complicates the discussion on resistance to slavery since those engaged in the practice were not against slavery per se but against the enslavement of certain individuals they thought should be protected from enslavement. Legal ransoming practices came to an end with the end of the legal slave trade and enslavement.

Ransoming Captives and Redeeming Slaves

The terms "ransoming" and "redemption" are often used interchangeably to refer to both the freeing of captives who were not enslaved and the freeing of slaves. For example, Sylviane Diouf uses the terms "redemption" and "ransom" as synonyms in discussing a concept she labels "captive redemption." In her article which focuses on the ransoming of Africans from European slave ships, even though Diouf does not specifically define the term "captive redemption," she refers to the term as the ability to "buy back someone's freedom" and "to buy the freedom of people slated for deportation."[23] Diouf argues that this process was a means for kin to rescue captives prior to enslavement and in particular their inclusion in the transatlantic slave trade.[24] Thaddeus Sunseri, in his work on German East Africa, uses the term

23 Diouf, "The Last Resort," 83.

24 Diouf, "The Last Resort," 81–100.

"slave ransoming" in a way that more closely resembles what I consider to be a form of slave redemption as it involved purchasing a person from slavery. He states that "slave ransoming was the basis of German abolition policy after 1900 . . . German policy allowed slaves who wished to end their bondage to be bought free or ransomed by third parties, especially German planters, who then had access to the slave's labor until the ransom debt was worked off. Thus ransoming gave slave men and women the choice of whether or not to sever their relations of bondage."[25] In his work on the Upper Congo, David Gordon uses the term "ransom" to refer to the practice of freeing captives from Zanzibar and East African slave traders and the term "redemption" to refer to the practice of Catholic missionaries purchasing individuals whom they identified as slaves "in order to end their alleged slave status and to gain converts for their missions."[26] Further confusing conceptual terms, Géza Dávid and Pál Fodor, in their edited volume on ransoming along the Ottoman and Austro-Hungarian border, use the term "ransom slavery" to refer to captives held by Ottoman forces who were released upon payment and permitted to return home with their social position intact. According to Fodor, "Prisoners of war and captives for ransom . . . were called *esir*/*tutsak*... Neither in law nor in actuality was the *esir* a slave but could easily become one if he or she was not sufficiently valuable to warrant a ransom demand, or if he or she could not raise the sum required."[27] The freeing of captives and the freeing of slaves through the payment of cash or kind, are, as Fodor agrees, two separate concepts.

In dealing with and acknowledging the differences between processes of captivity and enslavement in the Mediterranean world and those in the Atlantic world, Michel Fontenay differentiates between "captives" and "slaves" based on the captor's purpose in holding them. He distinguishes between "use-value" and "exchange-value" of the prisoner. For Fontenay, a "slave" was a person whose owner's purpose in holding them was to extract labor, whereas a "captive" was an investment to be treated primarily as a medium of exchange.[28] Daniel Hershenzon criticizes Fontenay's focus on "use-value" and "exchange-value." Unlike Fontenay, Hershenzon sees categories of "use-value" (slaves) and "exchange-value" (captives) as fluid, as family members

25 Sunseri, "Slave Ransoming in German East Africa, 1885–1922," 481.

26 Gordon, "Slavery and Redemption in the Catholic Missions of the Upper Congo," 578.

27 Fodor, "Introduction," xiv.

28 Fontenay, "Esclaves et/ou captifs:préciser les concepts,"15–24.

on both sides of the Mediterranean were concerned with obtaining the correct combination of money and specific individuals to secure the release of particular captives. In order to finalize a ransom payment someone initially categorized as "use-value" (slave) could be recategorized as "exchange-value" (captive). As Hershenzon points out, labor power ("use-value") and profit ("exchange-value") were not the only motivations for procuring prisoners, and often certain individuals needed to be located in order to exchange them for the freedom of others.[29]

Unlike Fontenay, in differentiating between captives and slaves, I place the emphasis not on the captor/owner's purpose but on the status of their victim. As I have stated elsewhere, I define ransoming as the practice of paying for the release of a captive at the time of capture or soon afterward. Ransoming is differentiated from redemption in that a redeemed slave remains in a subservient status in his/her owner's society whereas a ransomed captive returns to their previous status in their own society.[30] While I agree with Fontenay in that in many cases one can only tell if a person was being held for ransom or was enslaved once a payment has been made, my definition also distinguishes between the processes of "ransoming" and "redemption." Just like in West Africa and in other parts of Africa, there was a significant redeemed slave population in the Maghrib. European Christians who converted to Islam—"renegades"—whose freedom from slavery was purchased can be considered to be redeemed slaves. Renegades who had once been enslaved remained in Maghribi society in a subservient position to freeborn Muslim Maghribis. In many ways they had undergone what Orlando Patterson terms "social death."[31] They may have regained their freedom through payment of a fee or other means, but they had forfeited their original social status, family,

29 Hershenzon, "'[P]ara que me saque cabesea por cabasa," 18–19.

30 Lofkrantz, "Ransoming Policies and Practices," 1; Lofkrantz, "Protecting Freeborn Muslims," 109–10. Ojo, in his study of ransoming in nineteenth-century Yorubaland uses the term "ransoming" much like it is being used in this book. For him, ransoming "restored captives to freedom prior to enslavement." See Ojo, "'[I]n Search of their Relations," 56. Kaiser and Calafat also distinguish between slaves and captives by the outcome. For them, if a ransom was ultimately paid then the individual was a captive and not a slave. See Kaiser and Calafat, "The Economy of Ransoming in the Early Modern Mediterranean," 113.

31 Patterson, *Slavery and Social Death.* For renegades as cultural brokers see Bennessar and Bennessar, *Les chrétiens d'Allah;* also see Zemon Davis, *Trickster Travels: A Sixteenth Century Muslim between Worlds.*

religion, and name. A focus on the individual's social status after payment in determining whether a person was a ransomed captive or a redeemed slave takes this potential outcome into account.

The ransoming of a captive, therefore, is conceptually different from the redemption of a slave where an enslaved individual, upon payment of a fee raised either by themselves or by a third party, is declared free by their owner. A person who was ransomed, unlike an individual who was or had been enslaved, never underwent "social death." This is an important difference between captives who were marked for enslavement versus captives who were marked for ransoming. Captives who were enslaved were quickly moved away from the place of capture, communication with loved ones and potential rescuers was cut, and they were stripped of their public social identity as much as possible. The opposite was true for captives who were to be ransomed. A captive who was to be ransomed was ransomable because of their social identity. Captors who were willing to ransom their captives recognized and valued their captives' social identity and encouraged communication between the captive and those willing to pay a ransom in order to facilitate ransom negotiations. A captive's social status would have been a key factor in their ransoming. The ransomed captive, unlike a redeemed slave, is able to reclaim their previous status in their own society.

The difference between ransoming a captive and redeeming a slave can also be seen through examining the conceptual basis of ransoming and redemption in Islamic law. John Willis highlights the difference in his discussion of the ideology of enslavement in Islam. He uses the analogy of the debtor-creditor relationship. He demonstrates that on a theoretical and philosophical level, enslavement was the means through which "unbelievers" compensated the Muslim community for the loss of Muslim lives through warfare. In his use of analogy in describing the relationship between jihad, enslavement, and eventually redemption and manumission, he states, "In summary, it can be said that the jihad, in its effort to banish the humiliation of kufr, inflicted the shame of servility, and set in tandem a series of legal relations whichfixed the bond between master and slave. Slavery became a means of extinguishing the guilt of kufr—an expiation for the blood of Muslims spilt in jihad. Moreover, slavery was a grave debt as well as a deep humiliation, and it was only upon atonement of the debt that the humiliation could be removed. Thus the master was cast in the role of creditor, and the slave or dhimmi assumed the guise of debtor."[32] From this perspective,

32 Willis, "Jihad and the Ideology of Enslavement," 23.

the jizya—the tax levied on Christians, Jews, and other dhimmī—can be seen as a form of compensation for them not being killed (or in Willis's words as "a form of ransom for their failure to convert to Islam").[33] From this theoretical viewpoint the price paid in the ransoming of captives can be viewed as the immediate repayment of the debt incurred in the loss of members of the captor's community during warfare, while the redemption of a slave can be viewed as paying off the debt after a significant period; further, manumission can be seen as the cancellation of the debt. In this way, redemption, the cost of a slave's freedom, and ransoming the cost of a captive's freedom, can be viewed as related but different. As Mohammed Ennaji states, there was a vital difference in how a ransomed captive and a redeemed slave were viewed in Islamic society and law. This difference stemmed from the original Muslim community in Arabia and affected how ransomed captives and redeemed slaves were viewed, including Mālikī interpretations of law, which is what the madh'hab practiced in West Africa and the Maghrib. A ransomed captive bore no shame for once being held captive, but a freed slave always remained dishonored by their time spent enslaved.[34]

In practice also, a redeemed slave retained a low social status in their former owner's society. Prior to the British and French conquest of West Africa it was very difficult for redeemed slaves to leave the villages and cities of their former owners. Even for first-generation slaves who remembered their homes, it would have been difficult to return home, if it still existed, because of the distances involved and because the possibility of reenslavement was high. In the words of one former slave, Griga, born around 1847–48, who was held within the Saharan oasis of Gouram in present-day southern Algeria, "a freed [slave] is only free in his own village."[35] Claude Meillassoux makes an important distinction between manumission and enfranchisement. He argues that enfranchisement under Islam was, in reality, only manumission. According to him, "enfranchisement" meant that a freed slave acquires all the prerogatives of the freeborn including honors, and the stigma of slave birth or capture is removed. Enfranchised slaves, usually families, had the right to leave their former owners and settle on new land and enjoy all of the privileges of the freeborn.[36] There is a pre-Islamic Arabic word for full emancipation, "sa'ibah," which means to "flow away," whose sense and use disappeared

33 Willis, "Jihad and the Ideology of Enslavement," 23.

34 Ennaji, *Slavery, the State, and Islam*, 22.

35 Mercadier, *L'esclave de Timimoun*, 213.

36 Meillassoux, *The Anthropology of Slavery*, 121–23.

with the advent of Islam.[37] The concept of "sa'ibah" most closely resembles Meillassoux's conception of "enfranchisement." Using Meillassoux's terminology, most redeemed slaves in precolonial Muslim West Africa were manumitted slaves. The position of a manumitted slave contrasts drastically with the position of an enfranchised slave and certainly with that of a ransomed captive. A manumitted slave, either by redemption or by other legal means, even though free was usually viewed as a junior member of their former owner's family, was under their former owner's control, and was expected to perform certain duties for their former owner and give them gifts on certain occasions. A ransomed captive was free to return home, with their social identity and status intact and the right to rebuild a life after their traumatic experience. The concepts described by "redemption" and "ransoming" are fundamentally different and describe two different processes, as exemplified by the differing status of a ransomed captive and a redeemed slave. This book is focused on the ransoming of captives and how the intellectual discourse on legal and illegal enslavement, policies based on that thought, and actual practices mutually affected each other.

Approaches to West African Muslim Thought

In examining the intellectual discourse on ransoming and slavery in West African Muslim societies from the fifteenth through nineteenth century, this work draws upon Talal Asad's approach to Muslim intellectual discourse. In his short but influential publication, *The Idea of an Anthropology of Islam*, Asad provides a paradigm for studying religious, social, and cultural debate within Muslim societies that challenged the Western preoccupation and privileging of the Arab-Persian Islamic "center." For Asad, Islam is a "discursive tradition." Islam is "neither a distinctive social structure nor a heterogeneous collection of beliefs, artifacts, customs and morals" but a set of discourses "that seek to instruct practitioners regarding the correct form and purpose of a given practice."[38] Asad views Islamic discourse as a continuous engagement and reflection on the past and on previous scholarship in order to develop meaningful solutions to the problems of a particular time and place. In studies of contemporary African Muslim societies, the

37 Ennaji, "Sur la repudiation (divorce) qui montre le statut de la femme était lié à l'esclavage."

38 Hasad, *The Idea of an Anthropology of Islam*, 14.

concept of a "discursive tradition" has been used by anthropologists such as Adeline Masquelier to address how Muslim scholars and laypeople across Africa have navigated between "tradition," religious reform, and the modern world.[39] The concept of a "discursive tradition," however, is equally relevant to the historical West African scholarly discourse on slavery and ransoming. As Scott Reese has pointed out, until relatively recently, scholars studying African Islam have often accepted the assumption that African Muslim intellectuals and institutions are ahistorical and unchanging and that the religious nature of a text deprives it of any historical value.[40] However, in the past, just as in the present, the Islamic intellectual canon was a "living body of knowledge continuously employed and interpreted."[41] Applying Asad's concept of a "discursive tradition" helps address the criticism that the study of Muslim African scholarship is ahistorical and it allows for the examination of West African Muslim intellectual thought in its socioeconomic context.

Furthermore, adopting the viewpoint that African Muslims have been and still are participants in the Islamic "discursive tradition" means a rejection of the concept of an "Islam noir" in all its permutations. The term "Islam noir" was coined by French colonial officials to differentiate between what they viewed as "orthodox Arab Islam" of the Maghrib and the "syncretic African Islam" practiced south of the Sahara.[42] French colonial officials and scholars of the period viewed "Islam noir" to be both different and inferior to the "Islam central" of the Maghrib and Middle East. As J. L. Amselle states, the mindset of early twentieth-century French anthropologists was to "de-politicize, to de-historicize and de-islamize" sub-Saharan African Muslim societies."[43] The concept of an "Islam noir" outlived the colonial period with a slight twist. While historians and anthropologists dropped the idea that Islam as practiced south of the Sahara was an inferior form, many accepted that sub-Saharan Islam was fundamentally unique, local, and outside the dār

39 See, for example, Masquelier, *Women and Islamic Revival in a West African Town*; Loimeier, *Between Social Skills and Marketable Skills;* Tayob, *Islam in South Africa.*

40 Reese, "Introduction: Islam in Africa: Challenging the Perceived Wisdom," 3.

41 Reese, "Islam in Africa/Africans and Islam," 19.

42 André, *L'islam noir*; Monteil, *L'Islam noir*; Coulon, "Islam africain ou Islam arabe: Autonomie ou independence"; Triaud, "Giving a Name to Islam South of the Sahara."

43 Amselle and Sibeud, "Introduction," 13.

al-islām norm.[44] For example, Donal Cruise O'Brien argues that local sub-Saharan African practices of Islam, especially adherence to Sufi ṭurūq, developed out of a need to "counter the humiliation that spiritual subordination to an Arab religion might signify."[45] More recently, as Abdourahmane Seck and Cheikh Anta Babou have shown, contemporary West African thinkers have interconnected the ideas of Islam noir, négritude, and Afrocentrism to define sub-Saharan Islam as different but equal (if not superior to) Islam as practiced in the "center."[46] However, the concept of Islam noir, "with all its avatars and reincarnations, replenished and reappropriated in various forms"[47] including rejections of sub-Saharan African Islam as inferior, still puts Muslims south of the Sahara at the periphery of Muslim intellectual discourse and practice. The idea that precolonial sub-Saharan African Muslims were at the intellectual periphery of Islamic discourse has been disproven by recent scholarship on such topics as the medieval West African empires, the trans-Saharan book trade and isnād affiliations. Michael Gomez's recent book on the interior of West Africa from pre-Antiquity to the Moroccan invasion of the Songhay Empire demonstrates that from the introduction of Islam in West Africa, West African Muslims were fully enmeshed within the discourses and debates of the Islamic world. Indeed, he contextualizes the eleventh-century Almoravid expansion not as a North African movement but as a West African one.[48] The important collection of essays edited by Graziano Krätli and Ghislaine Lydon on the trans-Saharan book trade with their focus on the practicalities of book buying, trading, and borrowing and on which manuscripts were bought and where they were located across the Sudan region further gives concrete form to how sub-Saharan African intellectuals received and transmitted ideas to other intellectuals in other parts of the Islamic world.[49] Likewise, the examination of isnād affiliations, teacher-student relationships, and correspondence between intellectuals also demonstrate how intimately linked West African Muslim intellectuals were into

44 For a discussion on the anthropological treatment of Islam south of the Sahara see Launay, "An Invisible Religion?"

45 O'Brien, "La filière musulmane," 9.

46 Seck, *La question musulmane au Sénégal,* 181–83; Babou, *Fighting the Greater Jihad,* 177.

47 Triaud, "Giving a Name to Islam South of the Sahara," 15.

48 Gomez, *African Dominion,* 30–42.

49 Krätli and Lydon, *The Trans-Saharan Book Trade.* See also Last, "The Book in the Sokoto Caliphate."

the greater discourse of the dār al-islām. For example, as Stefan Reichmuth has shown in his study of the eighteenth-century Indian scholar Murtadā al-Zabīdī's correspondence with West African scholars, West African Muslims engaged in intellectual exchanges with their counterparts throughout the dār al-islām.[50] As Zachary Wright notes in the introduction to his coedited collection of West African Sufi writings, Muslim West African intellectuals drew upon both global Islamic and West African scholarship in forming their ideas.[51] Not only does the concept of a "discursive tradition," as opposed to "Islam noir" permit for a conceptualization of West African Muslim thinkers as being engaged with the events and ideas of their times, it also allows for the appreciation that they were doing so dynamically: transmitting knowledge and ideas across Africa and the Islamic world as well as receiving them.

Sources and Chapter Descriptions

This book examines the connections between scholarly opinion, policy based on interpretation of scholarly opinion, and actual ransoming practices. The types of sources used and the structure of the book reflects that interest. It is based on research conducted mainly in Mali, Niger, Nigeria, and France and on Arabic, French, and English language archival sources, treatises, personal correspondence, oral sources and testimony, biographical data, travel reports, and early colonial documents. For intellectual thought and debate on the issue of ransoming and the policies based on that thought and debate, I relied upon the intellectual treatises, poems, and personal correspondence of African scholars and policymakers. In an era of both the trans-Saharan and transatlantic slave trades, the question of who was and who was not legally enslavable was frequently debated by African scholars. In conjunction with that dispute was a debate among scholars and policymakers on preventives and remedies, such as ransoming, for what was deemed to be illegal enslavement. These debates played out in formal treatises and in personal correspondence and poetry. As well as an awareness that scholars were primarily writing in particular sociopolitical contexts and to address specific issues of their time and place, using texts written by scholars and especially

50 Reichmuth, "Murtadā al-Zabīdī (1732–91) and the Africans." For correspondence between Muslim West and North Africa see Maïga, "Letter Writing between West and North Africa."

51 Zachary Wright, "Introduction: The Sufi Scholarship of Islamic West Africa," 2.

by policymakers requires a cognizance of what Brinkley Messick refers to as "textual domination." He defines textual domination as the "interlocking of a polity, a social order, and a discursive formation."[52] An awareness of "textual domination" is especially important in using the treatises of scholars and policymakers of the postjihad states. The states that formed in the aftermath of the jihad movements were based on the promulgation and promotion of specific interpretations of Islamic law and justifications for overthrowing the preceding governments. Large bodies of treatises, letters, and poetry were written by scholars and policymakers to support and promote their viewpoints on law, belief, and politics. The scholars and policymakers of the Sokoto Caliphate were particularly profuse. However, while the texts produced during the jihads and their immediate aftermath were not without bias, they do provide an excellent window into the viewpoints, priorities, and concerns of these scholars and policymakers and how they justified their positions.

Analyzing actual ransoming practices was more complicated. Since no African nor European government nor agency kept central registers for West African ransoming cases, finding ransom cases required combing through African and European produced letters, personal correspondence, court registrars, political, economic, judicial and ethnographic reports, oral testimony transcripts, memoirs, and travel reports for mentions and descriptions of individual cases. Ransoming was discussed in both African and European sources. For example, specific ransom cases were discussed in both the official and private correspondence of Sokoto officials. An example of this is a letter written sometime between 1837 and 1842 by the third Sarkin Musulmi of the Sokoto Caliphate, Abūbakar Atikū, to the scholar Sīdī Mahmūd updating him on the status of a particular ransom negotiation. For a European source on the late nineteenth century, French colonial records located in the Niger, Mali, and Senegal national archives were particularly useful.[53] French colonial officials often recorded ransom practices that they witnessed or had heard about. In the immediate years after conquest, French colonial officials were frequently the recourse to which family members turned when their attempts to ransom a captive failed. However, in the early years of colonial

52 Messick, *The Calligraphic State*, 5.

53 I would like to thank Martin Klein here. When I was a PhD student, he permitted me to digitize his microfilm collection from the Archives Nationales du Sénégal (ANS). A copy of this collection is held at the Harriet Tubman Institute for Research on Africa and Its Diasporas, York University.

rule, French colonial officials and their British counterparts were operating in an environment where they were trying to assert their control, deny the reality of captive taking, enslavement, and slavery to the general European public, and form alliances with local power holders. While cases of ransoming were recorded, they were done so in an environment where French officials refused to use the word "slave" and instead used the word "captive" or "servant" to refer to enslaved individuals. They often conflated captives and slaves in their records. For both the French and British colonial officials, the emphasis was not on freeing already enslaved individuals but to stop captive taking and enslavement in order to demonstrate their governance and to placate abolitionists at home. In 1903, Governor-General Ernest Roume outlawed the legal recognition of slavery throughout French West Africa. Likewise, in what became northern Nigeria, in 1897, George Goldie of the Royal Niger Company abolished the legal status of slavery in company territories, which was the policy continued under Frederick Lugard when he became high commissioner of the Protectorate of Northern Nigeria in 1900 and continued the conquest of the Sokoto Caliphate.[54] These policies did not outlaw slavery but denied legal recognition of the status. Ransoming was tied to colonial policies since ransoming took place after an individual was taken captive and therefore, in writing about ransoming, officials were writing with an awareness of the official view on captive taking.

This book is divided into five chapters. Chapter 1 discusses what pre-nineteenth-century West African Muslim intellectuals wrote and argued about legal and illegal enslavement and the role of ransoming as a means to protect individuals from illegal enslavement. West African Muslim scholars wrote about the ethical, political, legal, and other issues of the time and place in which they lived. They were concerned with and influenced by the ideas, concerns, and events surrounding them. Moreover, policymakers of West African Muslim states based their policies and laws upon their understanding of intellectual thought and of influential scholars. This chapter focuses on the intellectuals and intellectual thought prior to the mid-eighteenth century, which influenced the leaders of the Sokoto jihad who founded the largest state in precolonial West Africa, the Sokoto Caliphate, and served as

54 For French policies on slavery see Klein, *Slavery and Colonial Rule in French West Africa*. For British policies on slavery in northern Nigeria see Lovejoy and Hogendorn, *Slow Death for Slavery*. The conquest of the Sokoto Caliphate and its division between the British, French, and German Empires was completed in 1903.

inspiration for later jihads. It is particularly concerned with the promulgation of "authoritative texts" and the development of consensus on ransoming issues.

Focusing on the pre-nineteenth-century period, chapter 2 discusses ransoming as a long-standing practice in the northern part of western Africa and in the Mediterranean world, and in relations between Christian Europe and the Maghrib particularly Morocco. The Maghrib and Muslim West Africa shared a common foundation in Islamic law—and the Mālikī madh'hab in particular—and drew upon the same intellectual tradition. Ransoming practices, nevertheless, differed. In both regions, ransoming was used to free freeborn Muslims from captivity. In the Maghrib, the economic benefits of ransoming back non-Muslims and how ransoming fit into relations with both Europe and the Sahara were emphasized. In Muslim West Africa, the emphasis was on the prudency of ransoming back non-Muslims. Moreover, in terms of ransoming, Morocco's relations with Europe were affected by its relations with its southern neighbors.

Chapters 3 and 4 concentrate on state or official ransoming policies and in particular those of the Sokoto Caliphate and of the Umarian states. One of the main causes of the jihads was the problem of the perceived illegal enslavement of freeborn Muslims. The Sokoto jihad was launched in large part to protect the perceived rights of freeborn Muslims. However, due to the importance of booty collection in warfare and the use of enslaved labor on Caliphate plantations, the jihad led to personal insecurity and to the captivity and enslavement of individuals whose capture was deemed "wrongful." Since the Sokoto Caliphate could not prevent the illegal captivity of freeborn Muslims, it encouraged ransoming as a practical way to rescue freeborn Muslims from potential enslavement. The Sokoto jihad and the establishment of the Sokoto Caliphate served as inspiration for subsequent jihads across the western and central Sudan, including that of 'Umar Taal in the 1850s that led to the formation of the Umarian states in the region. Even though Taal was a member of the Tijāniyya ṭarīqa instead of the Qādiriyya ṭarīqa favored in the Sokoto Caliphate, Taal legitimized his jihad in the western Sudan, especially against the Caliphate of Ḥamdallāhi, largely on Sokoto intellectual thought. Strong intellectual parallels can be made between the two movements including on policies concerning ransoming.

Chapter 5 focuses on the individual level rather than the state level and on the actual practices of ransoming among ordinary citizens. While intellectuals would view the implementation of their interpretation of doctrine as ideal and policymakers would view the full implementation of their policies as the ideal, there was often a gulf between the "ideal" and what actually happened. This chapter examines the motives for ransoming for the individual captor and captive, and the importance of communication links, social status, and the use of mediators in successful ransom negotiations. It shows that ransoming at the time of capture was related to the process of enslavement and that ransom and slave prices were therefore connected. It is argued that while the gain from selling a person on the slave market was the market value of that individual alone, a proportion of an individual's ransom price was based on what his or her family and friends were willing to pay for the return of that person in addition to the market value as a slave. In general, the ransom price was equivalent to twice the slave price value. It is clear from an analysis of the cost of ransoming and the price of slaves that the system of slavery capitalized on the fact that people valued freedom, especially of relatives, and, in order to achieve freedom were willing to pay more than the market value of the individual on the slave market.

Chapter One

Islamic Discourse on Slavery and Ransoming before 1800

In *Taj al-Din yajib 'ala-mulūk*, the treatise he wrote at the end of the fifteenth century for Sarkin Muḥammad Rumfa of Kano, Muḥammad al-Maghīlī advised that a good Muslim King preserves a surplus in the treasury for ransoming captives.[1] Indeed, issues surrounding legal and illegal enslavement and remedies for illegal enslavement, such as ransoming, had been debated in Muslim West African societies since at least a century before al-Maghīlī wrote his treatise. Subjects of debate included who was considered to be a Muslim, the onus for proving freeborn Muslim status, and the fate of illegally captive individuals. The issue of ransoming, as a remedy for potential enslavement, was closely linked to the question of captivity and enslavement. Captivity could result in both the ransoming of the captive and the enslavement of the captive as well as the execution, free release, and prisoner exchange of the captive. Therefore, the discourse on ransoming was strongly affiliated with the debate on who could and could not be legally enslaved and particularly with intellectual discussion on remedies for illegal captivity. The discourses on captivity, legal and illegal enslavement, and remedies for illegal enslavement are important as they provided the structure within which policy and practices were formed. A full understanding of captivity, ransoming, and enslavement policies and practices requires an understanding of the intellectual context from which they were derived.

The fact that slavery was being debated in West Africa is not surprising since the trafficking of enslaved people across the Sahara and across the Atlantic from West Africa increased starting in the seventeenth century. Due to the sources available it is difficult to estimate the number of enslaved Africans from south of the Sahara that were sold across the desert.

1 al-Maghīlī, *Taj al-Din yajib 'ala-mulūk*, 21.

The number of enslaved people from south of the Sahara trafficked throughout the trans-Saharan trade, including the eastern Sudan, are thought to have jumped from an estimated 5,500 people per year in the sixteenth century to an estimated 7,000 people per year in the seventeenth and eighteenth centuries. The central Sudan and in particular Bornu and the Hausa states provided slaves for the Tripoli and Tunis markets whereas the western Sudan supported the Algiers and Moroccan markets.[2] To meet demands for enslaved labor, in the seventeenth century, Morocco was importing approximately 2,000 enslaved people per year, Algeria 500 per year, and Tunisia 800 per year. In the 1780s, the slave trade out of Hausaland, especially Katsina, increased as Ghadames merchants expanded their activities in the region. Due to demand and increased trade links, the slave trade to Tunisia increased after 1780 to about 1,000 to 1,300 enslaved people per year.[3]

Moreover, with the growth of the Atlantic trade, the western and central Sudan, especially the region west of the Niger Bend, fed the Atlantic trade. The western and central Sudan did not provide as many enslaved individuals to the Atlantic trade as it could have. This is because over the course of the Atlantic slave trade some Muslim governments of the region sought to restrict the number of enslaved people trafficked outside of the dār al-islām even as the pull of the market encouraged traders to circumvent the law.[4] Indeed, fewer than 10 percent of the people sold into the Atlantic slave trade came from regions where Muslims were politically dominant, which means even fewer than 10 percent of people sold were Muslims. Yet, as the volume of the transatlantic slave trade increased in the eighteenth century so too did the number of trafficked individuals from the western and central Sudan region, including Muslims.[5] This is demonstrated through slave departures from Senegambian ports, which sold enslaved individuals from

2 Austen, "The Trans-Saharan Slave Trade:A Tentative Census"; Austen, "The Mediterranean Islamic Slave Trade out Africa: A Tentative Census." See also McDougall, "Discourse and Distortion: Critical Reflections on the Historiography of the Saharan Slave Trade."

3 Colvin, "Commerce of Hausaland, 1780–1833," 112–15; Montana, "The Trans-Saharan Slave Trade in the Context of Tunisian Foreign Trade in the Western Mediterranean," 28; Wright, "Morocco: The Last Great Slave Market?" 58. For more on the slave trade from the central Sudan to Tunisia, see Montana, *The Abolition of Slavery in Ottoman Tunisia.*

4 Lofkrantz and Lovejoy, "Maintaining Network Boundaries."

5 Lovejoy, *Jihad in West Africa*, 133–36. For more on the debate on why the western Sudan did not provide more slaves to the Atlantic slave trade see Lofkrantz and Lovejoy, "Maintaining Network Boundaries," 211–13.

the Senegal River Valley and from as far east as the Bambara states of Segu and Kaarta. Throughout the Atlantic slave trade era, various Europeans such as the French, English, Dutch, and Portuguese operated numerous ports along the Senegambian coast and river system including St. Louis, Gorée, Rufisque, James Fort, Cacheu, and Bissau among others. In the sixteenth century, from 1516 to 1600, total slave exports from Senegambian ports were 159,026 people. In the seventeenth century, from 1601 to 1700, that number dipped to 110,444 individuals. However, in the eighteenth century, from 1701 to 1800, the number of enslaved individuals trafficked from Senegambian ports jumped to 265,251.[6] What is even more revealing is when the eighteenth-century number is broken down by decade. As can be seen from table 1.1 the number of enslaved individuals sold across the Atlantic from Senegambian ports increased in the second half of the eighteenth century, in the years leading up to the jihads of the nineteenth century of the western and central Sudan.

In the second half of the eighteenth century, captives from the central Sudan, including the Hausa states, who were enslaved and sold into the Atlantic slave trade were trafficked through Bight of Benin ports, particularly through Lagos. Lagos became a major slave port in the mid-1760s. Although it is not possible to separate Muslims from non-Muslims who were sold to Europeans at Lagos, as faith is a matter of personal belief (as can be seen in table 1.2), the trend in slave exports from Lagos increased through the second half of the eighteenth century and into the first years of the nineteenth century leading up to the Sokoto jihad.[7]

6 *Voyages: The Atlantic Slave Trade Database* http://www.slavevoyages.org. These numbers do not include Sierra Leone ports. They include the ports of Senegambia and the offshore Atlantic. They are categorized in the database as Albreda, Bissagos, Bissau, Cacheu, Casamance, Galam Gambia, Goreé, Joal or Saloum, Portuguese Guinea, Saint-Louis, Cape Verde, Madeira, and Senegambia and offshore Atlantic port unspecified. Enslaved individuals from Fuuta Jalon were primarily exported through Sierra Leone ports, whereas Muslims from the central Sudan, including Hausaland (which is the focus of chapter 3), were primarily deported through Yoruba networks through Bight of Benin ports, especially Lagos.

7 There have been attempts using the recorded names of enslaved individuals in the transatlantic slave trade to count how many Muslims were sent across the Atlantic and where they went. See Domingues da Silva et al., "The Trans-Atlantic Muslim Diaspora to Latin America in the Nineteenth Century." However, not all Muslims would have had an identifiable "Muslim" name nor do names account for personal belief or unbelief.

Table 1.1. Number of Enslaved People Trafficked through Senegambian Ports, 1700–1800*

Decade	Number of Enslaved People Trafficked
1701–1710	6,589
1711–1720	13,129
1721–1730	19,603
1731–1740	24,871
1741–1750	15,952
1751–1760	39,734
1761–1770	44,679
1771–1780	44,263
1781–1790	33,140
1791–1800	23,291

* *Voyages: The Atlantic Slave Trade Database* http://www.slavevoyages.org. These numbers include the ports of Senegambia and the offshore Atlantic. They are categorized in the database as Albreda, Bissagos, Bissau, Cacheu, Casamance, Galam Gambia, Goreé, Joal or Saloum, Portuguese Guinea, Saint-Louis, Cape Verde, Madeira, and Senegambia and offshore Atlantic port unspecified.

Table 1.2. Number of Enslaved People Trafficked through Lagos, 1761–1805

Years	Number of Enslaved People Trafficked
1761–1765	269
1766–1775	4,721
1776–1785	6,032
1786–1795	18,263
1796–1805	24,694

Source: Mann, *Slavery and the Birth of an African City,* 38, table 1.2.

Enslavement, and particularly the enslavement of freeborn Muslims, provoked a response by West African intellectuals. The discussion of issues of captivity, enslavement, and ransoming were entwined since captivity could result in enslavement as well as ransoming among other fates. These scholars were responding to both an increase in enslavement in the eighteenth century and to a North African political argument that defined individuals identified as "black" as being enslaveable.[8] West African jurists agreed that freeborn Muslims should never be enslaved and that Muslims who came into possession of wrongly enslaved Muslims should release them. From the fifteenth century, many scholars acknowledged that ransoming was a useful tool for regaining the freedom of Muslims and should be utilized even though the legally preferred remedy was free release. Ransoming was regarded as a way to free captives and as an alternative and a preventative to enslavement. In order to show how ransoming fit into the West African intellectual discourse, this chapter will discuss the education system and transmission of ideas in pre-nineteenth-century Islamic West Africa, the debate on legal and illegal enslavement prior to the advent of the nineteenth-century jihad movements, and how ransoming was conceived as fitting into this debate as a remedy for illegal enslavement. In doing so, this chapter focuses on scholars whose texts became dominant in West Africa and would influence the beliefs and agendas of the nineteenth-century jihad leaders.

Islamic Scholarship in the Western and Central Sudan

Fifteenth- to nineteenth-century West African scholars, like their colleagues throughout the Islamic world, addressed the issues of their time and place and tried to influence local politics and rulers through their advice. Governance throughout the dār al-islām can be characterized as a balance between rulers who wanted to govern unhindered by religious authority and in accordance with local politics, and scholars who insisted that no one, not even the ruler, was above the law.[9] In pre-nineteenth-century West Africa, scholars sought to meet this challenge by advising the ruling elite on questions of law and policy. Throughout the Islamic world, and not just in West Africa, scholars and jurists had a tendency to insist that not only themselves but also rulers conduct themselves with piety. Muslim scholars and jurists often viewed themselves as the protectors and spokespeople for the disadvantaged and the nonelites. This was the role that both the fifteenth-century jurist Muḥammad al-Maghīlī (d. 1504) and the sixteenth-century jurist Aḥmad Bābā al-Tinbuktī (d.1627) carved out for themselves and the role that 'Uthmān b. Fodiye (d.1817) initially tried to fill in the Hausa city-state of Gobir before initiating his jihad at the beginning of the nineteenth

8 For a discussion of this debate, see El Hamel, *Black Morocco,* 60–108.

9 For a discussion on the tension between Muslim rulers and scholars see Hallaq, *The Origins and Evolution of Islamic Law*, 178–94.

century. Moreover, the average citizen often viewed scholars as role models for their piety, rectitude, and education and looked to them for guidance and practical advice on how to conduct themselves ethically, including on issues of enslavement. Even though they took different approaches to the relationship between a scholar and government, for al-Maghīlī and Aḥmad Bābā this adviser role can be seen in their career trajectories and the nature of their writings that were often in response to pressing issues raised by members of the political and trading elite.[10] Al-Maghīlī actively sought to advise rulers in Tuwāt, Songhay, and Kano and to be part of their courts. Indeed, al-Maghīlī's sojourn at the Songhay court in Gao revealed deep intellectual divisions between late fifteenth-century Gao court clerics, Timbuktu jurists, and himself. Bābā, by contrast, stayed true to the Timbuktu tradition and waited for rulers and policymakers to seek him out for advice.[11]

As Muslims, precolonial West African Muslim scholars of the southern Sahara, Sahel, and Sudan were tied into the intellectual discourse of the greater Islamic world yet were concerned with the problems of their particular place and time. These scholars were both influenced by and influenced intellectual thought throughout the Islamic world. Their intellectual thinking was dynamic and adaptable to the issues of time and place. West African scholars were fully a part of what Asad terms the Islamic "discursive tradition."[12] They employed the Islamic canon to develop solutions to issues in their societies and viewed the Islamic canon as Reese describes it as a "living body of knowledge continuously employed and interpreted."[13] Treatises of non-West African Muslim scholars that became influential in

10 See, for example, Hunwick, *Sharī'a in Songhay*; al-Maghīlī, *Taj al-Din yajib 'ala-mulūk*; Hunwick, "Al-Maghīlī and the Jews of Tuwāt"; Hunwick and Harrak, *Mi 'rāj al-Ṣu'ūd;* Lovejoy, "The Context of Enslavement in West Africa"; Cleaveland, "Ahmad Baba al-Tinbukti and his Islamic Critique of Racial Slavery in the Maghrib."

11 For more on the relationship between Gao and Timbuktu scholars in the Songhay Empire as well as a-Maghīlī's impact, see Blum and Fisher, "Love for Three Oranges, or, the Akiya's Dilemma"; Gomez, *African Dominion*, 193–257.

12 Hasad, *The Idea of an Anthropology of Islam.*

13 Reese, "Islam in Africa/Africans and Islam," 19. See also Kane, *Beyond Timbuktu*; Masquelier, *Women and Islamic Revival in a West African Town*; and Loimeier, *Between Social Skills and Marketable Skills* for more articulation of the idea of Islamic intellectual thought as dynamic response to the issues of a specific time and place.

West Africa did so because they resonated with the West African political/intellectual milieu and not because outside scholarship was deemed in any way as being superior. In this regard the Sahara was not a barrier nor indeed was it a bridge bypassing the desert and linking North Africa and West Africa.[14] In terms of intellectual exchange, a more useful conception of the Sahara is as a borderland region. As Evan Haefeli explains, a borderland is a region where "autonomous peoples of different cultures are bound together by a greater, multi-imperial context."[15] James McDougall draws upon conceptions of North American borderlands to help explain the connection between ecological and political change in the Sahara. As he points out the conception of a borderland as a region of competition for territorial sovereignty, access to resources, and jurisdiction over people, helps explain political and economic processes of the Sahara and also of the Sahel/Sudan.[16] The notion of the Sahara as a borderland region is also a useful concept for understanding the development and transmission of intellectual thought and ideas between the Maghrib, Sahara, and Sahel/Sudan. Unlike H. T. Norris, whose conception of Saharan intellectual discourse was about how Saharans accepted, rejected or negotiated with "Arab" (Maghrib) culture, and which is therefore hierarchal and privileges "Arab" thought, the concept of a borderland allows more room and more agency for indigenous Saharan, Sahel and Sudanese intellectual thought and their contributions to Islamic discourse.[17] Sahelian scholars such as Bābā in the sixteenth and seventeenth centuries and Sudanese scholars such as 'Uthmān b. Fodiye in the eighteenth and nineteenth centuries engaged with the scholarly discourse throughout West and northwest Africa and contributed to the scholarship of the greater Islamic world. West African scholars made a particularly strong contribution to the study of tafsīr (exegesis) with especially prominent texts being Muḥammad al-Yadāli b. al-Mukhtār b. Maḥam Sa'id al-Daymāni's (d. 1753) *al-Dhahab*

---

14 The concept of the Sahara as a bridge has primarily been utilized in terms of economic history. See Hopkins, *An Economic History of West Africa*, especially chapter 3, 78–124; Lydon, *On-Trans-Saharan Trails*; Austen, *Trans-Saharan Africa in World History*.

15 Haefeli, "A Note on the Use of North American Borderlands," 1224.

16 James McDougall, "Frontiers, Borderlands, and Saharan/World History." For other ways the Sahara has been conceptualized, see Horden, "Situations Both Alike? Connectivity, the Mediterranean, the Sahara"; and E. Ann McDougall, "On Being Saharan."

17 Norris, *The Arab Conquest of the Western Sahara*.

al-ibrīz fi tafsīr al-kitāb al-'azīz and 'Abdullāhi b. Fodiye's (d. 1829) *Ḍiyā' al-ta'wil fi ma'ānī 'l-tanzīl.*[18]

The vast majority of scholars in Islamic West Africa and the Maghrib, including al-Maghīlī who promulgated the Mālikī madh'hab in Hausaland, Bābā who wrote the most important African Islamic treatise on enslavement prior to the nineteenth century, 'Uthmān and 'Abdullāhi b. Fodiye who led the Sokoto jihad, and 'Umar Taal who led the Umarian jihad, were trained in Mālikī law. Mālik b. Anas's (d. 795) interpretation of law is one of the four surviving schools of Sunni Islamic law. The other surviving *madhāhib* are the Ḥanafī, Shāfi'ī, and Ḥanbalī schools of law. Mālik's treatise on Islamic law, *al-Muwaṭṭā'* (The smoothed path) was written about 767 and was the first book written on Islamic jurisprudence. Mālik wrote *al-Muwaṭṭā'* as a basic law manual but also to address the legal and political issues of the early 'Abbasid era. In formulating his law code, Mālik emphasized the Qu'ran, hadith (recorded deeds of the Prophet Muḥammad), and the ijma' (the consensus of jurists) of eighth-century Medina.[19] The fourteenth-century historian 'Abd al-Raḥman b. Khaldūn (d.1406) credits the popularity of the Mālikī madh'hab in the Maghrib to its straightforward and egalitarian principles and to the influence of Medina Mālikī scholars on early West African pilgrims performing the haj.[20] Mansour H. Mansour, in his study of the spread of Mālikī madh'hab in the Maghrib, categorically rejects Khaldūn's assessment. Instead, Mansour argues that the Mālikī madh'hab prevailed due to the early dominance of Mālikī scholars such as the ninth-century scholar Saḥnūn b. Sa'id al-Tanūkhī (d. c. 854) and the tenth-century scholar 'Abdullah b. Abī Zayd al-Qayrawānī (d. 996) at al-Qayrawan, the numerical superiority of Mālikī scholars in the Maghrib, due in part to the Mālikī dominance of al-Qayrawan, versus adherents to the other Sunni madhāhib; and ultimately the defeat of Khariji and Shi'a states in North Africa by the mid-eleventh century.[21] Joseph Schacht attributes the popularity of the Mālikī madh'hab and of the *Muwaṭṭā'* to the fact that Mālik took a centrist approach on disputed issues.[22] In West Africa, the Mālikī madh'hab was originally introduced in Ancient Ghana by the twelfth century by Almoravid traders

18 For a discussion of prominent texts in West Africa see Hall and Stewart, "The Historic 'Core Curriculum' and the Book Market in Islamic West Africa."

19 Mansour, *The Maliki School of Law*, 15.

20 Abd al-Raḥman ibn Khaldūn, *Kitāb al-ibar*, 1:810–11.

21 Mansour, *The Maliki School of Law*, 45–75.

22 Schacht, "Malik b. Anas."

and by the sixteenth century had spread throughout West Africa, initially through the religious and legal education system in the region. Al-Maghīlī is often credited with spreading the Mālikī school of law in Hausaland when he was an advisor to the Sarkin of Kano, Muḥammad Rumfa, in the late fifteenth century.

The importance of Mālik to the understanding and implementation of law in western Africa is exemplified by the minimum education requirements for teachers (karamoko) in the middle Senegal River Valley. These minimum requirements included a thorough understanding of Mālik's *al-Muwaṭṭā'*, which was his comprehensive corpus of his interpretation of all aspects of Islamic civil and criminal law.[23] Indeed, prior to becoming a Qu'ranic teacher in Satina, Fuuta Jalon, Taal's education had included manuals of Mālik's *al-Muwaṭṭā'*, other legal texts and the memorization of the Qu'ran and the hadith collections of al-Bukhārī.[24] Mālik's *al-Muwaṭṭā'* was also a basic education requirement for the Soninke Jakhanke clerical lineage. The Jakhanke, originating in the Ancient Ghana town of Jagha (Ibn Bāṭṭūṭa's Zāgha) but whose members had spread throughout the western Sudan, is considered to be one of the oldest groupings of clerical lineages in West Africa. The Jankhanke scholarly tradition is most associated with the late fifteenth- to early sixteenth-century scholar, al-Ḥājj Salīm Suwarī Sīse (Cissé). Sīse is credited with setting the basic education requirements for Jankhanke clerics. Along with Mālik's *al-Muwaṭṭā'* these also included the late fifteenth- to early sixteenth-century text *Tafsīr al-Jalālayn*, and the Almoravid Ceuta scholar and judge 'Iyaḍ b. Mūsā's, (d. 1149), *Kitāb al-shifā' bi-ta'rif ḥuqūq al-muṭṭafā*.[25] According to Muḥammad Kabā Sagnanughu, a member of the

23 See Wilks, "The Transmission of Islamic Learning in the Western Sudan"; and Levitzion, "The Eighteenth Century Background to the Islamic Revolutions in West Africa." It was Mālik's students who founded the Mālikī school of law that is followed throughout West and Northwest Africa. For more on the transmission of learning in the Islamic world see chapters in the same volume.

24 See Martin, *Muslim Brotherhoods in 19th Century Africa*, 68–69; Robinson, *The Holy War of Umar Tal*, 57; Al Habib, "Cheikh el-Hadj Omar Foutiyyu Tall (1794–1864)," 112–13. For a recent discussion of al-Bukhārī see Brown, *The Canonization of al-Bukhārī and Muslim.*

25 For more on the Jakhanke see Sanneh, *The Jakhanke Muslim Clerics*; see also Wilks "The Juula and the Expansion of Islam into the Forest." For more on Qāḍī 'Iyaḍ b. Mūsā's intellectual influence on the interpretation of Mālikī law in the Maghrib and West Africa see Gómez-Rivas, "Qāḍī 'Iyāḍ (d. 544/1149)." *Tafsīr al-Jalālayn* a popular Qur'anic commentary was written mostly by Jalāl

Sagnanughu clerical lineage whose members resided throughout the Upper Niger Valley, Mālik's *al-Muwaṭṭā'*, the *Tafsīr al-Jalālayn* and 'Iyaḍ's *Shifā'* were also important texts in his own education.[26] Comparatively, while the education requirements in Timbuktu were more flexible than that of Jakhanke scholars, they shared a common base. As 'Abd al-Raḥman b. 'Abd Allāh al-Sa'dī noted in the *Tārīkh al-Sūdān*, (1656) his own education in Timbuktu included not only a thorough study of Mālik's *al-Muwaṭṭā'* but also of his *Tas'hīl.*[27]

Yet, while full copies of Mālik's *al-Muwaṭṭā'* and of other foundational (or original) texts were available throughout West Africa, the more common way to study the material of foundational texts was through abridgements and versifications and by the exegeses of the abridgements and versifications. Three fiqh manuals that were particularly popular in West Africa were al-Qayrawānī's *Risāla*, the Egyptian scholar, Khalīl b. Isḥāq's al-Jundī (d. 1374) *Mukhtaṣar al-shaykh Khalīl,* and the Andalusian scholar Muḥammad b. Muḥammad b. 'Āṣim al-Gharnāṭi (d. 1427) *Tuḥfat al-ḥukkām fi nakt wa-'l-aḥkām*. The *Risāla* was a synopsis of Mālikī law. Khalīl's *Mukhtaṣar* is an abridgment of the prominent Mālikī jurist and grammarian 'Umar ibn al-Ḥājib's (d. 1249) *Mukhtaṣar al-far'i.* Āṣim's *Tuḥfat al-ḥukkām* was a popular manual of Mālikī fiqh. Popular commentaries on Khalīl's *Mukhtaṣar* included the one by al-Zurqāni's (d. 1688) *Sharḥ 'Abd al-Bāqī li-mukhtaṣar Khalīl,* and the commentary on al-Zurqāni's commentary by the Moroccan scholar Muḥammad b. al-Ḥasan al-Bannāni al-Fāsi (d. 1780), *Fatḥ al-rabbānī*

---

al-Dīn Muḥammad b. Aḥmad Maḥallī (d.1459) and completed by his student Abd al-Raḥmān al-Suyūtī after Jalāl al-Dīn's death.

26 Muḥammad Kabā Sagnanughu was a member of the Sagnanughu clerical lineage and belonged to the *Qādiriyya ṭarīqa*. Originally the Sagnanughu were considered to be Soninke but by the seventeenth century were considered Mandinke. Kabā Sagnanughu, who identified as Mandinke, was from the Tinkisso River Valley, which is a tributary of the Niger River. He was taken captive while en route to Timbuktu to continue his education in fiqh, sold to the Upper Guinea coast, and enslaved in Jamaica in 1777 where he wrote his memoir, *Kitāb al-ṣalāt* c. 1820. See Daddi Addoun and Lovejoy, "The Arabic Manuscript of Muhammad Kaba Sanghanughu of Jamaica, c. 1820" and Daddi Addoun and Lovejoy, "Muḥammad Kabā Saghanughu and the Muslim Community of Jamaica."

27 Hunwick, *Timbuktu and the Songhay Empire,* 65–66.

fī mā dhalala 'an-hu al-Zurqānī.[28] Indeed, even though Mālik's *Muwaṭṭā'* formed the base of a West African legal education, the abridgements and commentaries were especially important in the West African scholarly tradition. Commenting on the importance of Khalīl's *Mukhtaṣar* and the commentaries needed to study it, Muhammad Bencheneb stated that the "Mukhtasar, then, so obscure because of its conciseness that it can only be understood by means of a commentary, is the most renowned manual in the countries of the Muslim West, where, to some extent replacing the Muwatta' of Malik and the Midawwana of Sahnun."[29]

The authority of foundational texts and the promulgation of the dominance of certain texts were solidified through the system of educating scholars. Children received their basic education first at home and then at Qu'ranic schools.[30] However, throughout Muslim West Africa, advanced religious and legal education was based on a system of individual or small group tutorship where students usually learned from one or up to four teachers. In Timbuktu and its surrounding villages, scholars usually had no more than three or four teachers. For example, in the sixteenth century, the Tuareg Timbuktu scholar Bābā was educated by his father and by other members of his prominent scholarly family, the Aqīt, but his main teacher with whom he studied for ten years and from whom he learned Qu'ranic exegesis and hadith was the Juula scholar Muḥammad Baghayu'u.[31] Juula scholars, like scholars throughout West Africa, were usually educated through the isnād (sanad sing) system, where a student learned through a particular chain of authority through his teacher (who had been taught by a scholar before him) and formed an unbroken chain of scholarship into the past and preferably back

28 Hall and Stewart, "The Historic 'Core Curriculum' and the Book Market in Islamic West Africa," 132–33, 164–68. Hall and Stewart did a comprehensive study of literary works held in prominent libraries in West Africa in order ascertain common texts studied throughout the region.

29 Bencheneb, "Khalil b. Ishak." Saḥnūn b. Sa'id (d. 855) wrote the second book on Mālikī jurisprudence, *Al-Mudawwana*, following Mālik's *Muwaṭṭā'*. See Talbi, "Sahnun."

30 For a discussion of Muslim education in a sedentary agriculturalist West African setting, see Brenner, *Controlling Knowledge, Religion, Power and Schooling in a West African Muslim Society*; also see Ware, *The Walking Qu'ran*; and in a nomadic West African setting, see El Hamel, "The Transmission of Knowledge in Moorish Society."

31 See El Hamel, "The Transmission of Islamic Knowledge in Moorish Society," 78. See also footnote 57.

to the Prophet Muḥammad. In West Africa, isnād crossed both racial and ethnic lines. Biḍān (white) students often studied with sūdānī (Black) teachers and vice versa. Students were also willing to travel throughout West Africa to study with specific teachers. For example, an important teacher of the first Almamy of Fuuta Toro, Abdūl Qādir Kan, was the woman biḍān western Sahara scholar Khadīja b. Muḥammad al-ʿĀqil who specialized in Arabic grammar, theology, and Mālikī law.[32] In many ways the isnād system led to a decentralized educational process since teachers were free to develop their curricula according to their own belief of what was important. Yet, the system was also integrative since the most prestigious teachers shared a common educational background where the more advanced students, such as Kabā Saghanughu before his captivity, enslavement, and deportation to Jamaica in 1777 interrupted his education, moved on to the larger educational centers. In West Africa the vast majority of these isnād chains, certainly the most prestigious chains, trace back to Mālik and through him to the Prophet Muḥammad.[33] Moreover, the vast majority of eighteenth- and nineteenth-century members of the *Qādiriyya ṭarīqa*, of whom Kabā Saghanughu, the Fodiye, and Aḥmad Lobbo (1773–1845) (who led a jihad that founded the Caliphate of Ḥamdallāhi) were members, traced their isnād back to either the Qādiriyya saint Sīdī Mukhtār al-Kunti al-Kabīr (1729–1811) or to Sīdī Mukhtār's teacher, Sīdī ʿAli b. al-Najīb (1679–1757).[34]

This education system is also exemplified by the education of ʿUthmān b. Fodiye and his brother ʿAbdullāhi, who were educated in the Hausa city-state of Gobir in the latter half of the eighteenth century. The Fodiawa were a scholarly Fulbe family who traced their family roots to Mūsā Jokollo, who was said to have left Fuuta Toro in the fifteenth century due to religious persecution. Their name "Fodiye" means "learned man" in Fulfulde. The Fodiawa, who were part of the larger Fulbe migration from Fuuta Toro into the central Sudan region that began by the fifteenth century (at the latest), eventually settled in Gobir.[35] The brothers' principal teachers were their uncles ʿUthmān Binduri and Muḥammad Sambo and the scholars

32 Ware, *The Walking Qu'rān*, 130.

33 Saad, *Social History of Timbuktu*, 73.

34 Batran, *The Qadiryya Brotherhood in West Africa,* 58–91.

35 For a more detailed discussion of Fulbe settlement in Hausaland, see Adebayo, "Of Man and Cattle," 1–21. See also Last, *The Sokoto Caliphate*, xx–xxxiii; and Hiskett, *The Sword of Truth*, 15–17. ʿAbdullāhi b. Fodiye includes a history of his family and the Fulbe in *Tazyīn al-waraqāt* (1813).

Muḥammad b. Rāji and Jibrīl b. 'Umar. Through their teachers, the brothers were linked to the greater scholarship of the Islamic world. Not only did they receive the full corpus of a West African Mālikī education, but through the isnād that 'Uthmān received from Rāji and Jibrīl, their networks led back to Abu Ḥanīfa, the founder of the Ḥanīfa madh'hab, preponderant in the Mughal Empire and non-African Ottoman territories.[36]

However, the education system was flexible enough to integrate new scholarship. In the major urban centers such as Timbuktu, chains of learning were susceptible to outside influences, both local and foreign, through contact with the Maghrib and Egypt. It was always possible for local Timbuktu isnād to be overshadowed or usurped by newer or more prestigious outside ones. These chains of scholarship, however, linked scholars closely to their predecessors and provided a common basis of knowledge over wide geographic regions. Indeed, as Elias Saad states in reference to Timbuktu, "The lines of transmission [of learning] from one generation to another did not branch out in mutually exclusive directions, but rather crossed each other in complex patterns."[37] Moreover, as exemplified by both al-Maghīlī and Bābā, prominent scholars traveled throughout the region, teaching a number of students, and there was a constant exchange of views and scholarship. Furthermore, while ṭarīqa affiliation was important, whether it was the dominant Qādiriyya or, later, the less numerous Tījāniyya which was introduced to West Africa at the end of the eighteenth century, their influence on the education process was limited to the addition of their respective texts to the corpus of advanced study, and did not alter the shared foundation in Mālikī law, nor did it exclude the study of works produced by members of other ṭurūq.[38]

Throughout West Africa, it was the common training in Mālikī law through isnād that bound together scholars of different ethnic and educational backgrounds. Whether they were trained locally or had moved on to regional centers such as Walata or Katsina, or the major centers of Djenne,

36 For more on the received isnād of 'Uthmān and 'Abdullāhi and of their education and scholarly connection see Reichmuth, "Murtaḍā al-Zabīdī and the Africans"; and Hunwick, *Arabic Literature of Africa*, 2:53–57.

37 Saad, *Social History of Timbuktu*, 60. For more on education systems in the western and central Sūdān see Wilks, "The Transmission of Islamic Learning in the Western Sudan"; Hunwick, "Secular Power and Religious Authority in Muslim Society." For more on intellectual and information exchange see the articles in Wise, *The Desert Shore: Literatures of the Sahel.*

38 Saad, *Social History of Timbuktu*, 73.

Timbuktu, and Pir, the practice of Mālikī law, and the common association through the Qādiriyya or, later, the Tijāniyya, provided a basic foundation of intellectual analysis, a shared sense of important works and authors, and a common intellectual background for debate.[39] Basic training included tawḥid (theology), fiqh (Islamic legal theory/jurisprudence), tafsīr (exegesis/Qu'rānic commentary), hadith, and Arabic. By the late eighteenth century, common curriculum texts included Mālik b. Anas (d. 746) *Muwaṭṭa'*, Muḥammad b. Yusuf al-Sanūsī's (d. 1486) three creeds, Khalīl's *Mukhtaṣar* and al-Qaḍī 'Iyāḍ's *Kitāb al-shifā' bi-ta'rif ḥuqūq al-muṣṭafā*, al-Maghīlī's *Taj al-Din yajib 'ala-mulūk* and Bābā's *Mi'rāj al-Ṣu'ūd*.[40]

Demonstrating its textual dominance, Bābā's treatise on slavery was widely taught throughout West Africa and the Maghrib in the seventeenth and eighteenth centuries. 'Uthmān and 'Abdullāhi b. Fodiye's most influential teacher, the Tuareg scholar, Jibrīl b. 'Umar, relied upon Bābā's analysis and the analyses upon whom Bābā based his interpretations, to challenge the infringement of the rights of freeborn Muslims to protection against enslavement in eighteenth century Aïr and Hausaland. It is therefore not surprising that due to both the system of education and to the political and judicial interests of 'Uthmān and his relatives that references to both al-Maghīlī and Bābā as well as to the corpus of Mālikī jurisprudence can be found throughout the writings of both 'Uthmān and 'Abdullāhi and that these two scholars were influenced by their thought processes.[41] West African scholars shared a common corpus of foundational texts on which to base their opinions and to engage each other in intellectual debate.

39 Hunwick, "Secular Power and Religious Authority," 180–81. As the close relationship and shared common concerns between 'Umar Taal and Muḥammad Bello demonstrates, members of the Tijāniyya and Qādiriyya ṭurūq also shared a similar interpretation and knowledge base. See 'Umar Taal *Bayān mā waqa'a* for Taal's intellectual influences.

40 For more on common texts in circulation throughout West Africa see Hall and Stewart, "The Historic 'Core Curriculum' and the Book Market in Islamic West Africa."

41 See, for example, Uthmān b. Fodiye *Nūr albāb*, *Kitāb al-farq*, *Wathīqat ahl al-sūdān* and *Tanbīh al-ikwān*, Abdullāhi b. Fodiye *Tazyīn al-waraqāt* and *Ḍiyā' al-ḥukkām*; see also Lovejoy, "The Context of Enslavement in West Africa:Aḥmad Bābā and the Ethics of Slavery," 21.

Muslim Scholars and the Issue of Legal and Illegal Enslavement and Its Remedy

According to the Mālikī madh'hab, a person could only be a slave if they were born into slavery or if they were enslaved after they were captured during a jihad. A jihad, a legal war, is a war of self-defense conducted against non-Muslims. The Mālikī madh'hab also permitted a proselytizing war against non-Muslims if the target community refused to convert or, if they were ahl al-kitāb (people of the Book), refused to either convert or to pay the jizya (poll-tax).[42] Anyone, except a freeborn Muslim, could be enslaved if they were taken captive during a "legal" war. The Sunni Islamic schools of law agree, though, including the Mālikī madh'hab, that enslavement is only one option for dealing with prisoners of war, the others being execution, ransom, exchange against Muslim prisoners, taxation (applicable to the ahl al-kitāb) and free release.[43] Emphasizing that freedom was viewed as the natural condition of an individual, the nineteenth-century Indian scholar Syed Ameer Ali remarked that according to the Qur'an, the possession of a slave was only permissible with the capture of the person in a legitimate war against non-Muslims and that the enslavement was to serve the purpose of saving the life of the captive.[44] This was similar to Christian belief and justification of the enslavement of non-Christians.

From the founding of Islam there were scholars who argued against slavery. Arguments used by scholars against slavery included that there was no legal precedent for the forms of enslavement practiced during the expansion of the Caliphate; that while the Qur'an did not explicitly forbid slavery, the Prophet's example demonstrated that he favored manumission of slaves and the eventual abolition of slavery; and that the legal basis for war after the

42 Khalīl b. Isḥāq al-Jundī. *Abréjé de la loi musulmane selon le rite de l'imām Mālek*, 1:206–15.

43 Khalīl b. Isḥāq al-Jundī, 206–15. Further, the decision on what to do with one's share of captives rested fully with the owner. For example, after one battle during the Moroccan invasion of Songhay, the qadi 'Ali ben Abdallah chose to free his captives whereas the qadi al-Mustafa brought his to Timbuktu and sold them. See Abd al Rahmān al-S'adi, *Tārikh al-Sūdān*, 275–76. The *ahl al-kitāb* (or "people of the book") include those who believe in the monotheistic religions that preceded Islam: Zoroastrianism (subject of debate), Judaism, and Christianity.

44 Ali, *The Personal Law of the Mahommedans, According to All Schools*, 38.

Prophet's death was weak, which therefore undermined the Sunni madhāhib approved means of acquiring new slaves.[45] Indeed, jurists who argued that Islam was fundamentally against slavery interpreted chapter 47, verse 4, of the Qu'ran as recommending the freeing of war captives either through free release or the payment of ransom. "Now when you meet [in war] those who are bent on denying the truth, smite their necks until you overcome them fully, and then tighten their bonds, but thereafter [set them free] either by an act of grace or against ransom, so that the burden or war may be lifted."[46] This verse can be interpreted as encouraging the ransoming of prisoners held by one's forces. The Qu'ran forbade enslavement for the punishment of a crime or as payment for a debt, and it was forbidden for a free person to sell themself or their children into slavery.[47] According to those who argue for an antislavery bias in the Qu'ran and hadith, it was only later, with the development of the Sunni madhāhib (which included non-Qu'ranic sources of law), in conjunction with sociopolitical realities that encouraged the use of slave labor, that Islamic jurisprudence became more accepting of slavery. Jonathan Brockopp argues that it was in the centuries after the Prophet Muḥammad's death that the laws regarding slavery evolved substantially from the Qu'ran in terms of "vocabulary, emphasis and scope."[48] Yet, even if the Sunni madhāhib, and the scholars who established them, evolved in their thinking to permit enslavement and slavery, there continued to be scholars who argued against the legality of enslavement and slavery. Even though scholars who desired the outright abolition of slavery were always in the minority up until the twentieth century, even scholars who condoned slavery emphasized that the natural condition of a person is freedom and that enslavement could only be imposed on a select few under specific conditions.[49]

45 Clarence-Smith, *Islam and the Abolition of Slavery*, 22–45. See also Ghazal, "Debating Slavery and Abolition in the Arab Middle East."

46 Asad, *The Message of the Qu'ran*, 883–84.

47 See Lewis, *Race and Slavery in the Middle East*, 3–12.

48 Brockopp, *Early Maliki Law*, xviii. Unlike the Sunni madhāhib, Shi'i fiqh continued to view slavery as a temporary condition and recommended that slaves be freed after a maximum of seven years in slavery. See, for example, the writings of the twelfth-century Shi'i Iraqi scholar Ja'far ibn al-Hasan al-Muhaqqiq al-Hilli, *Droit Musulman:Recuil de lois concernant les Musulmans Schyites*, 2:109.

49 Clarence-Smith, *Islam and the Abolition of Slavery*; Ghazal, "Debating Slavery and Abolition in the Arab Middle East," 139–55. For a discussion of the interpretation of Mālikī law in terms of slavery in the nineteenth-century western

An important strain of Islamic thought viewed ransoming of prisoners as both a legitimate means for dealing with captives held by one's forces and as a useful way to free one's brethren from captivity and possible enslavement. Informing West African scholars' opinions on ransoming were the opinions of the aforementioned Egyptian scholar Khalīl and the Andalusian scholar Muḥammad b. Aḥmad b. Juzay (d. 1340) on the subject. Their texts were included in the general corpus for West African students. Uthmān b. Fodiye referred to both men in forming his own policies on ransoming in the late eighteenth and early nineteenth centuries. Both Khalīl and Juzay accepted the legitimacy of ransoming captives. They were concerned about who should pay for the ransoms. While al-Maghīlī would later emphasize the role of the state and of rulers in paying ransoms, Khalīl and Juzay distributed responsibility between the captive and their families and the community at large. Khalīl outlined his opinions on ransoming in his *Mukhtaṣar al-shaykh Khalīl,* which was a foundational text of jurisprudence in the core curriculum for Muslim scholars in West Africa and generated a number of commentaries that were also studies in the region. In *Mukhtaṣar al-shaykh Khalīl,* Khalīl devotes almost as much attention to the law regarding the ransoming of war prisoners as he does to their enslavement.[50] Juzay outlined his opinions in *Qawānīn al-aḥkām al-sharʿiya wa-masāʾil al-furūʿ al-fiqhiya.* Juzay and Khalīl shared similar views on the obligation of Muslims to ransom fellow Muslims but differed slightly on who was responsible for paying the ransom. Juzay argued that the payment of a ransom was first the responsibility of the captive. If the captive was unable to raise the ransom fee, then the imam became responsible for paying the ransom and should access the necessary funds first out of the State Treasury, second by raising the money from the Muslim community, and third by compelling non-Muslims to pay the fee. By contrast, Khalīl argued that the ransom fee should first be raised from the *fay'* (conquered peoples), second from among the Muslim community, and lastly from the captive's own assets. Khalīl reasoned that it was primarily the responsibility for the state and Muslims at large to pay the ransoms of Muslims because the ransom of an individual Muslim and his return to the community benefited the community more than the individual

Sahara/Sahel see Lydon, "Slavery, Exchange and Islamic Law: A Glimpse from the Archives of Mali and Mauritania."

50 Khalīl b. Isḥāq al-Jundī, *Mukhtaṣar,* 1:207–18; Khalīl b. Isḥāq al-Jundī, *Abréjé de la loi musulmane selon le rite de l'imām Mālek.*

captive Muslim and further that it was usually easier for the community to raise the ransom fee than an individual.[51]

Juzay and Khalīl also differed on the matter of compensation for individuals who paid the ransoms of Muslims. Juzay asserted that an individual who paid the ransom of another Muslim with the captive's consent could claim the amount from the freed captive. If the Muslim captive had not consented to being ransomed, the payer could still claim the ransom price from the freed captive if the captive was rich—or from the State Treasury if they were poor. However, if the person being ransomed was the spouse, father, mother, son, grandfather, paternal or maternal uncle, brother, sister, or nephew of the ransom payer, then the ransom payer could not claim compensation unless agreed to before the ransom had been paid. According to Khalīl, the ransom payer could claim compensation from the freed captive regardless of whether he or she was rich or poor unless the payment of ransom was intended to be an act of charity or if the person being ransomed was within the prohibited degrees of marriage.[52] The responsibility for the payment of ransom fees would be a subject of debate and disagreement in the nineteenth-century West African jihad states. However, it is clear, as the following chapters will show, that the ransoming of freeborn Muslims benefited religious authorities who had ethical and religious objections to the enslavement of freeborn Muslims, state officials who could not prevent illegal enslavement, the holders of wrongly captive freeborn Muslims who were compensated for the loss of their investment, and the captive freeborn Muslim facing enslavement who regained his or her freedom. Even though they disagreed on the order of responsibility for paying ransoms, the important point is that these two influential jurists in West Africa agreed that ransoming was an important and legitimate remedy for illegal enslavement.

West African scholars must have been aware of abolitionist arguments rooted in interpretation of Islamic law. However, the West African discourse centered on facilitating what was perceived to be legal enslavement while preventing what was considered illegal captivity and enslavement including the role of ransoming as a remedy for illegal captivity and potential enslavement. Informing the debate on legal and illegal enslavement in Islamic West Africa were not only local interpretations of Mālikī law but also the North African discourse on race and slavery. The West African debate on legal and

51 Muḥammad b. Aḥmad b. Juzay, *al-Qawānīn al-fiqhiyya*; Khalīl b. Isḥāq al-Jundī, *Mukhtaṣar*, 218.

52 Juzay, *al-Qawānīn al-fiqhiyya*; Khalīl b. Isḥāq al-Jundī, *Mukhtaṣar*, 218.

illegal enslavement was informed by the interpretation of core texts and by local spiritual and social contexts.[53] In the West African discourse surrounding captivity and enslavement, issues of debate included who was considered to be a Muslim, the onus for proving freeborn Muslim status, and the fate of illegally captive individuals. In the southern Sahara and in West Africa we see that scholars both rebutted a North African political argument that equated "blackness" with original unbelief and therefore "non-Muslimness" and enslavement and adamantly reiterated that the only reason for enslavement was personal unbelief in Islam.

North African discussions of racial difference and the meaning of racial difference were dominated by the Hamitic thesis and the theory of climes. Racial prejudice was emphatically condemned by the Prophet Muḥammad and in the Qu'ran, however, color prejudice was evident in the writings of early Muslim writers. Bernard Lewis argues that the racial prejudice aspect of the Hamitic thesis was innate to Arab culture whereas Chouki El Hamel argues that the Arab Muslim community picked it up from early Christian and Jewish converts to Islam.[54] Nevertheless, the origin in Arab Muslim thought, the Hamitic thesis as an explanation for color difference and color prejudice was evident from at least the writings of Abū 'Abd Allāh Wahb b. Munabbih (d. 728–32), a Persian convert to Islam from Yemen. According to the Baghdadi scholar Abū Muḥammad 'Abd Allāh b. Qutayba al-Dīnawarī (d. 889), Wahb b. Munabbih believed that the Hamitic thesis explained color difference. Accordingly, Wahb b. Munabbih believed that "Ḥām b. Nūḥ was a white man having a beautiful face and form. But Allāh (to Him belongs glory and power) changed his colour and the colour of his descendants because of his father's curse. Ḥām went off, followed by his children. They are the Sūdān."[55] For supporters of the Hamitic thesis, it is unclear as to what event led to Ham's curse. According to the medieval historian Shams al-Dīn al-Anṣārī al-Dimashqī (1256–1327) either Ham was cursed because he had sexual intercourse with his wife while on board Noah's ship during the flood or because Ham had seen Noah's genitals. Either way, according to the Hamitic thesis, Ham and his descendants were cursed and made black.[56]

53 Reese, "Islam in Africa/Africans and Islam," 23.

54 Lewis, *Race and Slavery in the Middle East,* 123; El Hamel, *Black Morocco,* 64.

55 Abū Muḥammad 'Abd Allāh b. Qutayba al-Dīnawarī, *Kitāb al-ma'ārif,* i15. See also Khoury, "Wahb b. Munabbih"; Dodge, *The Fihrist of Al-Nadim*m 1:42, 203, 2:1121.

56 "Shams al-Dīn al-Anṣārī al-Dimashqī," 212.

It was not much of a leap for Arab and Persian Muslim writers to turn the Ham story from an explanation of color difference to a justification for color prejudice and enslavement of "blacks." According to the Persian scholar, Abū Ja'far Muḥammad b. Jarīr al-Ṭabarī (d. 927) one of the most influential writers of his generation, "Noah prayed that the hair of Ham's descendants would not grow beyond their ears, and wherever his descendants met the children of Shem, the latter would enslave them."[57] Al-Ṭabarī considered Shem as the forefather of the Arabs, Persians, and Greeks; Japtheth as the forefather of the Turks, Slavs, Gog, and Magog; and Ham as the forefather of the Copts, Sudanese, and Berbers.[58] According to the Baghdad scholar Abū al-Ḥasan 'Alī b. al-Ḥusayn al-Mas'ūdī (d. 956), "the traditionalists say that Nūḥ, peace upon him, cursed Ḥām praying that his face should become ugly and black and that his descendants should become slaves to the progeny of Sām. [. . .] They are the various peoples of the Sūdān."[59]

In seventeenth- to nineteenth-century southern Sahara, Sahel, and Sudan, color difference was recognized, but the meaning of that color difference changed depending on place and time. Generally, in the Maghrib, the Sahara, and the Sahel conceptions of phonotypical difference as well as religion were used as a means to categorize difference. In the Sudan, generally, ethnicity and religious identity were used. James Webb argues that Saharans only developed a race-based identity in the seventeenth century as desertification forced migration to the southern desert edge and into closer proximity with the Sudanese. Webb views racial identity along the desert edge developing in tandem with nomadic Saharans asserting control over agricultural Sudanese with "white" owners and "black" slaves.[60] However, as shown by Bruce Hall, conceptions of race in the southern Sahara and Sahel region of West Africa changed over time as local populations integrated North African (and later European) ideas about race into their understandings of the significance of color difference.[61] As shown by Hall, after the seventeenth century, notions of racial difference became important to the social discourse

57 Brinner, *The History of al-Ṭabarī*, 2:21.

58 Brinner, 2:21.

59 Abū al-Ḥasan 'Alī b. al-Husayn al-Mas'ūdī (attrib), *Akhbār al-zamān* in Levtzion and Hopkins, *Corpus of Early Arabic Sources for West African History*, 34.

60 Webb, *Desert Frontier*, 47–55.

61 Hall, "The Question of 'Race." Also see Hall, *A History of Race in Muslim West Africa*.

of the region as some Berber and Tuareg populations became increasingly Arabized. Moreover, racial classifications had more to do with genuine or ascribed genealogy than actual phonotypical expression of skin tone. Those who had attached themselves to Arab genealogies, no matter their skin tone, were deemed "white," and those who had not were considered "black." Yet, even as the terms used to mark racial difference (and the social implications of that difference) changed, a common feature was the negative and servile connotation of those identified as "black."[62] However, just as Blackness was being more closely associated with social inferiority in the Sahara, there was a counter-discourse in the southern Sahel and Sudan arguing that skin color and the ability to trace one's genealogy to the original Muslim community in Arabia, ought not to denote social status nor one's standing as a Muslim. West African writers of the southern Sahel/Sudan, or those who had experience in the region, were dealing with a much more ethnically diverse population where an Arab forefather, whether real or imagined, did not denote social status. It is this counter-discourse that will shape the views of nineteenth-century policymakers of the western and central Sudan. While in the northern Sahel/southern Sahara a race-based justification for enslavement would gain more traction, in the southern Sahel/Sudan region enslaveability would remain dependent on freeborn Muslim status even though attitudes changed about who a freeborn Muslim was, based on their interpretation of Islam.

Four writers who probably had the most influence on seventeenth- to nineteenth-century West African Muslim ideas on race, religious belief, and slavery were Khaldūn, ʿAbd al-Raḥmān al-Suyūṭī (d. 1505), and the aforementioned al-Maghīlī and Bābā. All four emphasized that religious identity trumped racial identity. Khaldūn, the fourteenth-century historian from Tunis, whose *Kitāb al-ʿibar* (History of the Berbers) would provide later Arabized Berbers much of the historical material needed to connect local genealogies to important Arab Muslim figures in North Africa and the Arabian Peninsula, argued that adherence to Islam outweighed all other differences.[63] In the *Muqaddima*, he fervently argued against the popular idea

62 For more on the importance of race and ensleavability, see Hall, *A History of Race in Muslim West Africa,* 209–40.

63 For discussions on how Ibn Khaldūn's *Kitāb al-ʿibar* was used by later Sahelian and Sudanese writers see Austen and Jansen, "History, Oral Transmission, and Structure in Ibn Khaldun's Chronology of Mali Rulers," 17–28; Norris, *The Arab Conquest of the Western Sahara,* 13–14; Taylor, "Of Disciples and Sultans," 23.

among thirteenth- century Arabs that Blackness was related to descent from Ham, the son of Noah who had been cursed, which therefore suggested the subsequent inferiority of Blacks and their inherent enslaveability. Instead, Khaldūn accepted the theory of climes, that skin color and barbarism were directly related to geographic location, as the explanation of color difference. In the version of the theory of climes generally accepted in Mediterranean communities at the time, the farther one moves northward or southward, the more barbaric the population.[64] Therefore, both northern European paleness and African Blackness were associated with barbarism. Khaldūn however, rejected the direct correlation between skin color and climate and argued that the barbarism produced by climate could be ameliorated through the adoption of a revealed religion.[65] For Khaldūn, the real mark of civilization was not genealogy, climate, or skin color but religious identity.

Both the Cairo scholar al-Suyūṭī and the Tlemscen (Tilimsān) scholar al-Maghīlī were influential in the development of Islamic thought in West Africa even though they represented different sides of the orthodox spectrum. Al- Suyūṭī was admired in West Africa for his command of the Islamic sciences but also for his acceptance of syncretism and local traditions in Islamic practice. His *al-Kawkab al-sāti* was a popular commentary in West Africa on 'Abd al-Wahhāb b. 'Ali b. 'Abd al-Kāfī Tāj al-Dīn al-Subkī (d. 1370), *Jam' al-jawāmi' fi'l-uṣūl*, a foundational text on the sources of jurisprudence (uṣūl al-fiqh). He was also one of the coauthors of the popular commentary on the Qu'ran, *Tafsīr al-Jalālayn.* Moreover, throughout his career al-Suyūṭī carried out a vigorous correspondence with West African scholars from his home in Cairo.[66] By contrast, even though al-Maghīlī is known for his influence in spreading Islam and for the Mālikī school of law in Hausaland, he is also known for battling against syncretic and nonorthodox practices throughout West Africa and especially in the Songhay Empire. Yet both of these men, one approaching the question from a liberal interpretation of Islam and the other, from a strict legalistic interpretation of Islam, argued that belief was the great equalizer and that the largest factor in ascertaining religious status in society was personal religious belief. Al-Suyūṭī's writings on race are

64 For more on the theory of climes see Levtzion and Hopkins discussion in *Corpus of Early Arabic Sources for West African History*, xv–xix.

65 Ibn Khaldūn, *The Muqaddimah: An Introduction to History*, 1:167.

66 For more on the biography and correspondence of al-Suyūtī see Sartain, "Jalal ad-Din As-Suyuti's Relations with the people of Takrur," 193–98; Sartain, *Jalāl al-dīn al-Suyūṭī:Biography and Background.*

basically a repetition of the prolific twelfth-century Baghdadi scholar Abū'l Faraj 'Abd al-Raḥman b. al-Jawzī's (d. 1200) but were influential in West Africa because of his reputation.[67] Al-Suyūṭī used hadith to counter negative stereotypes of Blacks and while accepting that the genealogy of Blacks could be traced to Ham, he dismisses the idea that their Black skin was the result of a curse by Noah.[68]

For al-Maghīlī, race was also a nonissue. Al-Maghīlī, who was born in the central Magrhibi city of Tilimsān (Tlemcen) in modern-day Algeria traveled extensively throughout the Maghrib, Sahara, and Sudan advising several political leaders including the Askia al-hāj Muḥammad of Songhay, Sarki Muḥammad Rumfa of Kano and the political elite of Tuwāt.[69] Al-Maghīlī was heavily influenced by the political events in the dār al-islām of the late fifteenth century, especially the loss of al-Andalūs and the expulsion of Muslims and Jews from newly Catholic Iberia. Due to these events, he took a particularly rigid view of the rights and obligations of dhimmī, protected non-Muslims, living in Muslim territories and viewed the protection of freeborn Muslims as paramount. He divided people strictly on the grounds of personal belief and nonbelief. He heavily promoted the rights and protection of Muslims while advocating discrimination against non-Muslims. Al-Maghīlī's legal opinions and advice were grounded in the fundamental principle of Islamic jurisprudence that the natural condition, and hence the default status of an individual, is that of freedom. He shared the view that a person should be presumed free unless he or she is proven to be a slave.

Similar to al-Maghīlī, Bābā's scholarship of the late sixteenth and early seventeenth centuries, which was based on his training in Mālikī law, was also heavily influenced by the events surrounding him and his personal experiences. Bābā, a Timbuktu jurist of Sanhāja origin and member of the powerful

67 Hall and Stewart, "The Historic 'Core Curriculum' and the Book Market in Islamic West Africa," 164. See al-Jawzī, *Tanwīr al-ghabash fī faḍl al-sūdān wa-'l-ḥabash.*

68 Al-Suyūṭī's defense of Blacks is outlined in his treaty, *Raf' sha'n al-ḥubshān* (Raising the status of the Ethiopians) and the abridged version, *Azhār al-'urūsh fī akhbār al-ḥubūsh* (The flowers of the throne concerning information about the Ethiopians). See al-Suyūṭī, *Raf' sha'n al-ḥubshān*; and 'Abd al-Raḥmān al-Suyūtī, *Azhār al-'urūsh fī akhbār al-ḥubūsh*, ed.'Abd Allāh 'Īsā al-Ghazālī.

69 al-Maghīlī, *Taj al-Din yajib 'ala-mulūk*, For more on his personal history see Hunwick, *Shari'a in Songhay*; Hunwick, "Al-Maghīlī and the Jews of Tuwāt"; and Batran, "A Contribution to the Biography of Shaikh Muḥammad ibn 'Abd al-Karīm ibn Muḥammad 'Umar–A'mar al-Maghīlī."

and scholarly Aqīt family, wrote his treatise after his own "illegal" captivity in Morocco following Morocco's invasion of the Songhay Empire in 1591. Bābā was one of the many Timbuktu scholars who objected and organized resistance to the Moroccan invasion and occupation of Songhay on the basis that it was illegal for one Muslim state to invade another. Morocco reacted to the resistance of the Timbuktu scholars by arresting them, deporting them, and holding them captive in Marrakesh. Other scholars managed to flee. Bābā wrote *Mi'rāj al-Ṣu'ūd* (1615) in order to rebut North African ideas concerning skin color, religious belief and enslaveability. This text, which was a series of responses to questions posed to him about slavery, became the most famous and most important work on slavery in West Africa and the Maghrib in the pre-nineteenth-century period. This treatise not only revealed the thinking and interpretation of one of the most learned and respected scholars of Timbuktu but also exposed the internal debates about enslavement within the early seventeenth-century intellectual and ruling elite in the region.[70] It is important to note that Bābā was not against slavery or enslavement per se but was against the enslavement of freeborn Muslims. Bābā not only situated his judgments within the general corpus of Mālikī law but actively engaged the scholarship of those who came before him. This can be seen in his references to important scholars such as Maḥmūd b. 'Umar b. Muḥammad Aqīt and most importantly his discussion of Makhlūfi b.'Alī b Sāliḥ al-Balbālī's (d. 1533–1534) fatwa on legal and illegal enslavement.[71] Al-Balbālī was from Tabelbala in present-day southern Algeria, studied in Walāta and Fez, and taught in Kano, Katsina, Timbuktu, and Marrakesh. Concerning slavery, and again, showing the jurist emphasis on freedom rather than enslavement in his *fatwā fi 'l—'abīd al-majlūbin* al-Balbālī argued that enslaved individuals originating from predominantly Muslim territories should be freed in order to not mistakenly enslave a freeborn Muslim.[72] Bābā's reference to Maḥmūd Aqīt and al-Balbālī indicates not only Bābā's scholarly context but also the long tradition of debate on issues surrounding illegal enslavement and their remedies.

In *Mi'rāj al-Ṣu'ūd,* Bābā addresses two key points: the question of Blackness and enslaveability and the responsibility for proving a person's

70 For more on his personal history see Cleaveland, "Ahmad Baba al-Tinbukti and his Islamic Critique of Racial Slavery in the Maghrib," 42–44; Lovejoy, "The Context of Enslavement in West Africa," and "Introduction."

71 Hunwick and Harrack, *Mi'rāj al-Ṣu'ūd*, 1–2.

72 Hunwick, *Arabic Literature of Africa*, 2:25.

freeborn or nonfreeborn Muslim status.[73] Indeed, *Miʿrāj al-Ṣuʿūd* can be seen as a culmination of southern Saharan and West African Muslim intellectual thought up to the beginning of the seventeenth century on the nonequation of Blackness and enslavement. Bābā rebutted both the Hamitic thesis as justification for enslavement as well as the sixteenth-century North African argument that questioned the freeborn status of Black Muslims. The legitimate freeborn status of Black Africans from south of the Sahara, and therefore of Black Moroccans, was being questioned on the basis of how Islam spread in West Africa.[74] Basically, those who argued that "Black" African Muslims were enslaveable based their argument on the idea that since Black populations south of the Sahara had been forcibly converted to Islam (which was untrue), that meant their descendants were not true freeborn Muslims and were therefore enslaveable. To counter this argument, Bābā relied on accepted histories of the spread of Islam in West Africa and the undisputed Muslimness of West African states such as Ancient Ghana, Ancient Mali, and Songhay.

Yet, even so, there was an ethnic component to the West African discourse on enslaveability, as evident in *Miʿrāj al-Ṣuʿūd.* While Bābā insisted that personal belief and unbelief trumped all other considerations, he did include in *Miʿrāj al-Ṣuʿūd* lists of ethnicities that he considered to be mostly Muslim and non-Muslim. In doing so, Bābā was again following al-Balbālī's lead. However, where these two men differed significantly is that where al-Balbālī argued that no one from a known Muslim state should be enslaved for fear of enslaving a freeborn Muslim, Bābā acknowledged that not all people coming from known Islamic states were Muslims nor would all people claiming to be Muslim actually be freeborn Muslims.[75] In order to err on the side of freedom and not to mistakenly enslave a freeborn Muslim, al-Balbālī advised against enslaving anyone from lands that were predominantly Muslim. Bābā, on the other hand, advised using extreme caution to make sure one did not enslave nor purchase an enslaved or captive freeborn Muslim. This can be seen

73 Hunwick and Harrack, *Miʿrāj al-Ṣuʿūd,* 21–53.

74 In 1699, this discourse culminated in Morocco when Sultan Mawlāy Ismāʿīl ordered the enslavement of the entire free Black population in Morocco for his army on the basis that all Blacks, including freeborn Muslims, in Morocco were enslaveable on the basis of servile origin. For more detail see El Hamel, "The Register of the Slaves," 89–98; Hunwick, "Islamic Law and Polemics over Race and Slavery," 52–59; El Hamel, "Race' Slavery and Islam"; El Hamel, *Black Morocco,* 155–85.

75 Hunwick and Harrack, *Miʿrāj al-Ṣuʿūd,* 28–29.

in Bābā's reply to a question on the lawful enslavement of individuals from certain states posed by a Moroccan, Yūsuf b. Ibrāhīm al-ʻĪsī. He stated that

> what I think regarding your question is that you ought to know first that some of these groups (aṣnāf) are mixed together. Those whom we have ascertained to be Muslim are all of the people of Songhay and its kingdom [stretching for a distance of] some two months in length. Similarly all of Kano are Muslims since ancient times, likewise, Katsina and Zakzak [Zaria] and Gobir [?]. However, close to them are unbelieving people whom the Muslims may raid because of their extreme proximity, so we have heard, and they bring them to their place as unbelievers and slaves. As regards these people, if it is established among you that a slave woman or man is from these unbelievers and was merely raised in the city of Kano or Katsina or Zakzak or Kabi [Kebbi], and subsequently converted to Islam, then there is no harm in buying him, since he was taken captive while an unbeliever. Similarly, all the people of Bornu [Borno] are Muslims, but close to them also are unbelievers whom the people of Bornu raid. The ruling is as before.[76]

Hall argues that one of the reasons why *Miʻrāj al-Ṣuʻūd* became so popular with later scholars was because of Bābā's precise categorization of different types of "Blacks."[77] Both ʻUthmān b. Fodiye and Muḥammad Bello accepted Bābā's premise that ethnicity could be used as a tool for ascertaining an individual's religious status yet disagreed on which ethnicities were Muslim and which ones were not. Both ʻUthmān, the main leader of the Sokoto jihad, and his son, Bello, (d. 1837), who became Sarkin Musulmi of Sokoto in 1817, argued that by the late eighteenth century and early nineteenth century some of the ethnicities that Bābā had identified as being Muslims were not, in fact, Muslim.[78] According to ʻUthmān the people of Bornu, Kano, Katsina, Songhay, and Mali, whom Bābā considered to be Muslims, should not be considered as such because, according to ʻUthmān, they put state interests before the interests of Islam and therefore pretended to be Muslim when they were not. Basically since the sarakuna disagreed with ʻUthmān, ʻUthmān was making the argument that they were takfīr (declaring a self-professed Muslim to be an infidel) and extending that to their subjects.

76 Hunwick and Harrack, *Miʻrāj al-Ṣuʻūd*, 43–44.

77 Hall, *A History of Race in Muslim West Africa*, 84.

78 ʻUthmān b. Fodiye *Bayān wujūb al-hijra ʻalaʼ l–ʻibād*, 50, Muḥammad Bello, *Infāq al-Maysūr fī Tārikh bilād al-Takrūr*, 288–99. ʻUthmān b. Fodiye stated his injunction against the enslavement of Fulbe in his 1802 treatise, *Masaʼil muhimma*. See Lovejoy, "The Bello-Clapperton Exchange."

Not only was 'Uthmān disagreeing with Bābā's ethnic cheat sheet of who is most likely to be a Muslim, he was also disagreeing with Bābā's assertion that it was an individual's personal belief that mattered. Yet 'Uthmān, echoing al-Balbālī's caution against enslaving potential freeborn Muslims, insisted that all Fulbe were to be protected from enslavement even though he recognized that not all Fulbe were Muslim.

In *Mi'rāj al-Ṣu'ūd*, Bābā also addressed the question of who was responsible for proving a captive's freeborn or nonfreeborn Muslim status. One of the disagreements among Islamic jurists (and Bābā discusses the opposing opinions) was whether the onus to prove an enslaved person's original status was the responsibility of the slave or the owner. The general consensus was that it was the responsibility of the owner to prove that a captive was not a freeborn Muslim; however, there was a minority opinion that disagreed with this. To reiterate that point, and also showing the importance of the chain of scholarship, Bābā quotes the opinions of Abū'l—Asbagh b.Sahl Muḥammad b. Yaḥyā b. Zurb, and of Maḥmūd b. 'Umar Aqīt, the mid-sixteenth-century Timbuktu scholar and imam of the Sankoré mosque. Maḥmūd b. 'Umar Aqīt, argued that it was the responsibility of captors to prove their captives' nonfreeborn Muslim status and not the responsibility of the captive to prove their freeborn status.[79] For Bābā, Muslim status was based on the personal belief or unbelief of an individual. If a free person was a Muslim, then that person was not enslaveable regardless of ancestry or where he or she lived.

This question of who is and is not part of the Muslim community was answered differently depending on time and place. North Africans interrogating the freeborn status of Muslim Blacks were questioning the inclusion of Muslim Blacks in the Muslim community. Pre-nineteenth-century Sahelian/Sudan scholars pushed back on this questioning and narrowing of "Muslimness" and included as Muslim whoever considered themselves to be Muslim. For Sahelian and Sudanese scholars, religious identity was a matter of personal belief and unbelief. In nineteenth-century western and central Sudan we will see this question answered differently yet again by jihad leaders. Leaders such as 'Uthmān b. Fodiye and Taal will also reject a racialized argument, and they will also accept that membership in the Muslim community was based upon personal belief or unbelief but will argue that membership was limited to those who followed their particular interpretations of Islam.

79 Hunwick and Harrack, *Mi'rāj al-Ṣu'ūd*, 27–28.

As al-Maghīlī and Bābā exemplify, there was a pre-nineteenth-century West African consensus that only non-Muslims captured during war were potentially enslaveable, that Muslim identity was based on personal belief or unbelief, that the onus was on freedom, and that it was better to release a non-Muslim captive than to risk wrongly enslaving a freeborn Muslim. There was more disagreement on the use of ransoming as a preventative measure against enslavement of freeborn Muslims. As al-Maghīlī and Bābā again exemplify, scholars disagreed on the use of ransoming. Scholars like al-Maghīlī argued that rulers had the responsibility for ensuring the freedom of freeborn Muslims using whatever strategy would achieve that outcome including the payment of ransom.[80] Bābā argued that the enslavement of freeborn Muslims was illegal and that illegally captive freeborn Muslims should be freely released.[81] One scholar, al-Maghīlī, took a practical stance on a means to ensure the freedom of Muslims whereas the other, Bābā, based his viewpoint on a strict interpretation of law regarding the rights of freeborn Muslims and the ideal way to ensure their protection from enslavement.

Due to the loss of al-Andalūs and the expulsion of the Muslim population into the Maghrib, it is not surprising that al-Maghīlī emphasized the responsibility of the state in upholding the rights and status of freeborn Muslims and the freeing of captive Muslims. By the time he was advising the Sarki Muḥammad Rumfa of Kano (r. 1463–99) and had written *Taj al-Din yajib 'ala-mulūk*, al-Maghīlī was already known for his harsh interpretations of Khalīl's *Mukhtaṣar*, which laid out the Mālikī view of proper relations between Muslims and non-Muslims.[82] Al-Maghīlī interpreted the *Mukhtaṣar* to advocate the deep privileging of Muslims over non-Muslims. He also put the emphasis on ensuring the freedom of freeborn Muslims and was less concerned about how that was achieved. He advised in *Taj al-Din yajib 'ala-mulūk* that "if wealth abounds he [the prince] will preserve a surplus in the treasury for possible emergencies, for building mosques, *ransoming captives*, discharging debts, marrying women, aiding pilgrims and other necessities."[83] Here, he was not just answering a specific query about a point

80 al- Maghīlī, *Taj al-Din yajib 'ala-mulūk*, 21.

81 Hunwick and Harrack, *Mi'rāj al-Ṣu'ūd*, 29.

82 Hunwick, "Al-Maghīlī and the Jews of Tuwāt," 155–83. His negative attitude toward dhimmī was not helped when his son was murdered in Tuwāt, allegedly by members of the Jewish community. See also Hunwick, *Shari'a in Songhay*, 31–39.

83 al-Maghīlī, *Taj al-Din yajib 'ala-mulūk*, 21; my emphasis.

of law but advising on the duties of a Muslim political leader. For al-Maghīlī, Muslim leaders were responsible for ensuring the freedom of their Muslim subjects. This included paying their ransoms as needed.

While Bābā did not address the question of ransoming directly, it is possible to infer from his replies that he favored freeborn Muslims reattaining their freedom through free release. He believed that Muslims who could be proven to be freeborn Muslims should not be enslaved under any circumstances and should be freed immediately upon their free origin being verified. In his reply to a question posed by Sa'īd b. Ibrāhīm al-Jirārī of Tuwāt on the issue of unknown origins and enslavement, Bābā stated, "Whoever is enslaved in a state of unbelief may rightly be owned, whoever he is, as opposed to those of all groups who converted to Islam of their own free will, such as the people of Bornu, Kano, Songhay, Katsina, Gobir, and Mali and some of [the people of] Zakzak. They are free Muslims who may not be enslaved under any circumstance."[84] Further, he advised not to purchase a captive or a slave whose status was uncertain. He counseled al-'Īsī to only purchase slaves whose status was clear and not to buy a person whose origin or status was in doubt.[85] It is clear that Bābā thought that unbelief was the only reason for enslavement and that it was incumbent upon Muslims to ensure the freedom of captive freeborn Muslims. While al-Maghīlī put the onus on the state to ensure the freedom of freeborn Muslims, Bābā put the responsibility on the individual. Individual Muslims were responsible for ensuring the freedom of their fellow freeborn Muslims. From this line of thinking, freeborn Muslims who suspected that they might be in possession of a freeborn Muslim ought to freely release the captive or slave with no expectation for financial compensation.

Conclusion

The scholars who led the nineteenth-century jihads in the central and western Sudan were the inheritors of a rich intellectual tradition on the issue of legal and illegal enslavement, the role of the state in protecting freeborn Muslims from enslavement, and on the use of ransoming. Scholars of the

84 Hunwick and Harrack, *Mi'rāj al-Ṣu'ūd*, 27. See also Hunwick, "Islamic Law and Polemics over Race and Slavery," for a discussion of al-Jirārī's questions and Bābā's replies.

85 Hunwick and Harrack, *Mi'rāj al-Ṣu'ūd*, 53 and 21.

region shared a common background in foundational texts, including the works of Bābā and al-Maghīlī on Muslim identity, Muslim rights, and enslavement, and of Juzay and Khalīl on the payment of ransoms. The West African intellectual consensus by the end of the eighteenth century was that freeborn Muslims ought to be protected from enslavement and that freeborn Muslim status was based upon personal belief or unbelief and not on racial or ethnic identity. Ideally, the consensus recommended that freeborn Muslims ought to be freely released but that paying ransom was a legitimate strategy for preventing enslavement. Especially for the nineteenth-century jihadists, al-Maghīlī's emphasis on the responsibility of the state in protecting Muslim rights will be particularly resonant. This consensus did not develop in a vacuum. It developed amidst a North African discourse and a changing Saharan and Sahelian discourse on the relationship between racial identity, unbelief, and enslaveability and in a political environment where there was increasing demand for slave labor over previous centuries in North Africa and the Americas and a growing demand in West African markets. The nineteenth-century jihad leaders, in particular the Fodiawa, will draw upon this body of discussion to develop their policies concerning ransoming. The pre-nineteenth-century discourse provided the intellectual framework for the nineteenth-century Muslim West African policies and practices of ransoming. The following chapter will discuss the practice of ransoming in the Mediterranean World of the Maghrib and the Sahara; a region that shared the same legal tradition of the Mālikī school of law with West Africa yet will treat the issue of ransoming differently.

Chapter Two

The Policy and Practice of Ransoming in the Maghrib

The ʿAlawī Sultan of Morocco, Sayyīdī Muḥammad b. Abdallāh, also known as Sīdī Muḥammad, (r. 1757–1790) was known for restoring peace and stability in Morocco after thirty years of disorder following the death of his grandfather Mawlāy Ismāʿīl in 1727. He took the protection of his subjects and of Muslims in general very seriously. Indeed, his ransoming of Muslims held captive or enslaved in Christian European polities and his signing of peace treaties with those polities that included provisions for the return of each other's captives reflects this point.[1] Yet, his reign and policies concerning ransoming not only showcase the importance of the tradition of the Mālikī madh'hab and his desire to normalize relations with Europe but also demonstrate the changing relationship with southern Morocco and changing means of dealing with captives, in particular shipwrecked captives. Just as in West Africa, and indeed elsewhere in the Muslim world and beyond, the practice of ransoming in the Maghrib reflected the fact that people valued freedom. Ransoming practices in the Maghrib and the northern Sahara shared a common foundation in Mālikī law with ransoming practices in the western and central Sudan and Sahel. The same legal principles applied, yet while in West Africa the emphasis was on the usefulness of ransoming as a way to rescue freeborn Muslims, which will discussed in the following chapters, in the Maghrib ransoming was also utilized as a means for dealing with, and benefiting financially from, Christian captives. In the Maghrib, both the principle that Muslims should ransom freeborn Muslims and the legality of ransoming back captives held by Muslims was followed. This can be seen by examining the motives, government sanction, and the role of foreign and

1 Freller, "The Shining of the Moon"; Caillé, *Les accords internationaux*; Matar, *An Arab Ambassador in the Mediterranean World.*

internal relations in the ransoming practices of the Mediterranean world of the Maghrib and of the Sahara. With a focus on Morocco, this chapter will first discuss the Maghribi scholarly discourse on slavery, Maghrib ransoming policy in the context of Mediterranean and desert-edge politics, and actual ransoming practices.

Scholars and the Question of Slavery in the Maghrib

Similar to the Muslim states of West Africa, in Morocco there was tension between rulers, "the possessors of power," and scholars, "the possessors of knowledge." Vincent Cornell describes the medieval Muslim state, and Morocco in particular, as a "protection racket."[2] The Sultan protected the population from local violence and outside invasion in return for the population legitimizing the ruler's authority and paying taxes. Yet often the greatest threat to the citizenry was the state's overtaxation, corruption, and other predatory practices. Offsetting the power of the ruler in the Islamic state, however, was the prestige and influence of Muslim scholars who were viewed as upholders of the moral values of Islam and as bulwarks against the extremes of rulers. In theory, the Sultan's imperial edicts were not formally considered to be law but were instead considered as administrative orders. In principle, Muslim scholars who were appointed as judges in Morocco were responsible for the interpretation and application of Islamic law and were therefore the only ones who could introduce new legislation. Moreover, once a scholar was appointed as a judge, he was supposed to hold that position for life, even though their positions were sometimes revoked as was the case of the Qadi of Fez, Abu- 'Abdallāh Sidi Muḥammad al-'Arabī b. Aḥmad Burdulla (d. 1721), in his dispute with Mawlāy Ismā'īl over the enslavement of the Black population of Morocco.[3] Even though in practice, rulers often usurped judges' legal authority, especially in criminal and political matters, there remained the idea that Islamic law was the final authority and that rulers' edicts needed to be justified according to accepted interpretations of Islamic law. While in

2 Cornell, "Ibn Battuta's Opportunism."

3 Waterbury, *The Commander of the Faithful*, 23–26; Batran, "The 'Ulama' of Fas," 3. It is interesting to note that while Mawlāy Isma'īl never received the approval of the Fez scholars for the enslavement of the Black population, he tried to justify it legally by claiming that he had received approval from "Eastern" 'ulama.

Morocco rulers sought the approval of the scholars in Fez, in the Songhay Empire, the rulers in the political capital of Gao sought the approval of the scholars of Timbuktu. For example, when Muḥammad Tūrī seized power in Songhay in 1493 he was desperate to legitimize his authority through acceptance by Muslim scholars. He first turned to the Muslim establishment in Gao, then to Muḥammad al-Maghīlī, and finally, to the Muslim scholars in Timbuktu who had the most prestige in the region.[4] Askia Muḥammad knew that for his coup d'etat to survive and to be accepted, he needed the acceptance of religious scholars and for them to say that it was legitimate and legal. Likewise, Moroccan Sultans sought the approval of Fez scholars for their rule. As late as January 1908 when Mawlāy 'Abd al-Ḥafīẓ deposed his brother Mawlāy 'Abd al-'Azīz and proclaimed himself Sultan in Marrakesh, he sought the approval of the scholars of Fez in order to cement his rule and to end opposition to it.[5]

Similar to the West African Mālikī scholars and balking at political and social arguments that tried to equate Blackness with enslaveability, Maghribi Mālikī scholars, especially those of the religious center of Fez, reiterated that unbelief was the only justification for slavery and that an individual was to be presumed to be a freeborn Muslim unless he or she was proven to be a slave or a captive non-Muslim. Maghribi scholars, just like their Sudanese and Sahelian counterparts, argued that freedom was the default status and that the onus was on the captor/owner to prove that their captive/slave was not a freeborn Muslim instead of the captive/slave having to prove that they are a freeborn Muslim. For example, in his dispute with Mawlāy Ismā'īl who argued that "blacks" were enslaveable because they were descended from slaves regardless of their personal religious identity, the Qadi of Fez, Abu-'Abdallah Sīdī Muḥammad al-'Arabi b. Ahmad Burdulah stated that "the primary condition of man is freedom. Opinions do not differ on this . . . the 'Ulama' are unanimously agreed on this basic condition of man which cannot be reversed unless concrete evidence to the contrary is produced."[6]

Just as in Muslim West African societies that followed the Mālikī madh'hab, a person could only be a slave if they were a non-Muslim taken captive during a war and subsequently enslaved or if they were born into

4 Blum and Fisher, "Love for Three Oranges."

5 Burke, *Prelude to Protectorate in Morocco*, 99–127; Waterbury, *The Commander of the Faithful*, 18.

6 "Fatwa of Abu- 'Abdallah Sidi Muhammad al- 'Arabi ibn Ahmad Burdulah" in Batran, "The Ulama' of Fas," 14.

slavery to enslaved parents. The child of a slave woman and a free man is born free if the father recognizes his child. The children of a free woman are born free even if the father is a slave, but sex between free women and enslaved men was illegal. Just as in West Africa, the legal options for dealing with non-Muslim captives in the Maghrib were enslavement, free release, execution, prisoner exchange, taxation, and ransoming.

Maghribis not only held captives for ransom but also were themselves at risk of being taken captive and enslaved by their northern Mediterranean neighbors. Even though they were operating from a different canon of law and practice, the early-modern Christian societies of Mediterranean Europe held similar beliefs on captivity and enslavement as the Muslim societies of the Maghrib and West Africa. This is exemplified by the Castilian law code, *Las Siete Partidas*, (The seven sections) issued by King Alfonso X in 1265 to standardize and replace local laws including laws on slavery. As Castile expanded throughout the Iberian Peninsula, and later as Spain gained colonies throughout the world, this law code was also applied. Indeed, *Las Siete Partidas* continues to be the foundation of modern Spanish law, and its influences can be seen in the modern law codes of former Spanish colonies. With regard to slavery, *Las Siete Partidas* is similar to Muslim law codes in that noncoreligionists captured in war were enslaveable.[7] Where *Las Siete Partidas* and Muslim law codes differed is that under the Castilian law code, slave/free status was passed through the mother, whereas in Muslim law codes status was passed through the father. Under *Las Siete Partidas*, the children of enslaved mothers were born slaves whereas, according to the Muslim law codes, if the free father recognizes his child by a slave mother, the child is free and has the same status as the children of the father's wives. Moreover, while the Muslim slave codes forbade freeborn Muslims from selling themselves into slavery, *Las Siete Partidas* permitted self-enslavement under specific conditions.[8] More importantly, for a discussion on ransoming is that both Christian Mediterranean societies, as exemplified by *Las Siete Partidas*, and Muslim Mediterranean societies as exemplified by the Mālikī madh'hab, put an equal emphasis on freeing captives held by their enemies. King Alfonso X made clear that Christians were obligated to liberate from captivity and slavery, either through rescue, prisoner exchange, or ransoming, fellow

7 Portuguese canon law, Ordenações Manuelinas 1512–1603, and the Ordenações Filipinas 1603–1830, also allowed for a "just" war and enslavement of non-Christians.

8 Scott and Burns, *Las Siete Partidas*, 4:977.

Christians and all those they are connected to through lineage, agreement, sovereignty/vassalage, and benevolence.[9] The fact that both Christians and Muslims in the Mediterranean world shared the idea that nonbelief was the basis for enslaveability and that individuals had the responsibility to free their coreligionists from captivity either through ransoming or other means and were willing to negotiate with their enemies to do so, meant that they had a shared legal framework and belonged to the same "greater ransoming society."[10] There needed to be a large degree of cooperation, communication, and mutual protocol in order for ransom negotiations to be conducted.

Ransoming in the Mediterranean World

From at least the Middle Ages, the ransoming of prisoners between Christians and Muslims in the Mediterranean world was a central feature of Muslim/Christian relations. Moreover, since at least the conquest of Constantinople in 1453 by the Ottoman Turks and especially since the sixteenth century, the "golden age" of corsairing being the one hundred years between 1580 and 1680, Muslims from Morocco, the Regencies of Algiers and Tunis, and from other parts of the Ottoman Empire, and Christians from Europe participated in the capturing and enslaving of individuals with various degrees of governmental support. There were four main Mediterranean corsairing centers in the early modern period.[11] The first center was on the Adriatic where the *uskoks* (South Slav refugees) based their attacks on Venetian and Ottoman shipping with Habsburg and Papal support. The second center was the North African ports of Algiers, Tunis, and Tripoli, who with their growing independence from Constantinople, were able to use their economic and political power to raid land and ships from the western Mediterranean as far east as the Adriatic and the Levant and eventually west into the Atlantic. The

9 Scott and Burns, *Las Siete Partidas* 2:516–17. Marcel A. Boisard argues that European practices of ransoming may be based mainly on the Arab-Muslim tradition of ransoming. See Boisard, "On the Probable Influence of Islam on Western Public and International Law," 443.

10 For a discussion of shared legal logic across multiple legal jurisdictions see Benton, *Law and Colonial Cultures*. On captive taking and ransoming see 31–80. Meillassoux considered warring polities that had procedures for prisoner exchange or ransom as belonging to the "same" society. See Meillassoux, *The Anthropology of Slavery*, 103.

11 Fodor, "Maltese Pirates, Ottoman Captives and French Traders," 221–22.

third center was Malta where both the Knights of the Order of Saint Stephen and the Knights of the Order of Saint John based their corsairing operations from the late sixteenth century. The fourth center was western Europe. France and Venice had always been important in the corsairing activities of the Mediterranean, but they were joined by the English and Dutch after 1580.[12]

Captives were taken from land and from the sea. European corsairs primarily took captives from North African and Anatolian ships whereas most captives taken by Maghribi corsairs came from raids on Mediterranean Spanish, Italian and Greek, and occasionally French coastal and island villages as well as ships. As most ship crews and passengers were male, most captives taken from ships were men, although the occasional woman traveler was also taken. By contrast, women made up a much larger proportion of captives taken from areas on land, perhaps as much as just under 40 percent. According to Gillian Weiss it is not clear if corsairs who attacked villages on land were specifically targeting women captives for domestic and sex work or if women were easier to take captive because they were often slowed down by their refusal to flee without their children.[13] Captives taken from ships were viewed as more valuable for both ransom and for enslavement. Ship crew members usually had useful skills that could transfer well to galleys and to other skilled labor needed on both sides of the Mediterranean. Since traveling by sea was expensive, ship passengers were usually elites who could fetch a good ransom price. Oftentimes, when passengers realized that their ship was about to be boarded and that they would be taken captive, they tried to hide their wealth. They wanted to be viewed as wealthy enough to be held for ransom and not mistreated but also did not want to be viewed as so wealthy that their ransom price would be exorbitant. Indeed, we have more accounts of captives' experiences being taken from ships than from raids on land because most ship passengers came from merchant, noble, religious, or military backgrounds and were literate—therefore more likely to write about their experiences. Captives taken from ships had to wait until they reached a port for the opportunity to be ransomed. By contrast, a corsair ship would often stay near the raided coastline for up to a day to try to negotiate ransoms for their new captives with the remaining free people. Although still expensive and difficult to raise the fees in the aftermath of being raided and looted, it was cheaper and less complicated for the payers

12 For a discussion of the "northern invasion" of the Mediterranean, see Greene, "Beyond the Northern Invasion."

13 Weiss, *Captives and Corsairs*, 36.

of ransom to ransom their people immediately after a raid rather than after they had been transported to the Maghrib.[14]

Considering the ethnic and national diversity in corsairing and captive taking, estimating the number of enslaved and captive Europeans held in the Maghrib and of Maghribi Muslims that were held in Europe is challenging. European captives included British, Flemish, French, Spanish, Portuguese, Italians, and Swedes among others, while Muslim captives held in Europe came from across North Africa, Anatolia, and the Levant. Using qualitative sources and population projections, strategies reminiscent of the pre-*Voyages* database methodologies for producing population estimates for the transatlantic slave trade, Robert C. Davis, tentatively estimated that between a million and a million and a quarter European captives/slaves were held in the Maghrib between 1530 and 1780.[15] According to Christine Sears there were about seven hundred Americans held in the Maghrib between 1776 (the year of American independence from Britain) and 1830.[16] In 2001, Davis attributed the lack of interest in calculating the number of enslaved and captive Europeans and Muslims in the Mediterranean world to the "supposition that Mediterranean-based slaving was a pretty minor affair" and offered a challenge of sorts to assess the number of Muslims held in Europe.[17] A challenge that was subsequently taken up by Salvatore Bono who, while he lowers Davis's estimate of European captives held in both the Maghrib and the Ottoman Empire in total to one million, estimates that two million Ottoman and Moroccan subjects were held in Europe between the sixteenth and nineteenth centuries.[18] Demonstrating the economic desire for slave and captive labor in Europe, Alessandro Stella estimates that between 1500 and 1800, 150,000 captives and slaves were used to man Spanish galleys, rowing being the main use of slaves and captives in Mediterranean Europe. According to Stella, the majority of these rowers were from North Africa. He estimates that between three hundred thousand and four hundred thousand North Africans were enslaved or held captive in Portugal and Spain between 1450 and 1750.[19]

14 Davis, *Christian Slaves, Muslim Masters*, 27–39; Weiss, *Captives and Corsairs*, 27–38.

15 Davis, *Christian Slaves, Muslim Masters*, 23.

16 Sears, *American Slaves and African Masters*, 3.

17 Davis, "Counting European Slaves on the Barbary Coast," 89.

18 Bono, "Slave Histories and Memoirs in the Mediterranean World," 105.

19 Stella, *Histoires d'esclaves dans la Péninsule Ibérique*, 70, 78–79.

It is important to note that European captivity, use of European captive and slave labor, and ransoming of Europeans in the Maghrib took place in a context where captives and slaves were imported from across both the Mediterranean and the Sahara and that Maghribi polities were focused on their economic and political relationships with both their southern and northern neighbors. There is little quantitative data for the trans-Saharan slave trade to the Maghrib prior to the late eighteenth century. Ralph Austen estimates that by the late eighteenth century, Morocco was importing approximately two thousand enslaved West Africans per year while Algeria and Tunis imported less. An important difference between Morocco and the Regencies of Algiers and Tunis is that while Algiers and Tunis did not play a significant role in the trans-Saharan slave trade, Morocco emphasized maintaining an independent caravan link with the western Sudan in order to maintain a steady import of slaves.[20] In the Maghrib, enslaved West Africans could be found in all sectors of the economy, including agriculture, domestic service, and the military, and owned by private individuals and by the state. Moreover, in the Maghrib, the slave trade from West Africa was primarily a trade of women whereas the trade in Europeans was mostly a trade of men.[21]

Even though there was a political component in terms of resisting the Iberian Reconquista and curtailing European political expansion in the Mediterranean, for the Maghrib, privateering and captive taking in the Mediterranean were primarily a response to declining trade as the center of European economic power shifted from southern Europe to the north and as European trade with the Americas gradually reduced the amount of trade with the Maghrib while increasing European power within the Mediterranean.[22] With the opening up of the Atlantic trade route, just like their West African neighbors, the Maghribi polities had to adjust to changing political and economic relations. Morocco and the Regencies of Algiers, Tripoli, and Tunis used corsairing and captive taking as a means to gain hard currency and political leverage and to play a role in inter-European Mediterranean rivalry.[23] Indeed, Ismael Diadié Haïdara argues that Morocco invaded Songhay in 1591 mainly because

20 Austen, "The Mediterranean Islamic Slave Trade," 229–30.

21 For more on slavery in the Maghrib see Ennaji, *Soldats, Domestiques et concubines*; Montana, *The Abolition of Slavery in Ottoman Tunisia.*

22 Matar, "Introduction: England and Mediterranean Captivity," 12.

23 For a discussion of the connection between European, and particularly English economic and military expansion in the Mediterranean and captive taking see Matar, *British Captives from the Mediterranean to the Atlantic*, 160–91.

Morocco was hemmed in by growing European economic and political power on its Mediterranean and Atlantic borders. As a solution to his northern and western problem, Sultan Aḥmad al-Mansūr looked toward the south and the riches of the trans-Saharan trade routes and of the Songhay Empire.[24] In the aftermath of the invasion, Morocco enslaved thousands of Songhay captives and used them as rowers in the Moroccan navy, further demonstrating the link, for Maghribi rulers, of their Mediterranean and West African policies.[25] Even though, according to law, only unbelief justified enslavement and only when the nonbeliever was captured during a legal war, as discussed in chapter 1, in North Africa (especially in Morocco) race was also an important factor in enslaveability with many—especially rulers in search of labor—trying to argue that individuals who were identified as Black should not be considered freeborn Muslims no matter how they defined themselves.[26]

As the case of Morocco's invasion of Songhay and as Ismael Montana has shown for the foreign policy of Tunis, the North African polities were orientated to both the Mediterranean and West Africa. They tried to balance political and economic relations with both directions to improve their positions.[27] In the Mediterranean sphere, privateering and captive taking was a means for Morocco and the Ottoman Regencies of Algiers, Tripoli, and Tunis to compensate themselves for the shift of power in the Mediterranean. Moreover, at least for the Ottoman Regencies, having corsairing navies gave them autonomy from Constantinople rule. Privateering and captive taking forced European consuls and ambassadors into a weaker position as they sought to ransom captives, secure trade monopolies and exclusive access to ports, and gain access to munitions and other supplies during times of war.[28] By the seventeenth century, Algiers had overtaken

24 *The Manuscripts of Timbuktu.* See also Haïdara, *Jawdar Pasha et la conquête Saâdienne du Songhay.*

25 Le Tourneau, "Histoire de la dynastie sa'idide," 53.

26 For Black slavery in Morocco, see El Hamel, *Black Morocco;* and Ennaji, *Soldats, Domestiques et Concubines.*

27 Montana, *The Abolition of Slavery in Ottoman Tunis.*

28 Fontenay, "La place de la course dans l'économie portuare," 1321–334; Matar, "Introduction: England and Mediterranean Captivity," 12; Panzac, *Les corsaires barbaresques,* 11–23.

Constantinople as the most important center for Christian captives taken in the western Mediterranean.[29]

For European captives held in the Maghrib, there were four realistic options for freedom: escape, conversion to Islam, exchange against Muslim captives in Europe, and ransoming. Mālikī jurists favored the last three options. Indeed, paralleling Christian justification of the enslavement of non-Christians, one of the rationalizations for enslavement was to introduce Islam to nonbelievers. The release of captives and slaves who converted to Islam was encouraged. Escape was difficult but sometimes possible by stealing a boat, stowing away on a departing ship, or heading overland. While conversion to Islam did not always guarantee freedom, it usually guaranteed release from the more onerous work such as rowing. Estimates of the renegade population, captives who had converted to Islam, vary from between 30 percent and 80 percent of the captive and enslaved population.[30]

Europeans could also regain their freedom through exchange against Turkish and North African captives in Europe. Exchange was encouraged as a lawful means of regaining the freedom of freeborn Muslims. Captive exchange was the main means through which Maghribis secured the release of their loved ones held in Europe.[31] Unlike their European counterparts, Maghribis did not have formal institutions, equivalent to the Roman Catholic Church–sponsored Redemptionist orders, such as the Trinitarian and Mercedarian orders, through which to pursue the release of their kin.[32] This was due in part because European powers were reluctant to release captives for ransom; preferring their labor, especially on galleys, than the money they could receive in ransom.[33] Instead, Muslim kin had to rely on gaining

29 Rudt de Collenberg, *Esclavage et rançons des chrétiens en Méditerranée*, 29. According to Rudt de Collenberg, prior to 1600 Constantinople was the most important city European captives were ransomed from. This is based on his study of hortatoriae letters. Between 1570 and 1600 the Roman Catholic Church attempted to ransom 1,017 individuals held throughout the Ottoman Empire. Of this 312, or 30.7 percent, were ransomed from Constantinople. The next largest city from where captives were ransomed was Algiers with 127, or 12.5 percent. See p. 32.

30 Davis, "Counting European Slaves," 113–15.

31 Hershenzon, " '[P]ara que me saque cabesa por cabesa," 11–36.

32 On the Trinitarian and Mercedarian Redemptionist Orders see Friedman, *Spanish Captives in North Africa*; Martínez Torres, *Prisioneros de los infieles*; Barrio Gozalo, *Esclavos y cautivos*.

33 Weiss, "Ransoming 'Turks' from France's Royal Galleys," 39.

possession of a European captive who had the social and economic capital back home to encourage their state and family to arrange to exchange them for a particular captive. This system had its benefits and pitfalls. While Maghribi families were not hemmed in by state and Roman Catholic Church interests whose priorities and views of opportunity costs may not be their own, transactions could get very complicated.[34] This is exemplified by the 1642 case of the Flemish men Emmanuel D'Aranda, Rénier Saldens, and Jean-Baptiste Caloen. The three were on the same English ship en route from Saint Sebastien to England when it was taken captive by Algerian corsairs in August 1640. After two years in Algiers, they were freed in exchange for three Turks and one Algerian held in Bruges. This exchange was organized through a complicated set of transactions arranged by the fathers of the three men and the mother and grandmother of the captive Algerian, Mūstafa Inglis. Inglis's stepfather in Algiers arranged to buy D'Aranda, Saldens, and Caloen from their owner in order to use them to exchange for the men held in Flanders. The exchange of captives took place through the Spanish fort town of Ceuta and the Algerian town of Tetouan.[35] The European fortified towns on the Maghrib coast such as Ceuta and Oran were often used as transfer points for returning Christian and Muslim captives. The European enclaves in North Africa were a sort of borderlands region populated by European and Maghribi Christians, Jews, and Muslims interested in facilitating trade across the Mediterranean. They operated with varying degrees of autonomy and facilitated transactions that often could not take place in other jurisdictions including the exchange of captives.[36] In the case of Inglis, he was brought to Ceuta, while his mother, using the services of a hired intermediary, brought D'Aranda, Saldens, and Caloen to Tetouan, which is only twenty-two miles from Ceuta. The intermediary then arranged the exchange of the men in Spanish-held Ceuta.[37]

In the seventeenth century, ransoming was viewed as a benefit to both the European captives held in Morocco and the Ottoman Regencies and to their captors (both state agents and private captive and slave owners). European captives regained their freedom whereas captors gained financial compensation. Arrangements for the ransoming of European captives were

34 Lofkrantz and Ojo, "Slavery, Freedom and Failed Ransom Negitations," 35–36.

35 D'Aranda, *Les captifs d'Alger*, ed. Latifa Z'Rari, 11–43.

36 Kaiser, "Zones de transit," 251–72.

37 D'Aranda, *Les captifs d'Alger*, 11–43.

usually done by either Church organizations, the Redemptionist orders, or by European consuls. Algerian rulers actively courted ransom negotiators and offered them passports and certificates of safe conduct in order to travel to Algiers to conduct ransom negotiations.[38] Furthermore, while Algerian captors tried to maximize the labor output of their captives, they also tried to keep their captives alive and healthy so that they could be ransomed. In the Maghrib, just like their counterparts in Europe, most European captives and slaves worked as rowers on galleys. Otherwise, captives and slaves did required labor according to their captors/owners' needs such as skilled and unskilled labor on public works and carpentry, blacksmithing, farming, and household duties. Individual captives who could command the highest ransoms were sometimes not forced to work.[39] This process was somewhat formalized in Algiers where captives were divided into three groups. The majority of captives became public captives/slaves who were assigned hard labor and lived in the barracks. Depending on their nationality, rank, education, and skills, captives could also become part of the city's cadre of elite captives/slaves working in the Regency's bureaucracy. The smallest group was made up of elite individuals who had access to funds to pay a monthly fee to keep them from having to work or from living in the barracks as they waited to be ransomed. According to Sears, captive ship officers were assigned this third status.[40]

Although taking place in the neighboring Ottoman Regency of Tripoli, the treatment of the crew of the American frigate *Philadelphia* and the divergent accounts of two of its crew, the ship's doctor Jonathan Crowdery, and sailor William Ray, attests to the role of status in the categorization, treatment, and ransoming of captives.[41] The *Philadelphia* was captured on October 31, 1803, during the 1801–1805 war between Tripoli and the United States with 307 men on board. At the end of the war as part of the peace treaty,

38 Friedman, "Christian Captives at 'Hard Labor' in Algiers, 16th to 18th Centuries," 629. See also Clissold, *The Barbary Slaves*, 102–29.

39 Weiss, "Ransoming 'Turks' from France's Royal Galleys," Friedman, "Christian Captives at 'Hard Labor'," 618, 628; Davis, *Christian Slaves, Muslim Masters*, 69–102. See also Fontenay "Le maghreb barbaresque et l'esclavage méditerranéen," 17. This is obviously with regard to European slaves where there was a good chance of a ransom offer. According to Davis only 3 to 4 percent of European captives and slaves managed to escape or were ransomed or redeemed. See Davis, "Counting European Slaves on the Barbary Coast," 115.

40 Sears, "'In Algiers, the City of Bondage," 205.

41 Cowdery, *American Captives in Tripoli;* Ray, *Horrors of Slavery.*

Tripoli exchanged the surviving crew members for approximately one hundred Tripolitans held by American forces and a payment of sixty thousand dollars.[42] During their captivity Cowdery and the *Philadelphia*'s officers were housed in the former American consulate and at the castle, were given relative freedom to wander the city and enjoy the gardens; they also received provisions. Moreover, as a doctor, Cowdery was asked to treat the Pasha's family and was permitted to treat the *Philadelphia*'s crew.[43] Ray and the rest of the crew, however, received different treatment and indeed were treated in the more typical fashion for public slaves. According to Ray's account, they were kept in a prison and poorly fed and clothed. Skilled tradesmen such as blacksmiths and ship carpenters labored at their trades while those without useful skills did manual labor useful to the state.[44]

Reflecting the legality of ransoming, the ransoming of captives in the Maghrib had government sanction and involved the government bureaucracy. This is exemplified by the division of ransoming costs. In seventeenth-century Algiers and Tunis, ransoming costs involved not just the actual price of ransom but also payments to the government and agents, legal documents, and taxes.[45] In Morocco, ransoming also had government sanction. Before 1682, although ransoms were treated as a private matter between those holding the individual for ransom and those who wanted to pay ransom, all captured goods and people were subject to a ten percent tax. In 1682, ransoming officially became government business when Mawlāy Ismā'īl (r. 1672–1727) decreed that all goods and people captured on the sea should be remitted to him.[46] This government take-over had an impact as captives were used as part of government diplomacy. While the period between 1727, the death of Mawlāy Ismā'īl, and 1757, the date of Sīdī Muḥammad's accession to the

42 Lambert, *The Barbary Wars*, 169. For more on American-Maghrib relations in this time period, see Parker, *Uncle Sam in Barbary*, Allison, *The Crescent Obscured*.

43 Cowdery, *American Captives in Tripoli*, 7–15.

44 Ray, *Horrors of Slavery*, 59–60.

45 Fontenay, "Le maghreb barbaresque et l'esclavage méditerranéen," 26–27. See also Kaiser, "L'économie de la rançon en Méditerranée occidentale," 689–701, and Kaiser, *Le commerce des captifs*; Claude Larquie puts the average price of ransom at 2,104.96 réaux in Morocco and 2,032.52 réaux in Algeria. See Larquie, "La Méditerrannée, l'Espagne et le Maghreb au XVIIe. siècle," 82. See also Bachrouch, "Rachat et liberation des esclaves chrétiens à Tunis au XVIIe siècle," 131.

46 Vergniot, "De la distance en histoire," 99.

throne, was a period of political instability in Morocco it was also a period when most of the European captives remaining in Morocco were ransomed and released in a bid to normalize relationships between Morocco and European states. This continued under the reign of Sīdī Muḥammad who prioritized the ransoming of both European and Muslim captives in his commercial and peace treaties with European powers.[47]

The emphasis on ransoming back freeborn Muslims and allowing the ransoms of Christians is exemplified through the actions of Sīdī Muḥammad. His policies regarding ransoming were grounded in the same legal traditions regarding enslavement and ransoming as in the western and central Sudan. Sīdī Muḥammad considered himself to be acting in accordance with the Mālikī madh'hab, the school of law traditionally followed in Morocco and in West Africa, but was also influenced by Ḥanīfa and Shāfi'ī thought. He consolidated power in part by claiming and reinforcing religious doctrine.[48] Therefore, it is not surprising that he would emphasize the ruler's role in freeing captive Muslims. Sīdī Muḥammad's policies regarding ransoming were also rooted in Morocco's relationships with European states and likewise with Morocco's relationships with Wād Nūn and al-Sūs. Sīdī Muḥammad's pursuit of freeing freeborn Muslims either through exchange or ransom is exemplified by both the peace treaties he signed and the diplomatic missions he sent to negotiate and pay for ransoms. From the 1760s through 1780s, Sīdī Muḥammad negotiated a series of commercial and peace treaties with England, France, Spain, Denmark, Sweden, Venice, Tuscany, Portugal, the Netherlands, Sicily, Austria, and the United States.[49] An important issue for the European polities and the United States was the treatment of European and American captives in Morocco, who by this time were mostly sailors and passengers shipwrecked off Cape Juby, Cape Boujdour, and Cape

---

47 See the appendix in Caillé, *Les accords internationaux*, for copies of the treaties.

48 Matar, *An Arab Ambassador in the Mediterranean World*, 4; Sīdī Muḥammad was not the only Magrhibi rule to include the release of Muslims held in Europe in his European policy. See Hershenzon, " '[P] que me saque cabesa por cabesa' "; Belhamissi, *Les captifs algériens et l'Europe chrétienne*; and Weiss, *Captives and Corsairs*. Moreover, Algerian pashas felt obligated to offer support to the families of captives held in Europe. See Hoexter, *Endowments, Rulers and Community*, 27, 158.

49 See the appendix in Caillé, *Les accords internationaux* for copies of the treaties. For a discussion of Sīdī Muḥammad's diplomacy with the United States, see Roberts and Tull, "Moroccan Sultan Muhammad ibn Abdallah's Diplomatic Initiatives."

Blanc. For Sīdī Muḥammad it was the ransoming of Muslim captives that was key.[50] The exchange, freeing, and ransoming of Muslim captives were important components of Sīdī Muḥammad's 1777 and 1778 treaties with the Netherlands, Sweden, and Tuscany while the treatment of shipwrecked individuals and prisoners was prominent in the treaties with England (1760) and Spain (1767).[51]

Throughout his reign, Sīdī Muḥammad organized several missions to free captive Muslims in Europe. His interest was not just to ransom Moroccans but to ransom all Muslims being held in Europe and to arrange their transport home. He sent several officials to ransom captives; however, his two most notable envoys were his ambassador Aḥmad b. Mahdī al-Ghazāl and his diplomat Muḥammad b. 'Uthmān al-Miknāsī. In 1767, al-Ghazāl, upon signing a peace treaty with Spain was able to ransom sixteen hundred Algerians being held there. In 1779–1780 and again in 1781–1783, Sīdī Muḥammad sent al-Miknāsī on tours throughout southern Europe to conduct diplomacy and to ransom captives. In order to free Muslim captives, al-Miknāsī relied on his diplomatic skills, on large payments, and even organizing the exchange of Muslims captives held in Europe for European Christians held in other jurisdictions. Al-Miknāsī ransomed thousands of captives in Genoa, Naples, Malta, Sicily, and Spain but was not successful in ransoming all of them. During his stop in Cartegena, Spain, during his 1779–1780 tour where he was able to retrieve ninety-two Moroccan and Algerian captives, he told the remaining Algerian captives in the city that Sīdī Muḥammad had agreed to act as a mediator to negotiate to exchange them for Spanish captives held in Algiers.[52]

Sīdī Muḥammad was extolled (however exaggeratedly) by one nineteenth-century biographer, 'Abdallah Muḥammad b. Aḥmad al-Kanūsi, as having been so thorough in ransoming Muslims that by the end of his reign not one captive was left in Europe from either the Maghrib or the Mashriq.[53] He most likely won the hearts of many North Africans for his ransoming efforts. In describing the scene aboard one of the ships transporting the 813 captives he ransomed on Malta in 1783 to Morocco al-Miknāsī states: "You should

50 See Vergniot, "De la distance en histoire," 99; and Caillé, *Les accords internationaux* for more of Sīdī Muḥammad's diplomacy.

51 See Caillé, *Les accords internationaux*, 166, 184, 218, 220, 224.

52 Mater, *An Arab Ambassador in the Mediterranean World*, 6 ft. 27, 31–138; Freller, "'The Shining of the Moon,'" 307–26.

53 Mater, *An Arab Ambassador in the Mediterranean World*, 7.

have seen the captives on board the ships as men jostled with their shoulders, women ululating in gratitude, and men and boys responding by asking God's blessings on our master and lord."[54] As a Sultan, Sīdī Muḥammad acted on the ethic of protecting the rights of freeborn Muslims on a grand scale, but this ethic was also followed by more ordinary individuals in the Mediterranean basin. Even though government intervention was important, since at least the fifteenth century when Christian forces conquered Valencia, most captive Muslims in Mediterranean Europe, like Inglis, were ransomed or exchanged privately rather than by governments.[55]

The Atlantic Sahara and Ransoming

The Maghribi sphere of ransoming Europeans back to Europe stretched into the Sahara and included shipwrecked Europeans captured along the Saharan coast. By the late eighteenth century, most European and American captives in Morocco were sailors and passengers who were shipwrecked along the Atlantic coast. The survival of people who were shipwrecked along the Saharan coast was dependent on local fishers finding them. Usually the fishers and their families would feed and clothe the sailors and passengers until they could trade them for animals or other provisions such as goats, camels, cloth, flour, or iron.[56] After being exchanged numerous times, the captive would usually be shuffled northward but sometimes southward toward Ndār/St. Louis on the Senegal River, where they would eventually be bought by someone who had the interest and ability to trade them for ransom.

In the eighteenth and nineteenth centuries, sailors and passengers shipwrecked off Cape Juby, Cape Boujdour, and Cape Blanc were most often traded northward toward Wād Nūn and al-Sūs where arrangements were made to either to sell the captives to the Moroccan Sultan or to negotiate a ransom with a European consul.[57] Being able to control and ransom captive

---

54 Mater, *An Arab Ambassador in the Mediterranean World,* 100–101.

55 Blumenthal, *Enemies and Familiars,* 104–5. Mazur discusses a case where a Muslim slave in Naples converted to Christianity in order to be free and used his position as a freed Christian convert to help other Muslim Maghribi slaves escape and return home. See Mazur, "Combatting 'Mohammedan Indecency," 25–48.

56 Vergniot, "De la distance en histoire," 105.

57 Bennett, "Christian and Negro Slavery in Eighteenth Century North Africa," 72.

Europeans and Americans back to their homelands was an important political issue for Moroccan Sultans in both their relationships with European states and with Wād Nūn and al-Sūs. For the shipwrecked sailors, except for the fact that they had to be conveyed northward, the ransoming process for sailors shipwrecked off the Sahara coast differed little from the ransoming of European Christians in the northern Maghrib. Alternatively, but rarely, shipwrecked sailors for ransom could be transported southward to the French settlement of St. Louis at Ndār. Depending on where they were shipwrecked on the Atlantic coast and on their nationality, French subjects particularly preferred to be conveyed southward, and many captive sailors tried to convince their captors to ransom them at Ndār/St. Louis.[58] However, the choice of what to do with a captive always remained with the captor and was based on the captor's priorities and networks.

For Sīdī Muḥammad and his heirs, ransoming was not only an issue with regard to his obligation as a Muslim to free freeborn Muslims but was also a political issue in the context of his relationship with al-Sūs, located to the south of Morocco, and more importantly, with the southernmost portion of al-Sūs, Wād Nūn, Valley of Nūn, located at the foot of the Anti-Atlas Mountains on the northwestern edges of the Sahara Desert, about fifty kilometers from the Atlantic coast. For Sīdī Muḥammad, gaining control of shipwrecked sailors and being the one to return them to the European consuls was not only important in his relations with Europe but was also an indication of his authority over al-Sūs and Wād Nūn. Due to the growing importance of the Atlantic trade route, Sīdī Muḥammad redeveloped the port at Casablanca in 1760 and al-Ṣawīra (Essaouira/Mogador) in 1765 to facilitate and control European trade in the region. The Moroccans viewed al-Ṣawīra as the southernmost legitimate port of trade with Europe and as the nexus between the trans-Saharan and the Atlantic commercial systems.[59] This put them in conflict with the Tikna traders of Wād Nūn, from whom the Bayrūk would emerge as a powerful commercial family in the late eighteenth and early nineteenth centuries.[60] The Moroccan government viewed Wād Nūn

58 See, for example, De Brisson, *Account of the Shipwreck and Captivity of Mr. De Brisson*. De Brisson tried to convince his captor to bring him to Ndār (St. Louis), but he was ultimately conveyed northward where he was eventually ransomed in al-Ṣawīra.

59 Mohamed, *Between Caravan and Sultan*, 87.

60 For the importance of the Tikna trading network and the Bayrūk family see Lydon, *On Trans-Saharan Trails*, 160–205. For a discussion on the

along with the rest of al-Sūs and Tazerwālt as being part of the bilād al-sā'iba, "the land of dissidence or unruliness" in contrast to the territory of which the government had firm control, the bilād al-maghzan, or "the administered or conquered land."[61] Wād Nūn would remain largely autonomous until it was incorporated into the French Moroccan Protectorate in 1934.[62] Yet, al-Sūs and Wād Nūn were the lynchpin that connected the bilād al-maghzan with the bilād al-sūdān. Both the Moroccan government and Susian traders wanted to be in control of trade with Europeans on the Atlantic coast. This in part led Sīdī Muḥammad to close the port of Agadir and move the port north to al-Ṣawīra where he could better monopolize, derive profit, and control trade between European and Susian traders. Throughout the late eighteenth and nineteenth centuries, Sīdī Muḥammad and his heirs wanted to limit European traders to the port at al-Ṣawīra. His goal was to prevent them from traveling and trading directly with interior merchants outside his jurisdiction and to force Susian traders to trade at al-Ṣawīra if they wanted access to the Atlantic market and thereby accept the Moroccan court's dominance. Circumventing the court's control of trade relations between Europe and Wād Nūn was the motivator for the Bayrūk's multiple failed attempts to convince the British and the French to build a port at the mouth of the Asaka River.[63]

In dealing with the bilād al-sā'iba and in particular, the Wād Nūn, Sīdī Muḥammad and his successors, Mawlāy al-Yazīd (r. 1790–1792), Mawlāy Sūlayman (r. 1792–1822) and Mawlāy 'Abd al-Raḥmān (r.1822–1859) had to deal with the growing commercial and political power of the Bayrūk family. The Bayrūk family derives its name from Shaykh Bayrūk b. Abaydallah b. Sālam (r. 1815–1858). However, the successes of Shaykh Bayrūk were built upon the achievements of his father, Abaydallah b. Sālam. The Bayrūk family rose to prominence in the politics and economy of Wād Nūn in the first half of the eighteenth century. The authority of 'Abaydallah b. Sālam extended over the Tikna clans of the Aīt al-Jamal ('ahl al-sahil) and oversaw

---

interpretation and portrayal of the Bayrūk family see Mohamed, *Between Caravan and Sultan*. See also E. Ann McDougall, "Conceptualizing the Sahara."

61 Burke, *Prelude to the Protectorate in Morocco*, 267.

62 Gershovich, *French Military Rule in Morocco*, 160.

63 Cochelet, *Narrative of the Shipwreck of the Sophia*, 87; Pennell, *Morocco since 1830*, 45; Hodges, *Historical Dictionary of the Western Sahara*, 335; Marty, "Les tribus de la haute Mauritanie:Les Takna (Oued Noun)," 136–46.

the beginning of the Wād Nūn town of Guelmīm as a commercial center, but it was Shaykh Bayrūk who parlayed political power into an extensive commercial empire.[64] Bayrūk and his sons transformed Wād Nūn and Guelmīm into an epicenter of trade in western Africa through the negotiation of alliances with key Saharan groups such as the Tajakānit, the Rgaybāt, and the Ahl Barikallah; their patronage of Jewish traders and the Jewish community at Guelmīm; their friendly relations with the Trārza Emirate, which controlled access to the Senegal River trade and, after their founding in the mid-nineteenth century, to the 'Umarian States of the western Sudan; and their diplomacy and attempts to extend trade with Europe. Through their trade networks, they connected Wād Nūn and Guelmīm to both Atlantic and Mediterranean commerce. The Bayrūk commercial network traded in numerous goods including gum Arabic, cloth, animal products such as ostrich feathers, hides, and tanned leather; foodstuffs such as grain and dates; gold; goods imported through al-Ṣawīra such as sugar, green tea, firearms, and cotton cloth; and enslaved people and shipwrecked captives.[65] Indeed, the experiences of captive sailors demonstrate the interconnection of systems of Saharan economic exchange. The pillaging of wrecked ships for their goods and people by fishers and pastoralists, such as the Aīt al-Jamal, reflected the use of razzia as a means of resource redistribution in an environment of limited resources whereas the funneling of captives into the vast Tikna trade network that traded goods and people for profit from West Africa to the Maghrib reflected the system of long-distance commercial trade.[66]

Both 'Abaydallah and Bayrūk, were heavily involved in the ransoming of shipwrecked European and American sailors. Under 'Abaydallah, Guelmīm became an important collection center for European and American shipwrecked captives. As an indication of the number of captives passing through Guelmīm, in 1819, French captive Charles Cochelet counted the graves of

---

64 For more on the internal dynamics of the Tikna, see Mohamed, *Between Caravan and Sultan*, 67.

65 For the importance of the Tikna trading network and the Bayrūk family, see Mohamed, *Between Caravan and Sultan*; Lydon, *On Trans-Saharan Trails*, 160–205; and E. Ann McDougall, "Conceptualizing the Sahara," 369–86. For more on trans-Saharan trade between the Niger Bend and Morocco after the Moroccan invasion of Songhay to the nineteenth century, see Abitbol, "Le Maroc et le commerce transsaharien," 5–19. See also Miege, "Le commerce trans-saharien au XIXe siècle," 93–119.

66 For razzia as an economic system see Niang, "Deferred Reciprocity," 231–32. For Saharan long-distance trade networks see Lydon *On Trans-Saharan Trails*.

over fifty "Christian" captives in the town who had obviously not survived their captivity to be ransomed.[67] As indicated by the survivor accounts of the Frenchmen Adrien-Jacques Follie (1784), Saugnier (1783/1784) and Cochelet (1819), the Englishman James Irving (1789), and the Americans Robert Adams (1810) and James Riley (1815), the Bayrūk operated as regional wholesalers, purchasing shipwrecked sailors from coastal Aīt al-Jamal fishermen and pastoralists before negotiating with consuls in al-Ṣawīra and the Moroccan court for their ransom and release. The ransoming of Europeans especially illustrates the disagreements and power struggles between the Sultans of Morocco and the de facto rulers of Wād Nūn; the Bayrūk family.

Just as access to the Atlantic trade was a reflection of the political and economic relationship between the Moroccan court and Wād Nūn, so too was the control and ransoming of European and American captives who shipwrecked along the Sūs coast and points farther south. During his reign, Sīdī Muḥammad wanted to prevent captors in Wād Nūn and European ransom payers from negotiating directly and instead wanted to gain control of shipwrecked sailors and be the one to ransom them back. In order to do so, he usually used Jewish emissaries (who had trade contacts in Wād Nūn) and the governor of Taroudant as intermediaries to gain custody of shipwrecked sailors—but rarely sent officers into Wād Nūn directly.[68] After his release, Follie, a French colonial clerk who was on his way to Senegal when his ship, the *Deux-Amis*, foundered on the coast near the Rio de Oro region on January 17, 1784, complained that in Morocco, Sīdī Muḥammad tried to maintain a monopoly on ransom negotiations and persecuted those who bypassed him in organizing ransoms.[69] Indeed Follie only spent three months in captivity before he was ransomed in Guelmīm. His ransomers were the French vice-consul at al-Ṣawīra and the English directors of an al-Ṣawīra commercial house who arranged for an intermediary, known as Mohamed/David Bentahar, most likely a member of the prominent al-Ṣawīra Jewish merchant family, ben 'Aṭṭār, to negotiate and pay his ransom, and that of others, at Guelmīm and to bring them to al-Ṣawīra. This infuriated Sīdī Muḥammad, who had apparently "ordered" the release of the French captives in the spirit of the 1767 Treaty of Peace and Friendship he had signed with Louis XV of France when they were first captured, which was not obeyed in Guelmīm. In

67 Cochelet, *Naufrage du brick français La Sophie*, 322

68 Vergniot, "De la distance en histoire," 105–7.

69 Follie, *Voyage dans les deserts du Sahara*, 65–70.

a fit of pique, after Follie arrived in al-Ṣawīra, he ordered the arrest of those involved in negotiating the ransom, including the freed captives. However, upon reflection, he rescinded that order. For Sīdī Muḥammad, private ransom negotiations between captors in Wād Nūn and European consuls in al-Ṣawīra demonstrated his less-than-complete authority over the region.

The captivity and ransoming of Irving also demonstrate the role of shipwrecked captives in the diplomacy of Sīdī Muḥammad with both Wād Nūn and the European powers, in particular the British. Irving was the captain of the schooner *Anna,* which was en route from Liverpool to the West African coast in order to purchase slaves when it was wrecked on the Wād Nūn coast on May 27, 1789. Irving and his crew spent fourteen months in captivity—seven months as captives in Wād Nūn and seven months as captives of the Sultan, caught between the Sultan's diplomacy with Wād Nūn and the British. After being taken captive on the coast, within days, Irving was brought to Guelmīm, sold once, and a week later sold yet again to man he knew as Shaykh Brahim, who brought him to Talaïnt about thirty miles northeast of Guelmīm. It was Shaykh Brahim who bought Irving for the purpose of ransoming him and who put him in contact with the British Vice-Consul John Hutchinson at al-Ṣawīra. Throughout the months of June, July, and the first part of August, Hutchinson negotiated with Shaykh Brahim on the ransom price for Irving and the other two crew members that he held. This came to a full stop when Sīdī Muḥammad decided to get involved and to use the crew of the *Anna* for the purposes of his own diplomacy. He arranged first for a Jewish emissary and then for his son Mawlāy 'Abd al-Salām to negotiate the ransom of the *Anna*'s crew in place of the British officials. Sīdī Muḥammad did this in order to force the British to arrange for a doctor for Mawlāy 'Abd al-Salām since Mawlāy 'Abd al-Salām would not ransom the crew until a doctor arrived. In December 1789 Mawlāy 'Abd al-Salām ransomed Irving and brought him to Taroudant. According to Irving, once Mawlāy 'Abd al-Salām had ransomed all of the crew and they were brought to Marrakesh Sīdī Muḥammad told him that they would not be released until the British sent an ambassador to his court. Sīdī Muḥammad wanted concessions from the British government and was using the crew of the *Anna* to pressure the British to give them to him. While this diplomacy was going on the crew were permitted to reside in the European enclave at al-Ṣawīra. They were finally given permission to leave Morocco, in April 1790 after a settlement was reached between Britain and Morocco on the issue of tariffs. However, due to Sīdī Muḥammad's sudden death on April 11, 1790, and the ascension to the throne by Mawlāy al-Yazīd, the release of the crew was delayed until the end of July 1790.[70]

For Adams, it was only after being brought and sold in Wād Nūn by one of his last owners, who he knew as Abdallah Houssa, that ransom became a real possibility. Adams, an African American sailor, was on the ship *Charles* when it foundered about four hundred miles north of the Senegal River on October 11, 1810.[71] Adams and the rest of the crew were found by fishers and later sold. Instead of being funneled northward like some of the crew, Adams was instead enslaved in the desert, his differential treatment most likely due to his racial identity; he even took part in a raid in the Sahel that resulted in his and his owners' captivity in Timbuktu until they were ransomed by kin of Adams's owners. The fact that Adams was ransomed alongside his owners complies with Tuareg ransoming practices where slaves and low-status dependents were often ransomed by their owners and benefactors as a matter of personal honor.[72] Adams was then sold to Abdallah Houssa who had an interest in making money off of Adams by selling him for a profit to someone who could ransom him, instead of keeping him as a slave. Upon reaching Wād Nūn, Adams discovered that two of his shipmates, Stephen Dolbie and James Davison, had already been there for a year and belonged to "the sons of the Governor." The governor would have been 'Abaydallah b. Sālam. Abdallah Houssa first tried to sell Adams to 'Abaydallah b. Sālam but when no agreement could be reached, he sold Adams, to another Wād Nūn merchant, who Adams knew as Bel-Cossim-Abdallah, for the equivalent of seventy dollars. Adams resided in Wād Nūn for a year before he was finally

70 Schwarz, *Slave Captain, The Career of James Irving in the Liverpool Trade*, 7–64. See also Schwarz, "Ransoming Practices and 'Barbary Coast." 59–86.

71 Adams, *The Narrative of Robert Adams*, 31–58. Due to a lack of other employment options, seafaring was a popular vocation for free African American men in the eighteenth and early nineteenth centuries. Due to the egalitarian and cosmopolitan ethos of white seamen, while Blacks may not have been treated as completely equal, they tended to be accepted on the basis of their skills, contributions, and work ethic. Moreover, from 1796 onward the United States government issued free Black sailors with seamen's certificates attesting to their American citizenship, which is more recognition and rights than free African Americans had in the United States. See Bolster, *Black Jacks*. For African American sailors on slave ships see Christopher, *Slave Ship Sailors and Their Captive Cargoes*.

72 Personal communication with Ibrahim Amouren, Director of the Archives d'Agadez, March 2007.

ransomed by the English Vice-Consul in al-Ṣawīra.[73] Abdallah Houssa knew that the quickest way to make a profit out of an American captive like Adams was to sell him to those who had the expertise in negotiating a ransom, the Bayrūk family and their entourage, instead of investing the time and expense in either hiring a mediator or trying to negotiate the ransom himself. As it were, the negotiations for Adams's ransom and release took a year.

The capture and ransom of Irving, Follie, Saugnier, Riley, and Cochelet are good examples of the processes and practices of ransoming shipwrecked sailors. Due to the nature of the sources, the experiences of European/American men held captive in the region were most often recorded whereas those of sub-Saharan Africans, particularly of captive women, were not. Irving, Follie, Saugnier, Riley, and Cochelet were all captured soon after their ships foundered. All were subjected to harsh treatment and threatened with death; but they were also aware that they were valued as captives who could be exchanged for ransom. Irving wrote in his journal entry of June 2, 1789, that

> in the evening we were made to understand that I, the chief mate and my relation were now left alone . . . should be taken to the Emperor of Morocco and sold, that if they could not obtain a hundred dollars a head for us they would cut our throats. This information, horrid as it may appear, considerably eased our minds and excited a hope of still obtaining our liberty and a sight of our dear native country. Our hope was founded on a probability of an ambassador being at the court of the Emperor of Morocco, and that when he heard his countrymen were on sale he would certainly for so trifling a sum redeem [ransom] us and return us to our country.[74]

Riley was the captain of the American brig, *Commerce,* when it foundered on August 18, 1815. Besides Riley there was a crew of nine others: five officers, four seamen, one cook and two cabin boys. Initially, the crew tried to evade capture in their sailboat, but after twenty-three days, driven by starvation and thirst, they voted to return to shore, permit their capture, and hope that they would be traded north and eventually ransomed. Four of the crew, including Riley, spent two months as captives before being ransomed, whereas it took nineteen months for the others from the ship who were ransomed to be released. Of the decision to surrender, Riley wrote that "it was the 10th of September. I awakened my companions and told them we must now go forward and shew [sic] ourselves to the natives—that I expected they would seize upon us as slaves but had strong hopes that some of us would

73 Adams, *The Narrative of Robert Adams,* 66–88.

74 Schwarz, *Slave Captain,* 134.

escape with our lives. I also mentioned to them the name of the American Consul General at Tangier, and that if it ever was in their power, they must write to him, inform him of the fate of our vessel and her crew: to write, if possible to any Christian merchant in Mogadore, Gibraltar or elsewhere or to the Consul at Algiers, Tunis or Tripoli, if they should hear those places mentioned."[75] This demonstrated that Riley expected that he and his captive crewmates would be able to communicate with Europeans and Americans in the Maghrib who could arrange for their ransom. Indeed, as Sears argues, sailors knew that the only way that they would survive being shipwrecked along the coast was if they were found and taken captive by local people, usually fishers, who knew how to survive the desert and that their only chance at rescue was to be sold to someone willing to arrange their ransom at al-Ṣawīra.[76] Yet Riley and his crew denied this reality for as long as possible.

All four men were sold numerous times, at increasing prices, as they were moved up the coast toward al-Ṣawīra. For example, while Follie was traded twice and had three sets of captors, he was only held captive for four months before his ransom was arranged by the French vice-consul in al-Ṣawīra.[77] Before being ransomed, Follie's shipmate, Saugnier, had at least seven sets of captors, and it appears that his third and fourth captors both "flipped" him for profit. His third captor held him for only a few days while his fourth captor traded him the day after he got him.[78]

Riley had only two owners. About eighteen days after his capture, he and his crewmates, second mate Aaron Savage and seamen James Clarke and Thomas Burns, were sold to Sīdī Hamit of the Awlād Bū al-Sibā' and brought to Guelmīm. This accounts for their only months-long captivity as Sīdī Hamit was affiliated with the Bayrūk family. Once in Guelmīm, Riley was encouraged and was able to make contact, through an exchange of letters, with the English Consul, William Willshire, in al-Ṣawīra who arranged for his ransom and that of Savage, Clarke and Burns and where they were brought and released.[79] The fact that Sīdī Hamit was a member of the Awlād Bū al-Sibā' is important. Unlike the Tikna the Awlād Bū al-Sibā' never had a

75 Riley, *Loss of the American Brig Commerce*, 71.

76 For more on American sailor experiences while awaiting ransom in the western Sahara see Sears, *American Slaves and African Masters*, 109–35.

77 Follie, *Voyage dans les deserts du Sahara* 52–56.

78 Saugnier, "Récit du naufrage du Moghreb," 140–44.

79 Riley, *Loss of the American Brig Commerce*, 346.

distinctive or permanent "homeland." However, from a 1596 truce between them and the local Awlād Tidrārīn, the Awlād Bū al-Sibā' claimed territorial rights on the western Saharan coast from Imrīgli south to a place just north of the mouth of the Senegal River near the caravan passageway of Ndiago. Although contested by other groups from Trārza Emirate with similar territorial claims, the Awlād Bū al-Sibā' territorial claim included the right to the Atlantic coast and the small island of Tidra, which was accessible by foot at low tide and that contained a source of fresh water. This territorial claim put members of the Awlād Bū al-Sibā' in the perfect position for collecting shipwrecked sailors. Moreover, the Awlād Bū al-Sibā' had a long-standing relationship with the Tikna, Wād Nūn and the city of Guelmīm, which dates from at least the fifteenth century. One Awlād Bū al-Sibā' ancestor from the fifteenth century, 'Amrān, became an established saint commemorated at the yearly fair of Guelmīm's neighboring town, Liksābī. The Tikna and Awlād Bū al-Sibā' were close commercial and political allies and a member of the Awlād Bū al-Sibā' usually held the position of imam in Guelmīm's main mosque.[80] Riley claimed that Sīdī Hamit was the "son-in-law" of the "governor" of Wād Nūn. This is most likely a reference to Bayrūk's father, 'Abaydallah. Whether or not Riley is correct on the exact relationship between Sīdī Hamit and 'Abaydallah, it does indicate the closeness between the Awlād Bū al-Sibā', the Tikna and the Bayrūk family.

Whereas it was when Irving was sold to Shaykh Brahim in Talaïnt that Irving was ordered to make contact with the British vice-consul; an order with which Irving was happy to comply. On June 24, 1789, Irving wrote in his journal that was told by one of the Jewish men who was under the protection of his captor that he must "write to Mr. Hutchinson, the British Vice-Consul at Mogodore [sic], informing him of my misfortune and situation as he (the Jew) had occasion to dispatch a courier for that place distant only about six days journey. The Jew also assured me that the Vice-Consul would send and purchase me, and that myself and crew (if alive) would be returned to our native country."[81] Except for the interference of Sīdī Muḥammad, who at the time was trying to maintain a monopoly on the ransoming of Europeans and to use their presence for his own diplomacy with

80 For more on the Awlād Bū al-Sibā' see Lydon, *On Trans-Saharan Trails*, 186–93.

81 Schwarz, *Slave Captain*, 141.

both Europe and Wād Nūn, Irving would have probably been ransomed and released soon after reaching Talaïnt.

Conclusion

For the Maghrib, Mediterranean ransoming encompassed the immediate Mediterranean basin, the Atlantic coast and into the Sahara desert. Biography and individual stories, even though these sources are mostly about men, permit a deeper understanding of how race, class, gender, and particular political circumstances affected whether and how an individual was ransomed. On the macro-level ransoming was not just viewed as an obligation to protect Muslims from potential enslavement but was also viewed as a tool and a measurement to gauge political influence and control in both Mediterranean and Saharan affairs. For Morocco in particular, gaining control and ransoming back European captives was an important component of engagement with European powers and in its relationship with al-Sūs and Wād Nūn. Europeans were able to be ransomed from North Africa because ransoming was permissible under Mālikī law, Maghrib governments viewed the money gained from ransoming as more beneficial than European labor and because these governments established processes for the ransoming of captives. The same was not true for Muslim captives held in Europe. For the most part, European governments preferred to maintain control over the labor of Muslim captives and enslave them rather than benefit from their ransom money. Most Muslim captives held in Europe were freed through privately arranged prisoner exchanges, although governments, especially Sīdī Muḥammad's, actively used diplomacy to arrange the ransom, exchange, and free release of Muslim captives. As will be seen in chapters 3 and 4, the governments established by the nineteenth-century West African jihadist states were not motivated by financial or political gain to ransom back enemies that they held. However, what they did share with many Moroccan sultans was the belief that it was the duty of Muslim rulers to free captive freeborn Muslims and that ransoming was a useful and legitimate tool for doing so.

The ransoming of Muslims in Europe ended with the abolition of slavery in that region. For Morocco, the abolition of slavery in Malta by Napoleon in 1798 was of special importance since it had been a main nexus of the trade in Muslim captives. However, the holding of Europeans for ransom and the organizing of ransoms through Morocco continued into the nineteenth century despite the 1818 ban on corsairing activities instituted by Mawlāy

Sulaymān. In the last half of the nineteenth century the Bayrūk family continued to hold Europeans for ransom in Wād Nūn. For instance, when he was in Wād Nūn in the mid-nineteenth century, as part of his overland trip between Senegal and al-Ṣawīra, Leopold Panet overheard plans to kidnap him and demand a ransom for him from the French Consul in al-Ṣawīra.[82] In another case, an Englishman, W Butler was held in Wād Nūn for eight years, from 1866 to 1874.[83]

82 Panet, "Relations d'un Voyage du Senegal a Souiera (Mogador)," 168. Panet was a biracial orphan born on Goreé Island. He was educated at a French school and became involved in the gum trade along the Senegal River. After participating in Colonel Raffanel's expedition to Kaarta, he became, in 1850, the third "Christian" to cross the western Sahara, albeit disguised as a Muslim, when he volunteered to go overland between Senegal and Morocco. According to E. F. Gautier, Europeans who shipwrecked or crashed along the Atlantic coast of the Sahara were still being held for ransom as recent as the 1930s. In discussing the Toulouse to Dakar flight route he states, "There are occasional crashes, in which case the aviator is made prisoner by the Moors and while neither killed nor tortured is held for ransom." Gautier, *Sahara: The Great Desert*, 230. See also Vergniot "De la distance en histoire," on Moroccan ransoming practices in the nineteenth and early twentieth centuries, 114–24.

83 Lenz, *Timbouctou Voyage au Maroc, au Sahara et au Soudan*, 1:274, 360.

Chapter Three

Jihad, the Sokoto Caliphate, and Ransoming

In a song he composed on the late eighteenth-century social strife in Hausaland, ʿUthmān b. Fodiye blamed the divisions in society in large part on the capturing and enslavement of free individuals.[1] In West Africa, unlike in the Maghrib, ransoming was primarily viewed by government officials as a means to free captive freeborn Muslims and not as a way to benefit financially from captives that they held. Like many West African scholars, ʿUthmān was interested in addressing the problems of his time through interpretation and application of Islamic scholarship. While he would eventually lead a jihad, along with his brother ʿAbdullāhi b. Fodiye and his son Muḥammad Bello that would overthrow the various kingdoms of the central Sudan and establish the Sokoto Caliphate, ʿUthmān first tried to use moral suasion and to advise political rulers to effect change and to protect the rights of freeborn Muslims.

The Triumvirate, as ʿUthmān, ʿAbdullāhi, and Bello became known, came from a long line of Fulbe scholars and teachers. As descendants of an eighteenth-century scholarly Fulbe family in the central Sudan, the Triumvirate's education included tawḥīd (theology), fiqh (Islamic legal theory/jurisprudence), tafsīr (Qu'rānic commentary), hadith, and Arabic. It included a mixture of the basic texts of the Mālikī madh'hab, the Sufi Qādiriyya ṭarīqa and of major West African scholars including al-Maghīlī and Bābā. ʿUthmān and ʿAbdullāhi's principal teachers were their uncles ʿUthmān Binduri and Muḥammad Sambo and the scholars Muḥammad b. Rāji and Jibrīl b. ʿUmar. The Triumvirate grounded their scholarship in the Mālikī madh'hab, and the

1 ʿUthmān b. Fodiye, "Boneji Hausa" as translated in Saidu, "The Significance of the Shehu's Sermons and Poems in Ajami," 205. "Some of its troubles are capture of a free man, not a slave; then follow this (action) with enslavement."

Sufi Qādiriyya ṭarīqa. ʿAbdullāhi has often been described as the ideologue of the movement whereas ʿUthmān has been described as the teacher and spokesperson.[2] In evaluating his own, his brother's, and his son's intellectual strengths, in an 1813 text, *Najm al-ikhwān yahtadūna bihi bi-idhn Allāh fi umūr al-zamān*, ʿUthmān described ʿAbdullāhi as an expert in jurisprudence, Bello as an expert in administration and himself as an expert in both.[3] In addition to these three men, another figure who was instrumental in the consolidation of the Sokoto Caliphate was ʿUthmān's daughter Asma'u b. Fodiye, a well-respected scholar who established the education system in the Caliphate.

Indeed, considering Asma'u's instrumental role in the establishment of the Sokoto Caliphate and the perpetuation of the Sokoto intellectual tradition it is more accurate to refer to the Sokoto Tetravirate rather than the Triumvirate. Asma'u was integral to the maintenance and reproduction of the prestige of the Fodiye family and the acceptance of the Sokoto interpretation of Islam. Asma'u was still a child at the beginning of the jihad but helped with battlefield logistics and supplies as she grew older. Just like her father, uncle, and brother, Asma'u was a well-established scholar who wrote over five dozen works in Tamajek, Fulfulde, Hausa, and Arabic.[4] Her greatest contribution to the establishment of the Caliphate was the creation of an education system and curriculum for women. She established a cadre of teachers, known as the ʿYan Taru who spread the teachings of the Fodiye throughout the Caliphate.[5] The Fodiye believed in educating their daughters as much as they educated their sons. Indeed, even though ʿUthmān advocated the separation of unrelated men and women in daily life, from the time he was a young preacher, and despite the backlash he received from other men, ʿUthmān supported women's education. According to Muhammad Ahmad Khani both ʿUthmān and ʿAbdullāhi believed that leaving women

2 Khani, *The Intellectual Origin of Sokoto Jihad*, 29–31; Fillitz, "Uthmân dan Fodio et la question du pouvoir en pays haoussa," 209–20.

3 Gwandu, "A Pragmatic Administrator's Approach to Fiqh–The Case of Amir al-Mu'minin Muhammad Bello."

4 See Mack and Boyd, *One Woman's Jihad:Nana Asma'u, Scholar and Scribe*; Boyd and Mack, "The Essential Nana Asma'u"; Bivins, *Telling Stories, Making Histories*, 111–27.

5 For more on Asma'u and the ʿYan Turu see Boyd and Mack, *Educating Muslim Women*, 94–121.

in "ignorance" was a greater "evil" than their mixing with men.[6] Given her family and her strong intellect, it is not surprising that Asma'u held such an important position. Asma'u's education system was the means through which the Tetravirate's interpretation of Islam was promulgated and passed down to subsequent generations and was therefore instrumental in the success of the jihad as women were their children's first teachers. Moreover, as a woman intellectual, who worked with enslaved women in elite households in a society where the vast majority of enslaved people were women, she offers a unique perspective on the issue of legal and illegal enslavement and the rights of freeborn Muslims.

This chapter focuses on the problem of what was perceived by many Muslims as illegal enslavement in Hausaland and Sokoto Caliphate policies concerning ransoming as a strategy to free captives prior to enslavement. First, it considers the issue of the enslavement of Muslims prior to the beginning of the Sokoto jihad and its role in instigating political reform. Second, it examines the Sokoto Caliphate's political, social, and economic context and its policy toward enslavement. Finally, it examines Sokoto's policies concerning ransoming as both a remedy for illegal enslavement and as an option for dealing with captives held by their forces.

The Hausa City-States, the Enslavement of Muslims, and Intellectual Responses

In the seventeenth and eighteenth centuries, the region that eventually became the heartland of the Sokoto Caliphate, Hausaland, was divided into many kingdoms of which the most important included Katsina, Kano, Gobir, and Zamfara. The Hausa states were large entities, larger than their counterparts on the Swahili coast, but relatively smaller than West African forest-zone states such as Asante or Oyo. Some were organized around urban towns and markets, with surrounding settled agricultural and commercial zones. The economic life of the Hausa states was dominated by textile production, which involved growing cotton and indigo and other trades such as leather working, iron working, and pottery making, as well as control of the southern end of trans-Saharan trade routes. While those who identified as Hausa were mostly urban or settled agriculture producers whose products supported local, regional, and long-distance trade and who considered

6 Khani, *The Intellectual Origin of Sokoto Jihad*, 31–34.

themselves to be Muslims, the Hausa states also had large populations of bori-practicing Hausa farmers and of Tuareg and Fulbe, known locally as Fulani, pastoralists. By the late seventeenth century most of the rural Fulbe population considered themselves to be Muslim.

While the spread of Islam in Hausaland was a complex process, it is commonly accepted that the Maghribi scholar al-Maghīlī introduced the Mālikī madh'hab to the region when he was at the Kano court of Muḥammad Rumfa in the late fifteenth century. By the end of the seventeenth century, Islam was the religion of most of the Hausa royal courts, and there were a growing number of adherents among the general population. By the end of the eighteenth century, Hausa kings were navigating a complex religious environment of bori practitioners and of Muslims. Both Hausa society and Muslim society were divided into two. Hausa society was divided between a bori rural population and an urban Muslim population. The Muslim community was also divided between the urban Hausa Muslim community focused on the palace courts and a rural Fulbe and Tuareg Muslim population focused on individual teachers. The growth of Islamic education throughout the eighteenth century, due in large part to the schools established by the Kunta scholars of Timbuktu throughout the western and central Sudan and Sahel to promulgate the Qādiriyya, especially among the rural population, led to a questioning of the traditional religions, values, and customs, including bori, upon which the structure of the eighteenth-century states were based. Throughout the eighteenth century, the rural Muslim community complained that rulers were enacting unislamic laws and participating in bori rituals.[7] For example in the first part of the eighteenth century, in order to raise funds for wars, the Sarkin Kano, Muḥammad Sharefa dan Dadi (1703–31) introduced new taxes on the main market, Kurmi, on women upon marriage, and on Muslim scholars.[8] These taxes went against allowable taxes under Mālikī law. Instead of interpreting these taxes as a desperate attempt to raise revenue for the war effort, many Muslims viewed them as an attack on their rights as freeborn Muslims to not be subjected to "illegal" taxes.

One of the most important complaints of the Muslim community, especially of rural Muslims, toward the prejihadist states was their inability or

7 El-Masri, "A Critical Edition of Dan Fodio's Bayān wujub al-hijra 'ala 'l-'ibad," 521–22.

8 Adeleye "Hausaland and Bornu 1600–1800," 517. For more on the prejihad political situation in Hausaland see Fuglestad, "A Reconsideration of Hausa History before the Jihad," 219–29.

their unwillingness of their governments to protect them from enslavement during border wars. These wars were caused by disputes over control of trade routes, especially as long-distance trade in West Africa shifted from a focus on the Sahara to a focus on the Atlantic, and as the region became more integrated into the Atlantic economy. Many of these captives were sold into the trans-Saharan and transatlantic slave trades. Many rural captives were Fulbe, which has led to past interpretations of the jihad as an ethnic conflict between the Fulbe and Hausa, despite the fact that 'Uthmān's followers included significant numbers of Hausa and Tuareg, or as a conflict between rural pastoralists and urban agriculturalists.[9] Yet, the enslavement of freeborn Muslims was an issue throughout eighteenth-century West Africa and involved Muslims from multiple ethnicities and political jurisdictions. As mentioned in chapter 1, Muḥammad Kabā Saghanughu was a freeborn Muslim student who was kidnapped while traveling from the Upper Niger Valley to Timbuktu and sold to Jamaica in 1777.[10] Other prominent freeborn Muslims who were taken captive, not ransomed, and who were trafficked to the Americas include Ayuba b. Sulayman Ibrahima Diallo, also known as Job ben Solomon, and Big Prince Whitten. Diallo who was from Fuuta Bundu was kidnapped in 1731 and sold to a commercial partner of his family, the English slave trader, Captain Stephen Pike. Even though Pike and Diallo knew each other, Pike did not release Diallo nor delay his sailing to Maryland to wait for Diallo's father to send his ransom.[11] Whitten, also known as Juan Bautista, was Mandinka, probably from Kaabu on the Gambia River, who was enslaved in the Gambia River Valley in the 1770s and subsequently sold to Charleston, South Carolina. Later he escaped to St. Augustine in Spanish Florida and served twenty-six years in the Spanish militia.[12]

Throughout the eighteenth century, there were significant and increasing numbers of Hausa, Fulbe, and other Muslims from the central Sudan sold southward toward Yorubaland and Asante and into the transatlantic

9 See, for example, Last, *The Sokoto Caliphate*; Hiskett, *The Sword of Truth*, Adeleye, "Hausaland and Borno 1600–1800"; Trimingham, *A History of Islam in West Africa*.

10 See Daddi Addoun and Lovejoy, "Muḥammad Kābā Saghanughu and the Muslim Community in Jamaica," and Daddi Addoun and Lovejoy, "The Arabic Manuscript of Muhammad Kaba Saghanughu of Jamaica c. 1820."

11 Lofkrantz and Ojo, "Slavery, Freedom, and Failed Ransom Negotiations," 29. For more on Diallo's life history including his eventual ransom from Maryland see Naylor and Wallace, "Author of this own Fate?"

12 Landers, *Atlantic Creoles in the Age of Revolutions*, 15–19, 38–41, 51–54.

slave trade. Muslim slaves were retained in Oyo and formed a significant contingent within the military. By 1817, there were enough Hausa slaves—many (if not most) of whom were Muslim—in Oyo that they constituted an important component of that year's rebellion in northern Yorubaland. Similarly, large numbers of Muslims were held in Asante.[13] By the mid-eighteenth century there had been an increase of Hausa, Nupe, and "Bornu" slaves in the Americas over previous periods. This increase of enslaved Hausa in Yorubaland, Asante, Dahomey, and the Americas corresponded not only with the wars between the Hausa states but with the increase in general trade between the central Sudan and the Atlantic world. The increase in trade between Hausaland and the Bight of Benin was facilitated by Oyo opening a direct trade route to the coast and establishing control over the ports of Porto Novo and Badagry. This allowed for direct trade between Hausaland and European traders on the coast. The enslavement of Muslims and their deportation to Oyo and to the Americas as well as northward across the Sahara was alarming to freeborn Muslims in Hausaland concerned with their own safety and to Muslim intellectuals and leaders concerned with issues surrounding legal and illegal enslavement.

Throughout the late eighteenth century, based on (and building upon) the scholarship on the issue, intellectuals in the central Sudan tried to use moral suasion to persuade political leaders to uphold the rights of freeborn Muslims and, especially, to protect them from enslavement. Scholars complained that freeborn Muslim captives taken in the wars between the Hausa states should be able to expect that the Muslim governments of these states would uphold their right to freedom. The failure of Hausa kings to properly navigate expectations, especially in terms of protections by the state, had led to rural indifference and urban disgruntlement among Muslims by the late eighteenth century. There was a growing call, outside of royal circles, led by noncourt clerics but with growing mass support, to reorganize society according to a more "orthodox" interpretation of Islam: one with an emphasis on protecting Muslim "rights" rather than the "syncretic" interpretations favored by the Hausa elites. In the central Sudan, in the years leading up to the Sokoto jihad and throughout the nineteenth century, various scholars

13 The 1817 rebellion was an important event in the disintegration of Oyo and the integration of Ilorin into the Sokoto Caliphate. See Verger, *Trade Relations between the Bight of Benin and Brazil, 17th-19th Century*, 186–90; Fisher, "A Muslim William Wilberforce?" 537–55. See also Lovejoy, *Transformations*, 99, Adamu, "The Delivery of Slaves from the Central Sudan," 178–79.

repeated the injunction against enslaving freeborn Muslims and attempted to free captive freeborn Muslims.

The Tetravirate was at the vanguard of the movement to protect Muslims from enslavement. However, they were not alone. ʻUthmān and ʻAbdullāhi developed an interest in social activism through their teacher: the Tuareg scholar Jibrīl b. ʻUmar. Throughout the late eighteenth century in both Aïr and Hausaland, Jibrīl had been an agitator for Muslims rights and especially for the protection of freeborn Muslims from enslavement. He divided non-Muslims into five categories: those who do not know the Qu'ran, those who mock the Sunna, those who practice false religions, those who do not pray, and those who sell free individuals without a just reason. Jibrīl further equated the selling of free men with adultery, the drinking of wine, and manslaughter, which he viewed as serious moral and religious sins.[14] Although he died before the start of the jihad, in their writings, both ʻUthmān and ʻAbdullāhi discussed Jibrīl's influence on them.[15] Oral history from Adār in the modern-day Niger Republic confirms the close relationship between Jibrīl and the two brothers. According to oral tradition, Jibrīl had wanted to conduct a jihad in Hausaland but did not because God had told him that this task was reserved for ʻUthmān.[16] This oral tradition indicates both the close relationship between teacher and student and Jibrīl's desire to influence his students toward activism. Similarly to Jibrīl, ʻUthmān's contemporary and friend, the Fulbe scholar Muḥammad Tukur also condemned the enslavement of freeborn Muslims.[17]

Prior to resorting to war, ʻUthmān repeatedly tried to convince Hausa political leaders to institute policies to protect the Muslim community. While

14 See Khani, *The Intellectual Origin of the Sokoto Jihad*, 30–31; Bivar and Hiskett, "The Arabic Literature of Nigeria to 1804," 143.

15 For example, ʻAbdullāhi b. Fodiye *Tazyīn al-waraqāt* (1813), ʻAbdullāhi b. Fodiye, *Īdā' al-nusūkh man akhdhtu ʻanhu min al-shuyūkh* (1812), ʻUthmān b. Fodiye *Naṣā'iḥ al-umma al-Muḥammadiyya* (undated). Together, ʻUthmān, ʻAbdullāhi, and Bello, wrote 279 works in Arabic, Hausa and Fulfulde, not including letters, other informal writing, and compositions that were never written down. For a discussion of these works, see Last, "The Book and the Nature of Knowledge," 208; and Last, "The Book in the Sokoto Caliphate," 135–63. For a listing of many of ʻUthmān b. Fodiye ʻAbdullāhi b. Fodiye and Muḥammad Bello's writings see Hunwick, *The Writings of Central Sudanic Africa*, 2:52–149.

16 Hamani, *L'Islam au Soudan Central*, 196.

17 Tukur, "Busuraaʻu," verses 8–15.

he was never a court cleric, up until hostilities erupted between him and Gobir's Sarki (king), Yunfa, in 1804, 'Uthmān was a frequent visitor to the Gobir court pressing for reform and also taught some members of the royal family, including Yunfa. From the time he started preaching around 1774, 'Uthmān regularly visited the Gobir court throughout the reigns of Bawa Jangwarzo, Yakuba, Nafata, and finally Yunfa. Indeed, upon the death of Nafata in 1801, 'Uthmān supported Yunfa's succession to his father's throne against claims by other male family members.[18] During this time, 'Uthmān's writings frequently addressed the issue of illegal enslavement. In *Masā'il muhimma* (1802) (Important matters) written two years before the jihad, 'Uthmān forbade the sale of any Fulbe on the basis of the Fulbe having been long recognized as Muslim.[19] During the jihad, he reiterated the importance of protecting free persons from enslavement. In a Fulfulde poem, *Tabbat hakika* (Be sure of that) written sometime between 1809 and 1812, either near the end or just after the first phase of the jihad, 'Uthmān proclaimed, "And the one who enslaves a freeman, he shall suffer torment/ The Fire shall enslave him, be sure of that!"[20] 'Asma'u b. Fodiye restated her father's opinion twenty years later in her revision and translation of the poem into Hausa. In her version she states, "The Enslaver of a freeman who inflicts on him harsh treatment/The Fire will enslave them all/ Be sure of God's Truth."[21]

Uthmān twinned his diplomatic efforts with concrete activism. In the immediate years prior to the jihad, he regularly sent his students to intercept caravans and rescue trafficked Muslims.[22] Indeed, 'Uthmān was not unique in this behavior. In 1770, six years before the Denyanke ruling class was overthrown and the Almamate was established in Fuuta Toro in 1776, the Fulbe scholar who initiated the jihad, Sulaymaan Baal, forcefully rescued a Muslim man who was being transported by boat on the Senegal River to the coast to be sold into the transatlantic slave trade. In order to free the man, Baal first demanded that his captors release him since he was a freeborn Muslim. When that did not work, Baal tried to ransom him. Only when his money was refused did his students attack the captors to effect the

18 Hiskett, *The Sword of Truth*, 46–49.

19 Hiskett, *The Sword of Truth*, 77.

20 Hiskett, *The Sword of Truth*, 77; Jean Boyd and Beverly B. Mack date the poem to 1812. See Boyd and Mack, *Collected Works of Nana Asma'u*, 44.

21 Asma'u b. Fodiye, "Be Sure of God's Truth," 51.

22 Nicolas, "Détours d'une conversion collective," 83–105.

release of the captive.[23] This is important. Both Muslim and non-Muslim Africans preferred to pay ransom for the freedom of their captive kin and friends instead of using physical force since a violent altercation risked the death of not just the captive but also the death or capture of the rescuers. As in this case, physical force was usually a strategy of last resort that would only be used when there was a reasonable chance of success.[24]

The enslavement of freeborn Muslims was universally condemned by the Fodiye and their circle. However, they held a relatively narrow view of who they considered to be a Muslim. In defining who was and who was not a Muslim, the Tetravirate drew upon al-Maghīlī's definition. Al-Maghīlī defined as non-Muslim those who denied the existence of God and the prophecy of the Prophet Muḥammad; those who behave in ways that an "unbeliever" behaves even though those actions on their own are not acts of unbelief, such as the drinking of alcohol, forcible seizure of property, abandonment of obligatory religious practices, and denial of anything in the Qur'an, and making statements only a non-Muslim would make.[25] Following this definition, in *Nūr-al-albāb* (undated but most likely predating the jihad), his treatise on "blameworthy" practices in pre-reform Hausaland, 'Uthmān divided the population of the Sudan into three categories. The first group consisted of people who followed "pure" Islamic law. The second category included individuals who followed a mixture of orthodox Islamic practices and bori practices while the third group consisted of people who have never accepted the "truth" of Islam. 'Uthmān considered it fully permissible to enslave members of the last two groups, along with their children, and to confiscate their property.[26] In *Wathīqat ahl al-Sūdān*, 'Uthmān argued that it was obligatory to make war on any ruler who was an "apostate"

23 Kamara, *Florilège au jardin de l'histoire des noirs,* 316–17. Rudolph Ware argues that the enslavement of freeborn Muslims and this instance in particular was a major cause of the Fuuta Toro jihad. See Ware, *The Walking Qu'rān,* 115–26. Indeed, after the jihad, in a 1785 treaty with France, the Fuuta Toro government that articulated the terms of trade and the access of French traders to the upper Senegal River Valley, made clear that it was illegal for freeborn Muslims to be enslaved and for French traders to buy illegally enslaved freeborn Muslims for the transatlantic slave trade. See Barry, *La Senégambie du XVe au XIX siècle,* 156.

24 Lofkrantz and Ojo, "Slavery, Freedom, and Failed Ransom Negotiations," 35–42.

25 Hunwick, *Sharī'a in Songhay,* 74.

26 'Uthmān b. Fodiye, *Nūr-al-albāb,* 300–303.

and on any backsliding Muslims in order to protect the rights of freeborn Muslims who he defined as individuals who complied with his interpretation of Islam.[27] Indeed as Kota Kariya has shown, the Tetravirate's willingness to enslave "apostate" Muslims was controversial. 'Uthmān acknowledged that the majority of scholarly opinion opposed the enslavement of "apostates." However, 'Uthmān justified the enslavement of "apostates" on the basis that ikhtilāf (difference of opinion) existed on the topic and that where ikhtilāf existed it was acceptable to follow any previous legal opinions of one's choosing unless they were contrary to accepted interpretations of the Qu'ran, Sunna, and ijmā' (consensus of jurists). In this regard, as Koriya argues, 'Uthmān was consistent, as he had long advocated the free choice of which opinion to follow when scholarly opinion was divided on a legal issue.[28]

Not all Muslim scholars in Hausaland supported the Tetravirate. Many Muslim scholars associated with the royal courts unsurprisingly backed their governments rather than the Tetravirate. It was these scholars who were the primary target of 'Uthmān's criticisms during his speaking tours in the years preceding the jihad.[29] 'Uthmān's criticisms centered on their "syncretic" practices such as being producers and purveyors of magical objects such as charms, amulets, and gris-gris, and their unwillingness to condemn the Hausa rulers' failure to uphold the protections afforded to Muslims according to Mālikī law. This attack on "syncretic" practices was exemplified in an 1810–1812 exchange of a series of letters between 'Uthmān, Bello, and Muḥammad al-Kānimī of Bornu. The scholars debated about whether or not the prevalence of syncretic religious practice within a community made the entire community non-Muslim. 'Uthmān and Bello argued that it did. Al-Kānimī argued that while "syncretic" practitioners might be "bad" Muslims they were nevertheless still Muslims and worthy of the protections given to freeborn Muslims.[30] This concern for "pure" Islam continued throughout the existence of the Caliphate. Writing in the 1820s Asma'u counted consulting with diviners, observing bori, and practicing "witchcraft" among her list of "dangerous habits" that needed to be abolished.[31] However, as well as its attack on "syncretic" practice, the Tetravirate also had a tendency to attack and declare as apostates or non-Muslims any scholar who disagreed

27 'Uthmān b. Fodiye, *Wathīqat ahl al-Sūdān*, 240.

28 Kariya, "Free Choice Theory and the Justification of Enslavement," 3–4.

29 Bello, *Infāq al-maysūr*, 65.

30 This correspondence was reproduced in Bello, *Infāq al-maysūr*.

31 Asma'u b. Fodiye, *Tanbīh al-ghāfilīn*, 24–25.

with them. For example, early in the jihad, Bello attacked and destroyed the intellectual town of Yandoto, south of Katsina, because its scholars refused to support his cause.[32] Indeed, Sokoto justified its attack on Bornu on the concept of taqlīd, the emulation of an ideal Muslim leader. According to Sokoto forces, Fulbe in Bornu who were rebelling against the Mai of Bornu were doing so because they were emulating 'Uthmān as an ideal Muslim leader. Thereby, according to Tetravirate reasoning, 'Uthmān was correct to declare the Mai of Bornu and his supporters, who viewed themselves as defending Bornu against an internal rebellion, as takfīr (declaring a self-professed Muslim as an infidel), making Bornu a legitimate venue for jihad.[33]

For the Tetravirate and their supporters, the Sokoto jihad was a response to attacks on Muslim rights, especially the right to protection from enslavement. According to 'Uthmān, he embarked upon jihad against Gobir in defense of the Muslim community. He stated that, "self-defence and defence of dependants and possessions is a righteous act, according to received opinion. We went to meet those who were harrying us—horsemen of evil purpose."[34] This view was supported by an anonymous Hausa poem describing the raid that led to 'Uthmān and his followers' migration, known as the "Sokoto hijra," from Degel to Gudu on the western border of Gobir in 1804. The withdrawal precipitated the declaration of jihad later in the year. The poem referred to the attack and captive taking by Gobir forces on a Muslim community living in the village of Gimbana on the Zamfara River, southwest of present-day Sokoto, under the leadership of the Hausa scholar 'Abd al-Salām and their subsequent rescue by jihadist forces. The poem describes the attack by Gobir as follows: "They captured freemen and their war captives. They burned all the books you understand, And likewise, the Koran reading boards, scattering them on the ground."[35] Accounts differ on whether or not it was Yunfa or one of his commanders who ordered the attack and whether it was 'Uthmān or 'Abdullāhi who ordered the rescue of the captives who were being brought back to Yunfa's capital at Alkalawa to be sold as slaves. However, the incident resulted in Yunfa ordering 'Uthmān and his family into exile and 'Uthmān responding by migrating, along with

32 Bello, *Infāq al-maysūr*, 105.

33 Lofkrantz, "Intellectual Discourse in the Sokoto Caliphate," 391–92. For more on the history of Bornu see Hiribarren, *A History of Borno*.

34 'Uthmān b. Fodiye, *Tanbīh al ikhwān alā arḍ al-sūdān*, 191. For an early account of the jihad see Salih, *Takyid 'Akhbar*.

35 Hiskett, "The Song of the Shaihu's Miracles," 95.

his followers, to Gudu.[36] After the Gimbana incident, and the migration of 'Uthmān and his followers to the outskirts of Yunfa's political authority, it was clear that there was little chance for a peaceful resolution between the Gobir state and 'Uthmān's Muslim community. Yunfa viewed 'Uthmān and his followers as rebellious subjects, whereas 'Uthmān viewed his former student as an apostate who would neither respect nor uphold the legal rights of freeborn Muslims. Both sides prepared for the war which started when Gobir troops attacked Gudu, which 'Abdullāhi had already evacuated in anticipation of hostilities.

The war with Yunfa sparked rebellions elsewhere throughout Hausaland and drew people who were motivated by religious, political, social, and economic reasons. 'Uthmān, 'Abdullāhi and Bello were motivated by what they perceived to be a need to protect freeborn Muslims from antagonistic state structures and were supported by many who shared their ideals. However, other supporters were drawn to the jihad not just because they shared the Fodiye's ideals but also due to complex sociopolitical and economic factors operating in Hausaland at the time. Many people saw the jihad as an opportunity to alter ethnic, political, and economic relationships. Peter Waterman attributes the support for the jihad to economic factors as the regional economy changed from what he viewed as a tribute mode of production to one based on trading, raiding, and slave-produced agriculture. Economic change then led to changes in ethnic relationships and political organization.[37] Certainly, starting in the sixteenth century, Hausaland became more integrated into both the trans-Saharan and Atlantic economies, which led to greater competition over resources and trade between the Hausa states and greater participation in the external slave trades.[38] Besides being at risk for captivity and enslavement, the rural populations—nomadic and sedentary, pastoralist and agriculturalist—bore the brunt of the costs of these conflicts as governments sought to raise revenue to fund military expeditions. Yet, urban populations were also called upon to fund the conflicts through increased taxation. Environmental crises also drove young men to the jihadist cause.[39] Due to epizootic disease outbreaks in cattle around Gobir and

---

36 For a discussion of the different accounts of the Gimbana incident see Hiskett, *The Sword of Truth*, 70–73; Last, *The Sokoto Caliphate*, 14–16.

37 Waterman, "The Jihad in Hausaland as an Episode in African History," 141–52.

38 Adeleye, "Hausaland and Bornu 1600–1800."

39 Last, "Towards a Political History of Youth in Muslim Northern Nigeria," 4.

Bornu, in the last decades of the eighteenth century many Fulbe youth were without cattle. Previously, their choices under such circumstances would have been to join Hausa courts as either soldiers or palace retainers; however, the jihad gave these men a new opportunity for social and economic advancement. Indeed, as Mahmoud Hamman has demonstrated, for the Middle Benue River region in the mid-nineteenth century local politics and economics were important factors in whether or not people supported the Sokoto cause.[40]

The Sokoto jihad, therefore, was underpinned by a concern to protect the rights of freeborn Muslims against enslavement. However, the jihad was sustained in part by people who joined for more pragmatic reasons, such as needing a job, than the ideals outlined by the scholars they followed. The tension between the ideals of the scholars and the more practical concerns of their followers would shape not only the form of governance within the Sokoto Caliphate but also policy toward enslavement and remedies for illegal captivity and enslavement.

The Establishment of the Sokoto Caliphate

The state that the jihadists established between 1804 and 1810, the Sokoto Caliphate, became the largest state in sub-Saharan Africa in the nineteenth century, with a population of between eight and ten million people.[41] Its founders envisioned a state grounded in Islamic precepts, the Mālikī madh'hab, and the Sufi Qādiriyya ṭarīqa. By the mid-nineteenth century, the Caliphate encompassed an estimated 150,000 square miles. It stretched from Hausaland in modern-day northern Nigeria westward to modern-day Burkina Faso, eastward to the Central African Republic, northward into modern Niger, and southward into Yorubaland. It was a four-month journey from east to west and a two-month journey from north to south. As it grew

---

40 Hamman, *The Middle Benue Region and the Sokoto Jihad 1812–1869*, 136–37.

41 These estimates are uncertain due to a lack of census data for the nineteenth century and complications in the data arising from the division of the Sokoto Caliphate into British, French, and German spheres at the time of conquest. For a discussion on the difficulty of determining the population of the Sokoto Caliphate see Lovejoy, *Slavery Commerce and Production*, 1–2.

from its Hausaland heartland, it became a multiethnic, multicultural, multilinguistic state with significant non-Muslim minorities.[42]

The Sokoto Caliphate did not have a strong central government. It was a confederation whose unity was dependent on cooperation between emirate and central elites; respect for the intellectual foundations of the jihad; the prestige of 'Uthmān, 'Abdullāhi, Bello, and their successors; and the willingness of the emirs and local power holders to be governed by them and the central government. Asma'u acknowledged the importance of the continued respect for the intellectual legacy of the Fodiye in maintaining unity when she threatened in an 1844 poem that "anyone who leaves the community of the Shehu has left the Sunna and is doomed."[43]

The relationship between the central government and the emirates was established during the jihad period. The jihad had attracted individuals who supported the Tetravirate's goals but also individuals who wanted to effect political and economic change for other reasons. Many of 'Uthmān's students, who were the people who most closely shared the Tetravirate's ideals and supported the jihad for ethical reasons, had died in the initial stages of the jihad due to lack of proper military training. Asma'u commented on this in her account of the jihad when she stated that "many of the reciters of the Qu'ran were killed and also the students among his [Uthmān] community."[44] The fighters who were left and who helped establish the emirates were mostly young cattle-less Fulbe who joined the jihad for a job and for social advancement. 'Uthmān's approach to unifying the rebellions against the Hausa governments and to assert his leadership and his ideals had been to give flags to individuals who had his blessing and support to lead the jihad in different parts of Hausaland and beyond. Once a territory was conquered, the flag-bearer and his supporters were able to establish governance and systems of rule that suited their interests with oversight from 'Uthmān, 'Abdullāhi, Bello, and subsequent Sarakuna Muslimi. To maintain a unified state, the government in Sokoto had to work with the emirs, taking into consideration the political, economic, and strategic concerns of the emirate governments.

---

42 For more on how on the intellectual debates among Sokoto leaders as they transitioned from leading a rebellion to governing see Naylor, *From Rebels to Rulers*.

43 Asma'u b. Fodiye, "Te-Medde Jewgo Fu-nbara," 192.

44 Asma'u. b. Fodiye, "Filitago/Wakar Gewaye," 143.

The stability of the early Caliphate, however, was jeopardized by competition within the senior leadership. For example, in order to maintain unity, 'Abd al-Salām, the Hausa Muslim leader whose rescue by jihadist forces predicated the hijra and who had a strong following, was given administrative control of territory south of Sokoto. So as to reduce tension between Abdullāhi and Bello, 'Uthmān, upon his retirement from active governance in 1812, divided the Caliphate into two provinces which were governed by 'Abdullāhi and Bello. 'Abdullāhi received the western and southern sections (the west) with headquarters at Gwandu and Bello received the eastern and northern sections (the east) with headquarters at Sokoto. 'Abdullāhi and Bello were responsible for the emirates in their respective province and for advising their emirs.

The tension and competition between Bello and 'Abdullāhi were primarily centered on who would become Sarkin Musulmi upon 'Uthmān's death. This tension played out in a series of writings by 'Abdullāhi and 'Uthmān in 1812 and 1813. In *Ḍiyā'al-sulṭān wa-ghayrihi min al-ikhwān fī ahamm mā yuṭlabu 'ilmuhu fī umūr al-zamān* (1812), his advice for new rulers, 'Abdullāhi warned against the dangers of kingship and the succession from father to son. 'Uthmān responded a year later in *Najm al-ikhwān* (1813) by stating that there was nothing legally wrong with a son inheriting a position of power as long as he possessed all the qualities necessary for leadership.[45]

Following 'Uthmān's death in 1817, there was a danger of the Caliphate splitting into two as 'Abdullāhi refused to accept Bello's election as Sarkin Musulmi. The rift was not rectified until after Bello helped 'Abdullāhi pacify the rebellion at Kalambayna, a few miles southeast of Gwandu, in 1820–21, and the two men were able to settle their differences with 'Abdullāhi accepting Bello's ascension to the position of Amīr al-Mu'minīn/Sarkin Musulmi.[46] In establishing the Sokoto Caliphate, the Tetravirate, therefore, adapted the constitutional frameworks of the Umayyad and 'Abbāsid Caliphates who also had to deal with governing a state over a large geographic region. Local emirs were chosen from and by local leaders with the approval of the governments at Sokoto and Gwandu, and when once again unified, by Sokoto only. An emissary from the capital supervised each local emir. In total the Caliphate was composed of at least thirty-three emirates, which were also divided into

45 Minna, "Succession and Legitimacy"; Balogun, "Succession Tradition in Gwandu History, 1817–1918," 17–33.

46 For more on the debate on the succession see Lofkrantz, "Intellectual Discourse in the Sokoto Caliphate," 398–99.

smaller political jurisdictions.[47] The central government had oversight over the activities of the emirates but lacked a means to take direct action. There was no central standing army. It was reliant on the emirates to provide troops for campaigns for the protection of Caliphate territory and subjects.

One of the criticisms leveled at the Caliphate's political structure is that over the course of the nineteenth century, it took on, especially at the emirate level, the former Hausa forms of government. For example, under the reign of Ibrahim Dabo (1819–46) in Kano Emirate, a number Hausa title and political institutions were readopted. M. G. Smith argues that this was necessary in order to entrench the position of the new ruling class.[48] Indeed, in many ways, even the division of the Sokoto Caliphate into western and eastern jurisdictions is a reflection of prereform Hausaland, where state politics had revolved around western and eastern axes since at least the seventeenth century.[49] A further example of the adoption of Hausa ways of being, according to Stephanie Zehnle, was the adoption of the Hausa worldview of the division of the world, and humanity, into two separate animal worlds of the domesticated and the wild. According to Zehnle, Sokoto forces used the Hausa conception of the animal world and the classification of people as belonging to either the domestic/civilized or the wild/uncivilized to justify their southward expansion and slave-raiding.[50] Indicating that in the early years of the establishment of the Sokoto Caliphate, the readoption of prereform and of Hausa political organization and ways of being was viewed not as a pragmatic necessity but as a choice, in 1807, 'Abdullāhi almost abandoned the Sokoto Caliphate for Mecca because he was disgusted with what he viewed as the materialistic goals of many jihad leaders and preferred to live a religious life in Mecca rather than live in a state that he viewed as having abandoned the ideals of the jihad. Indeed, one of the reasons that Bello was elected upon 'Uthmān's death as Sarkin Musulmi instead of 'Abdullāhi was that Bello, like 'Uthmān (and unlike 'Abdullāhi) was viewed as realistic,

47 For a much larger discussion on the constitutional framework of the Sokoto Caliphate see Hiskett, *The Sword of Truth*, 134–46 and Burnham and Last, "From Pastoralist to Politician: The Problem of a Fulbe Aristocracy," 315–19.

48 M. G. Smith, *Government in Kano*, 225–27

49 Adeleye, "Hausaland and Bornu, 1600–1800," 485–517.

50 Zehnle, "War and Wilderness," 216–37. For more on Sokoto worldviews see Zehnle, *A Geography of Jihad.*

flexible, and capable of brokering compromise and unity between different interest groups.[51]

Economically, from the beginning of the jihad, the Caliphate was reliant on booty, including captives, as an important source of income. In *Kitāb al-farq*, ʻUthmān stated that booty was one of the seven income sources for the public treasury: the others being the fifth, the land tax, the poll tax, the tithe, inheritance, and property with missing or no owner.[52] In *Usulul-adliliwullatil umuri wa ahlil-fadli*, a treatise on the principles of justice, ʻUthmān asserted that proper uses of the government's and imam's share of the booty included defense spending, the payment of government employee salaries, the welfare of the poor and needy, the building of mosques, and the freeing (ransoming) of prisoners of war.[53] Indeed, Moses Ochonu argues that Caliphate expansion south of the Benue during the reign of Bello was not motivated by ideology and territorial gain but by the soldiers' desire for booty, captives, and tribute.[54] Indicating the importance of booty to state funds, Asma'u warned against its improper use. In her 1842 text warning against committing sin, "Godaben Gaskiya" (The path of truth), Asma'u stated that the "embezzler of booty . . . will not get salvation in the Next World from Ahmada [Prophet Muḥammad]."[55] Booty was also an important means for paying soldiers as it had been in the region since at least the sixteenth century.[56] During the jihad and subsequent warfare Sokoto forces made use of the common military technique of the region of raiding villages

51 Abdullāhi b. Fodiye, *Tazyīn al-waraqāt*; Balogun, "Succession Tradition in Gwandu History."

52 See Hiskett, "Kitab-al-farq: 'A Work on the Habe Kingdoms Attributed to ʻUthman dan Fodio," 571.

53 ʻUthmān b. Fodiye, *Usulul-Adliliwullatil Umuri wa ahlil-fadli*, 15.

54 Ochonu, "Caliphate Expansion and Sociopolitical Change," 133–76.

55 Asma'u b. Fodiye, "Godaben Gaskiya," 181. In a translation and reworking of ʻUthman's 1809/1812 text *Tabbat Hakika*, Asma'u stated that "those who steal booty from those who first captured it will be seized by the Fire, Be sure of God's Truth/Captured booty must definitely not be hidden: War trophies must be taken to the leader. There are those, without doubt who conceal booty. Those who deny the poor their rightful share will receive the Fire as their share, Be sure of God's Truth." Asma'u b. Fodiye, "Tabbat Hakika," 52. Abdullāhi b. Fodiye, *Ḍiyā' al-ḥukkām*, 2. For an Arabic edition, see Abdullāhi b. Fūdī, *Ḍiyā' al-ḥukkām* (Zārīya: Maktab Nūlā, 1956).

56 Es Soudan, *Tadhkirat al-Nisyān*, 300–303.

and towns and taking captive whoever was not killed in the fighting.[57] In describing the first attack on Gobir, ʻUthmān stated, "We met them and put them to flight, and burnt their houses. We killed their males and took their women and children. They scattered."[58] Indicating the importance of booty in Caliphate warfare, in *Tanbīh al ikhwān alā arḍ al-sūdān*, ʻUthmān disagrees with the ninth-century jurist ibn ʻArafa's qualification of who could be considered a mujāhid. This is significant since the Sokoto leadership regularly relied upon ibn ʻArafa opinions in forming their policies.[59] According to ibn ʻArafa, a person who fights for the sake of booty or to show bravery cannot be considered a mujāhid, whereas ʻUthmān argues that "aiming to get booty should not be counted against a man if he has fought to make God's law supreme."[60] The disagreement about who could be considered a mujāhid had ramifications for the taking of booty, including captives and the profits to be made from prisoners. In making his statement, ʻUthmān acknowledged the reality of the situation: while his fighters supported his vision of a just society, they were also motivated by payment. After one expedition in Gobir, Bello's troops were ready to desert if they did not receive what they perceived to be a more equitable share of the captives.[61] Demonstrating the continued importance of booty, at the close of the nineteenth century in an undated letter (most likely from the 1890s), the Emir of Katsina wrote to the Sarkin Musulmi after a successful raid that "Allah granted the power to go to the country of Maradi and I myself went with my army to a village called Ungwar Mata, which we sacked and burnt, and in which we found much booty by Allah's will and your blessing."[62]

The economic engine of the Sokoto Caliphate was plantation agriculture. In order to support this sector, Sokoto officials facilitated the purchase of slaves. Plantations had long existed in the central Sudan, especially in Kano, but in the eighteenth century this sector had suffered due to the

57 Abukar, 7th Emir of Katsina to the Sultan of Sokoto, the Sarkin Musulmi Abderrahman, n.d.; Backwell, *The Occupation of Hausaland 1900–1904*, 34.

58 Uthmān b. Fodiye, *Tanbīh al ikhwān alā arḍ al-sūdān*, 191.

59 See Hiskett, "An Islamic Tradition of Reform in the Western Sudan from the Sixteenth to the Eighteenth Century," 592

60 ʻUthmān b. Fodiye, *Tanbīh al ikhwān alā arḍ al-sūdān,* 180.

61 Es Soudan, "Histoire de Sokoto," 306–7, 313.

62 Abukar, 7th Emir of Katsina to the Sultan of Sokoto, the Sarkin Musulmi Abderrahman, n.d., 34.

intra-Hausaland warfare and periodic drought.[63] The founding of the Sokoto Caliphate unified Hausaland for the first time, which led to a solidification of a regional economy that was based on slave-produced plantation agriculture. The expansion of plantations was also stimulated by government policy that encouraged the development of plantations near rubuṭ (ribāṭ sing) defensive centers, in order to ensure a stable food supply.[64] Agricultural products also formed an important component of the Caliphate's trade. Grains such as millet and sorghum were traded northward to the Sahel and southern Sahara in exchange for livestock and salt while cotton and indigo were traded from the countryside to the urban dye works within the textile belt of southern Kano and northern Zaria. Other plantation-produced agricultural products included rice, tobacco, locust beans, cowpeas, peanuts, sugar cane, kola nuts, and shea nuts. Internationally traded products included indigo, tobacco, dried onion leaves, and finished goods such as cotton textiles.[65] Increased agricultural production supported the flourishing Caliphate population. The population of Kano city, the most important economic center of the Caliphate, for example, rose from 30,000–40,000 people in 1824, to 60,000 in 1851, and to 100,000 in 1900.[66] Key to this plantation agricultural economy was enslaved labor. Enslaved people constituted between 20 percent and 45 percent of the total population.[67] The concentration of enslaved people, though, varied across emirates with the core emirates having the higher slave populations. In nineteenth-century Kano, the economic hub of the Caliphate, in the early to mid-nineteenth century the enslaved population was estimated as being between one-third and one-half of the total

63 For a thorough summary on the debate about the usage of word "plantation" in reference to the Sokoto Caliphate see Salau, *The West African Slave Plantation*, 1–14. Paul Lovejoy argues that enslavement was a crucial institution and that the political order was based on systematic enslavement. See Lovejoy, "Slavery in the Sokoto Caliphate," 201–3. See also M. G. Smith, *Government in Kano*, 107–72; Mahadi, "State and the Economy," 220–23; Lovejoy and Baier, "The Desert-Side Economy of the Central Sudan," 551–81.

64 Salau, "Ribats and the Development of Plantations," 30–31.

65 Lovejoy, "The Characteristics of Plantations in Nineteenth-Century Sokoto Caliphate," 1282–83.

66 Bovill, *Missions to the Niger*, 4: 650; Barth, *Travels and Discoveries in North and Central Africa 1849–1855*, 1:510; Charles Henry Robinson, *Hausaland or Fifteen Hundred Miles*, 113.

67 Lovejoy, *Slavery Commerce and Production*, 9.

population, with a significant number working on plantations. There were similar ratios for Katsina and Zaria.[68] The government had to balance their policy concern of preventing illegal enslavement with economic imperatives and the interests of individual emirates.

Sokoto Policy Toward Enslavement, Slavery, and Manumission

The Sokoto jihadists and the founding scholars of the Sokoto Caliphate wanted to facilitate legal enslavement while preventing illegal enslavement. However, the Caliphate's constitutional framework, the importance of booty as a source of government revenue, and the dependence of the plantation sector on enslaved labor limited their ability to institute their preferred policies toward slavery. The Tetravirate argued that non-Muslims could be enslaved through legal warfare. (As discussed earlier, they held a narrow view of who was a freeborn Muslim and considered the warfare undertaken for their cause as legal.) They did not agree with the argument that was gaining popularity in the nineteenth-century Ottoman Empire that there had been no legal warfare since the time of the Prophet Muḥammad and therefore no legal enslavement since the time of the Prophet Muḥammad.[69] The scholars of the Sokoto Caliphate favored the free release of freeborn Muslims. They favored Bābā's argument that a freeborn Muslim who suspected that he was holding another freeborn Muslim should freely release the individual and accept the economic loss. Bello, for instance, freed captives that he suspected might be freeborn Muslims.[70]

The acceptance of the viewpoint that it was better to permit a non-Muslim to go free than to wrongly enslave a freeborn Muslim can be seen in Sokoto's policies concerning the enslavement of Fulbe. Two years prior to the start of the jihad, in *Masā'il muhimma* (1802), 'Uthmān had forbidden the enslavement of any Fulbe on the basis that the majority of Fulbe had long been

68 Denham, Clapperton, and Oudney, *Narrative of Travels and Discoveries in North and Central Africa,* 2:251; Barth, *Travels and Discoveries,* 1:510, 523; and Robinson, *Hausaland or Fifteen Hundred Miles,* 112–33. See also Lovejoy, *Transformations in Slavery,* 202.

69 Ghazal, "Debating Slavery and Abolition in the Arab Middle East," 139–54.

70 Es Soudan, "Histoire de Sokoto," 303.

recognized as Muslims.[71] This injunction continued after the founding of the Sokoto Caliphate even though both 'Abdullāhi and Bello did not consider all Fulbe to be Muslims. In 1813, 'Abdullāhi described some of his fellow Fulbe Muslims as being sellers of free men, which according to the Sokoto intellectuals made them non-Muslims.[72] In *Miftāh al-Sadād fi aqsām hādhihi 'l-bilād*, (undated) his classification of the people of Hausaland according to their degree of Islamization, Bello made clear that he did not consider all Fulbe to be Muslims, yet he also repeated the ban on enslaving Fulbe.[73]

Moreover, once the Caliphate was established, the leadership made numerous attempts throughout the nineteenth century to stop the trafficking as slaves of freeborn Muslims. For example, in the 1830s, there were efforts to inspect northbound caravans for enslaved recognized freeborn Muslims, and searches were also conducted in Katsina, Agadez, Tassaoua, and Damergou. Caravans found to be exporting illegally enslaved people could have their merchandise confiscated.[74] Attempts were also made to place similar restrictions on the southern slave trade. One of the justifications for enslavement was to encourage the conversion of non-Muslims to Islam. Selling slaves, especially illegally enslaved freeborn Muslims (and also enslaved individuals who had converted to Islam) outside of the dār al-Islām was condemned by the Sokoto leadership. It was against Sokoto Caliphate law to sell enslaved people to Christians. Bello affirmed this law to the British envoy Hugh Clapperton during Clapperton's 1824 visit to Bello's court. Indeed since at least 1812 Bello had routinely condemned Oyo, the major Yoruba state to the south of the Sokoto Caliphate, for selling enslaved people to Christians on the Atlantic coast.[75] As discussed earlier, it was through ports controlled by Oyo that many enslaved freeborn Muslims from the central Sudan were sold into the Atlantic trade. Despite the injunctions and the searches, the enslavement of recognized freeborn Muslims continued to be a problem throughout the nineteenth century. Export checks and export prohibitions reduced the export of illegally enslaved individuals but did not help individuals trafficked within the Sokoto Caliphate. Sokoto officials could not

71 Hiskett, *The Sword of Truth*, 77.

72 'Abdullāhi b. Fodiye, *Tazyīn al-waraqāt*, 142.

73 Bello, *Miftāh al-Sadād fi aqsām hādhihi 'l-bilād.*

74 Lovejoy, "The Bello-Clapperton Exchange," 219–20. For more on the relationship between the Sokoto Caliphate and the Sultanate of Agadez and Sokoto's expansion into Adār see Rossi, *From Slavery to Aid*, 42–57.

75 Lovejoy, "The Bello-Clapperton Exchange," 206–11.

completely safeguard the population they considered to be freeborn Muslims from being taken captive especially within its borders.

As a state claiming to be founded on a more orthodox interpretation of Islam and on fair enslavement policies, the Sokoto government encouraged slave owners to manumit their slaves and to follow a generous interpretation Qu'ranic exegis on manumission. In discussing slavery, the Qu'ran is biased toward the liberation of slaves. There were several means through which an enslaved person could be freed. Enslaved people could become lawfully free if they were manumitted. Manumission was viewed as an act of benevolence, and many pious owners manumitted people they owned for that reason. Manumitting slaves was also viewed as a way to make amends for committed sins. Owners could also permit slaves to buy their freedom or pledge to free the person they owned at a later date or after the owner's death. The Qu'ran recommends that owners permit people they own to purchase themselves or to permit a third party to purchase their freedom. Indeed murgu, where slaves and owners could enter into a contract for slave self-purchase (fansar kai), was an important component of slavery in the Sokoto Caliphate.[76] A judge could also order an owner to free a slave due to mistreatment. A concubine who gives birth to her owner's child, thereby acquiring the title of *umm walad* (mother of children), gains certain legal rights that eventually lead to her freedom. An enslaved person, who subsequently converts to Islam but is owned by a non-Muslim, must be freed or sold by his or her owner since a non-Muslim is forbidden to own a Muslim (although a Muslim is permitted to continue to own an enslaved individual who converts to Islam).[77] While the chances of a particular individual being manumitted by their owner were low, the emphasis on manumission meant that there was a continual need for new captives to be enslaved to fulfill the desire for enslaved labor.

The fact that there was legal enslavement meant that there was space for illegal captivity and enslavement. Warfare was the only legal way to gain new captives either to enslave or to ransom. However, individuals were often taken captive and either ransomed or enslaved through illegal raiding and

---

76 For more on the institution of murgu see Lovejoy, "Murgu: The Wages of Slavery in the Sokoto Caliphate," 168–85.

77 On the treatment of slaves and the avenues of manumission advocated in the Qu'ran see, for example, passages 4:92, 5:89, 16:71, 24:32, 24:33, and 90:13. For Malik ibn Anas's opinion, the founder of the Mālikī school of law (which was the school of law followed in Islamic West Africa) see Bewley, *Al-Muwatta of Iman Malik ibn Anas*, 320–26. See also Lewis, *Race and Slavery in the Middle East*, 3–12; Schacht, *Introduction to Islamic Law*.

criminal activity. Caravans were often targeted. One of the inherent risks of being a caravaner was the possibility of being raided. Wealthy merchants in particular were a target for kidnapping. The insecurity of the trade routes was acknowledged in government correspondence. For example, in an undated letter, Bello acknowledged the problem of raiding on the northern trade routes especially by the Tuareg Kel Gress.[78] In the 1850s, to the north, the roads in and out of Zinder especially gained a reputation for being attacked.[79] In 1902, French officials were demanding that Gobir officials stop the Gobirawa from attacking caravans that indicates that security on the northern trade routes was still a problem fifty years later.[80] In 1904 there were reports of one bandit who operated between Gobir and Maradi holding approximately 250 enslaved women and an unknown number of free women at his compound who were kidnapped during his raids. The free women were possibly eligible to be ransomed.[81] Likewise, in 1907, five years after British forces had captured Kano, the security situation in Nassarawa was summed up in a report as "slave raids very common, kidnapping was an everyday occurrence."[82] Baba of Karo recounts that when she was a child in the 1890s, Ibrahim Nagwamase, also known as Mai Sudan, continuously raided the Katsina-Zaria region and also sent raiders into her region of southern Kano. According to Baba, Nagwamase was willing to ransom his captives. If he could not negotiate a ransom, he would sell his captives as slaves.[83] In another example, Ṣāliḥ, a freeborn Muslim, was captured in a raid by an army from Madaka in about 1891 and was sold northward.

78 Muḥammad Bello to Wachar, n.d., 282–283; ANN Bouba Hama "Journal de 2 mars 1968 au 6 mai 1969," Muḥammad Bello to Sīdī Mahmūd, n.d., 284. Boubou Hama is one of Niger's preeminent scholars. In the 1960s he collected primary documents from around the country that were of interest to him and stored them by collection date in journals. These journals are now stored at the ANN and at the Institut de Recherches en Sciences Humaines, Université Abdou Moumouni, Niamey. Sokoto's trade routes to the south were also affected by banditry. See Akinwumi, "Princes as Highway Men," 333–50.

79 Richardson, *Narrative of a Mission to Central Africa*, 2:225.

80 ANN 1E1.16 1902 Rapport politique sur les sultanats du Tessaoua, du Gober et du Maradi (mois du Janvier).

81 ANN 1E1.34 1904 Cercle de Zinder, Residence de Tessaoua. Rapport politique du mois de Juin.

82 NAK SNP 7/8 3039/1907 Report on the Nassarawa Province.

83 Smith, *Baba of Karo,* 66–75.

Similarly, both Halīma and Khadīja were free women from Kano who were taken captive during the 1893–1895 Kano civil and sold as slaves.[84]

Young Sokoto nobles also engaged in illegal raiding, which often resulted in the captivity of freeborn Muslims. Throughout the nineteenth century, the number of nobles greatly increased. In 1820 the typical household may have consisted of a *mai sarauta* and his wives, concubines, and children, yet by 1900 a typical elite household could number a thousand adult men. Finding work for elite men became a challenge. Culturally legitimate occupations for nobles were scholars, soldiers, and governors. Throughout the nineteenth century, young noblemen were often sent to the frontier where they engaged in activities away from the direct supervision of scholars, senior officials, and their elders who usually resided in Sokoto and near other main cities. These nobles were supposed to be defending the border and occasionally raiding enemy territory. Often, however, in order to make a living, since raiding across the border was not sufficiently lucrative, they raided the local population, including Muslims.[85]

The Sokoto government wanted to enforce what it considered to be legal enslavement while eradicating what it considered to be illegal enslavement. Yet, the central government was too weak to assert its policy regarding the free release of suspected freeborn Muslims against a myriad of political, military, and economic interests. Despite its desire to limit enslavement to nonfreeborn Muslims, and instead of decreasing the number of people enslaved, the founding of the Sokoto Caliphate actually led to an increase in slavery within the region that included the enslavement of freeborn Muslims (as it became a slave-based economy). The central government was too weak to stop the captive taking of freeborn Muslims either through warfare or illegal activity. It was also too weak to enforce the preferred remedy of free release for suspected captive freeborn Muslims. Instead, the government condoned ransoming as a means for preventing the enslavement of captive freeborn Muslims.

Condoning Ransoming and Shifts in Ransoming Policies

Despite its inability to limit enslavement, the Tetravirate viewed the return of wrongly enslaved Muslims and of captured Sokoto followers and citizens as a key priority of the Sokoto jihad and the Caliphate. The legally preferred

84 Christelow, *Thus Ruled Emir Abbas*, 118, 124, 127.

85 Last, "1903 Revisited," 63–66.

remedy was the free release of illegally captive and enslaved individuals; yet due to the Caliphate's social, political, and economic structures, this remedy could not be enforced. Instead of simply releasing freeborn Muslims taken captive and facing enslavement, the Sokoto Caliphate condoned and facilitated having illegally captive freeborn Muslims attain their freedom through ransoming by their families and friends.

In their writings, 'Uthmān, 'Abdullāhi, and Bello emphasized the importance of ransoming as a strategy for freeing their followers who had been taken captive. In *Bayān wujūb al-hijra 'alā 'l—'ibād* (1809) 'Uthmān stated that the "redemption [ransoming] of Muslim captives is obligatory."[86] In *Risāla ilā ahl al-ḥaramayn al-sharīfayn wa ilā ahl al-mashriq*, Bello writes that it was the responsibility of Muslims to free fellow Muslims.[87] In *Ḍiyā' al-ḥukkām* 'Abdullāhi indicates that the protection of Muslim rights was a government priority, that ransoming should be used to free wrongly captive Muslims and that ransoming could be used as an option for dealing with captives held by their forces.[88] The founding scholars of the Sokoto Caliphate viewed ransoming as a useful way to rescue people from captivity and possible enslavement. Further indicating the importance Sokoto scholars and officials placed on the strategy of ransoming was that in the mid-nineteenth century, individual ransom cases were discussed in the correspondence of the Sarakuna Musulmi.[89] As will be discussed more thoroughly in chapter 5, Sokoto officials helped facilitate ransom negotiations for the return of Sokoto freeborn Muslims. Information on captives for ransom could be exchanged in market towns throughout the Caliphate. Government officials were available to mediate ransom negotiations, and some funding was available to pay the ransoms of poor Muslims.

The issue of responsibility for the payment of ransoms was a subject of debate and concern among government officials. They agreed that ransoming should be used as a means to free captive freeborn Muslims. Sokoto officials acknowledged that the state had a role in paying ransoms. However, the Sokoto and emirates governments preferred to offload the cost to private families. Both 'Uthmān and 'Abdullāhi placed the onus on individuals and their families to look after themselves and that the state should

86 'Uthmān b. Fodiye, *Bayān wujūb al-hijra 'alā 'l – 'ibād*, 123.

87 Bello, *Risāla ilā ahl al-ḥaramayn al-sharīfayn wa ilā ahl al-mashriq*, 42.

88 Abdullāhi b. Fodiye, *Ḍiyā' al-ḥukkām*.

89 ANN Bouba Hama "Journal de 2 mars 1968 au 6 mai 1969" Abūbakar Atikū to Sīdī Mahmūd, n.d., 279.

only intervene if self-sufficiency was not possible. This can be seen in how 'Uthmān paraphrased and interpreted Muḥammad b. Aḥmad b. Juzay and Khalīl b. Isḥāq al-Jundī's opinions on ransoming in *Bayān wujūb al-hijra 'alā 'l—'ibād* (1809) and *Irshād al-'ibād ilā ahamm masā'il al-jihād* (undated) and in 'Abdullāhi's discussion of ransoming in *Ḍiyā' al-ḥukkām* (c. 1807).[90]

'Uthmān interpreted both Juzay's *Qawānīn al-aḥkām al-shar'iya wa-masā'il al-furū' al-fiqhiya* and Khalīl's *Mukhtaṣar* as indicating that while the state ought to be helping its citizens, especially the poor, that both Juzay and Khalīl were also directing that kin should be primarily responsible for paying the ransoms of their relatives. According to 'Uthmān's interpretation even though Khalīl argued that the payment of ransoms was a communal responsibility and not an individual one, that Khalīl was indicating that kin should be responsible for kin by forbidding a claim for compensation from a close relative.[91] This is notable since this interpretation of Khalīl seems to go against the spirit of Khalīl's advice as discussed in chapter 1. In his synopsis of Juzay 'Uthmān emphasizes Juzay's comment that rich captives ought to pay their own ransoms and that the state treasury should fund the ransoms of the less fortunate.[92] Similarly, in *Ḍiyā' al-ḥukkām*, Abdullāhi, while appearing to be following Khalīl when he states that the community was responsible for ransoming Muslims, actually agrees with 'Uthmān's emphasis on family and not state responsibility. 'Abdullāhi, however, did add the caveat to his assessment by stating that while the wealthy should pay for their own ransoms, the local imam should organize the ransoms of poor Muslims.[93] These interpretations of Khalīl and Juzay supported the Sokoto Caliphate policy that rich captives and their families should pay for their own ransoms, whereas the state should be responsible for the ransom payments of poor Muslims. This Sokoto policy was still in force at the end of the nineteenth century when Baba of Karo's aunt and her children were taken captive by Mai Sudan's forces. The Emir of Katsina ordered Baba's uncle's senior brother to raise the ransom fee. The Katsina government was aware of the captivity of Baba of Karo's aunt and her children. They were aware of the ransom demand. They were also aware that the family was having trouble raising the ransom fee.

90 See chapter 1 for a thorough discussion of Juzay and Khalīl's thoughts on ransoming.

91 Uthmān b. Fodiye, *Bayān wujūb al-hijra 'alā 'i-'ibād*, 123.

92 NAK A/AR/43/2 'Uthmān b. Fodiye, *Irshād al-'ibād ilā ahamm masā'il al-jihād*, 44–45.

93 Abdullāhi b. Fodiye, *Ḍiyā' al-ḥukkām*, 5.

Even so, the government did not want to use government funds to pay the ransom fee but instead insisted that the family raise it. It took the family three months to gather the money and some family members went into debt in order to contribute.[94] However, the fact that the matter of who should be responsible for ransom payments was discussed at length also indicates that it was most likely a matter of debate within Sokoto society.

Sokoto officials were in agreement on the usefulness of ransoming as a means of freeing recognized freeborn Muslims and were in agreement that families should bear the cost ransoms and only resort to state funds as a last recourse. The issue of debate for Sokoto officials, especially in the early years of the Sokoto jihad, was on the efficacy of ransoming prisoners held by Sokoto forces. This was not a new debate in the Sunni schools of law. Both Hānafi and Mālikī scholars debated about whether Muslims should permit the ransom of captives held by their forces. Early Hānafi scholars forbade ransoming and prisoner exchange. The fifteenth-century Maghribi Mālikī scholar b. Sirāj approved of prisoner exchange but was against ransoming back prisoners because they could bring back important information to their side.[95] According to the Mālikī madh'hab followed by Sokoto intellectuals, ransoming was one of the lawful means of dealing with prisoners. However, it was not mandatory and not always viewed as being militarily strategic. In his circa 1789 admonitory poem "Busuraa'u" on the treatment of prisoners, Muḥammad Tukrur, the scholar and close friend of 'Uthmān, did not mention that captives could be ransomed but instead suggested that they could be kept as slaves, sold for horses, or made to pay tribute.[96] Yet in prejihad Hausaland it had been common for captured sarakai (nobles) to be escorted home by an armed escort who would then be "compensated" by a "large present."[97] Moreover, Sokoto did ransom back enemy prisoners. After an attack on Nupe in c. 1813, 'Abdullāhi stated that the army seized many fortresses, killed many people, took many others prisoner, and "gave safe-conduct to some of the unbelievers if they asked for it."[98] While 'Abdullahi does not say why certain "unbelievers" were given safe conduct while others were not and were kept prisoner, it seems likely that those given

94 Mary F. Smith, *Baba of Karo*, 70.

95 See Clarence-Smith, *Islam and the Abolition of Slavery*, 26.

96 Tukrur, "Busuraa'u'," verses 759–61.

97 Adamu, "The Delivery of Slaves from the Central Sudan," 166–67.

98 'Abdullāhi b. Fodiye, *Tazyīn al-waraqāt*, 130.

"safe-conduct" were sent to help arrange their own ransoms and those of their comrades left behind.

The debate on whether or not to permit the ransoming of captives held by Sokoto forces is exemplified by Bello and 'Abdullāhi's official opinions on the subject. The issue of contention was on the prudency of permitting the ransoming of enemy captives. This was dependent on the particular political and military situation. In advising Bauchi Emirate, Bello was strongly against the ransoming back of prisoners. He stated this opinion in an undated letter addressed to Ya'qūb b. Dādi, the founder of Bauchi Emirate (r. 1808–1845). Considering the subject matter and the fact that a compilation of questions and answers between Ya'qūb and Bello has been dated to the 1809–1817 period, it is likely that this letter was also written at a similar time.[99] By contrast, Abdullāhi, in *Ḍiyā' al-ḥukkām* and *Tazyīn al-waraqāt* (1813), supported the ransoming of enemy prisoners.

The letter in which Bello outlined his opinion on ransoming appears to be a response to Ya'qūb's request for advice on what to do with war prisoners captured by his forces. In this letter Bello retold the story of the victory over Tabūk and the discussion over the fate of the prisoners. According to Bello, the Prophet Muḥammad told his Companions that with regard to the captives, there were three possible choices that were acceptable to the interests of Islam. First, they could permit the ransoming of their prisoners. Second, they could enslave them. Third, they could kill the captives. According to Bello, the Prophet Muḥammad initially favored allowing the prisoners to be ransomed. However, the Prophet's Companion, 'Umar, argued that the prisoners should be killed. 'Umar reasoned that the prisoners deserved neither ransoming nor enslavement and that they should be executed so that they would no longer pose a threat to Islam. In Bello's retelling of the story, after a vigorous debate of the issue among the Companions, God descended with a Qu'ranic verse that said to kill all the prisoners. In advising the Sarkin Bauchi on what to do with the prisoners in his custody, Bello counseled that his decision must be based upon the will of God, and the interests of Islam and

99 According to Ismail and Aliyu, *al-qawl al-mawhūb fī ajwibat as'ilat al-amīr Ya'qūb*, was most likely written between 1809 and 1817. See Ismail and Aliyu, "Muhammad Bello and the Tradition of Manuals of Islamic Government and Advice to Rulers," 65–102. However, it is possible that the letter was written sometime before Bello's death in 1837.

of justice.[100] From this it can be inferred that Bello had advised Ya'qūb to kill his prisoners instead of ransoming them.

By contrast, on at least two different occasions, in *Ḍiyā' al-ḥukkām* written immediately after Kano Emirate was secured, and a few years later in *Tazyīn al-waraqāt,* Abdullāhi argued in favor of permitting the ransoming of war prisoners held by Sokoto forces. In *Ḍiyā' al-ḥukkām,* his legal treatise that he wrote for Kano's rulers, he stated that ransoming was a legitimate means for dealing with prisoners of war.[101] He listed five options for dispensing with male "infidel" prisoners in accordance with the public interest. The prisoners could be executed, freed, ransomed, forced to pay the jizya (poll-tax paid by non-Muslims), or enslaved. He left the fate of the prisoners to the discretion of the local imam. 'Abdullāhi reiterated his point that the ransoming of prisoners was a legitimate option in *Tazyīn al-waraqāt,* his narrative of the jihad's military campaigns. In this treatise, he stated that prisoners should be permitted to pay ransom and that the ransom money should be included in the booty.[102]

One of Abdullāhi's main concerns was how the options dealing with war prisoners affected the division of the ghanīma (war booty). According to Abdullāhi's understanding of Mālikī law, the fate of the prisoner would affect booty distribution. If the prisoner was executed his value would be deducted from the total amount of the booty. The financial loss caused by the execution of the prisoner would thereby be divided among all those receiving a share of the booty. If the prisoner was freed his value would be deducted from the khums (the share that went to the state treasury—a fifth of the total booty). If the prisoner was forced to pay the jizya, the value of the prisoner would be deducted from the imam's fifth affecting the amount of booty that the imam received but not the other recipients. If the prisoner was enslaved the profit from the sale would be added to the main booty and divided accordingly. If the prisoner was ransomed, then the ransom money would also be added to the main booty before being divided. However, if the ransom was in the form of Muslim prisoners—in other words, a prisoner exchange—then the

100 ANN Boubou Hama "Journal novembre 1961 à mars 1965" Bello to Bauchi, n.d., 397–400. The story of the battle of Tabūk is important in the oral tradition of the central bilād al-sūdān. See Muhammad, "The Tabuka Epic (?) in Hausa: An Exercise in Narratology," 397–415.

101 Abdullāhi b. Fodiye, *Ḍiyā' al-ḥukkām*, 1–2.

102 Abdullāhi b. Fodiye, *Tazyīn al-waraqāt*, 122–30. Asma'u does not discuss possible the fate of war prisoners in her history of the jihad. See Asma'u. b. Fodiye, "Filitago/Wakar Gewaye," 134–54.

value of the ransom would be deducted from the imam's fifth. For women and child prisoners 'Abdullāhi advised that they could be freely released, enslaved, or ransomed.[103] 'Abdullāhi seems to have taken it for granted that a certain number of captives would be ransomed. As an expert in jurisprudence, 'Abdullāhi was concerned with explaining the legitimate options for dealing with war prisoners according to Mālikī law. He wanted to make sure that like for any other fate, the "worth" of a ransomed captive was properly accounted for in the division of booty. In his view, ransoming was only one of many options for dealing with war prisoners. According to him, the imam was responsible for deciding what to do with each captive.

Bello and 'Abdullāhi based their opinions on ransoming on their training in intellectual thought and law and also on the specific situations that they were addressing. Bello and 'Abdullāhi both wrote their opinions in a context of political uncertainty, but they were radically different situations. In Bauchi, the situation that Bello was addressing, Sarki Ya'qūb was well respected by his fellow jihadists, but the new political class did not have firm control. Between 1808 and 1837, Ya'qūb was conquering the region and then solidified his control as he was fighting off rebels and outside attackers. While Ya'qūb became Sarkin Bauchi in 1808, he did not achieve effective control until 1811 though fighting persisted throughout the emirate. Like Kano and Zaria, Bauchi had to repel raiders originating from Ningi, a mountainous region situated between Kano, Zaria, and Bauchi, inhabited by non-Muslims who did not want to join the Sokoto Caliphate.[104] Ya'qūb also had to deal with large swaths of unconquered territory within Bauchi's borders, especially in the rugged southern plateau region. Moreover, Bauchi was on the frontlines of the dispute between the Sokoto Caliphate and Bornu, and indeed Ya'qūb successfully repelled Bornu's army in 1826.[105] When Bello was advising Ya'qūb on what to do with war prisoners it may not have been prudent to release them even for large amounts of money.

The situation in Kano was different. The jihadists had firm control of the commercial capital of Hausaland but were bereft with inside bickering. The new governing class could not agree on how to govern themselves, let

103 Abdullāhi b. Fodiye, *Ḍiyā' al-ḥukkām*, 2. Here he is referring to the authority of Muḥammad b. Aḥmad b. Juzay al-Kalbī al-Gharnāṭī's (d. 1340) *Qawānīn al-aḥkām al-shar'iyya*.

104 For more details on Sokoto's relationship with the Ningi region see Patton, "An Islamic Frontier Polity," 193–213.

105 Smaldone, *Warfare in the Sokoto Caliphate*, 36, 57, 75; and Johnston, *The Fulani Empire of Sokoto*.

alone the conquered population. Unlike in Bauchi where Ya'qūb was viewed as a strong leader, and was supported by the local jihadist forces, Kano's sarki, Sulaymanu, was unpopular and politically weak. 'Uthmān appointed Sulaymanu as emir/sarki because he had been the imam, and there had been no one else from among the surviving leaders who had the social capital and resources to rise above the others to be a respected emir. 'Uthmān's flag-bearer, Malam Dan Zabuwa, was dead and his son, 'Abdullāhi, was a generation younger than the other surviving fighters. Other possible candidates were just as politically weak as Sulaymanu but did not have his religious credentials. Even though he lacked the support of the local jihad leaders, Sulaymanu was the legally correct choice since he was the imam.[106] 'Abdullāhi wrote *Ḍiyā' al-ḥukkām* as a manual for an audience that was in firm control of the new Kano Emirate but that needed clarity on issues of law and governance. Militarily, 'Abdullāhi viewed Kano as being able to afford and indeed could benefit from ransoming back captive enemies.

As the Sokoto Caliphate consolidated its power, the ransoming of non-Muslims and enemies became more frequent. This was due to the changing political conditions. By 1820, the ideological phase of the jihad was over; it was evident the jihad would succeed and that the leadership was into the consolidation period of their rule. Warfare and raids continued to be conducted throughout the rest of the nineteenth century on the frontiers of the Sokoto Caliphate and individual emirates as a means to expand territorially and consolidate power.[107] In the latter half of the nineteenth century, the Sokoto Caliphate was firmly established; it was militarily safe to ransom back enemies throughout the Caliphate, including outlying emirates and emirates that had earlier faced internal rebellions. This is exemplified by ransoming in mid-nineteenth-century Ilorin, the southernmost emirate. Oral history suggests that captives in Ilorin who wanted to convert to Islam would refuse to be ransomed.[108] This suggests that at this time Ilorin was willing to ransom non-Muslims. On the Sahel side of the Caliphate, according to oral history,

106 M. G. Smith, *Government in Kano*, 200–18.

107 Umaru, 4th Emir of Bauchi to Sultan Sarkin Musulmi 'Abd al-Raḥmān, n.d.; Abubakr, 7th Emir of Katsina to the Sultan Sarkin Musulmi Muhammadu Attahiru, n.d., 22–23, 35; ANN 1E1.21 1903 Résidence de Tessaoua Rapports Politiques mensuels 1903 Mois de Mars 1903; Richardson, *Narrative of a Mission to Central Africa*, 2:221; Mockler-Ferryman, *Up the Niger*, 99, 169; Staudinger, *In the Heart of the Hausa States*, 2:26.

108 O'Hear, *Power Relations in Nigeria*, 39.

captors in the late nineteenth century deliberately targeted the children of high-status non-Muslims in order to ransom them back to their families.[109]

However, the emphasis remained on ransoming as a tool to prevent the illegal enslavement of freeborn Muslims. This can be seen at the end of the nineteenth century when it was still easier to ransom back freeborn Muslim captives than non-Muslims. According to Dan Rimin Kano, an informant to the 1970s Economic History Project, in mid- to late nineteenth-century Kano, while many prisoners brought to the city were executed at the various city gates, Muslim captives were, for the most part, ransomed.[110] In another case, at the close of the century, in an undated letter written between 1891 and 1897, Umaru Bakatara, the Emir of Gwandu informed the Sarkin Musulmi ʿAbd al-Raḥmān, that he had captured some men who had "joined the heathen in a rebellion" and while he was keeping the slaves and captured goods, he was sending the captured Muslim men to Sokoto.[111] There was no mention of the fate of the captured free men but ransoming or free release was a possibility. According to Baba of Karo, toward the end of the nineteenth century, if one was captured by someone from Maradi (in other words, by Muslims), it was possible to be ransomed.[112]

Conclusion

The Tetravirate and their supporters undertook the Sokoto jihad in large part to stop the enslavement of people whom they considered to be freeborn Muslims. However, due to the political, social, and economic realities of the state they established, they were unable to institute full protection for the individuals they wished to protect nor enforce the legally correct and preferred method of the free release of freeborn Muslims. Amidst the strife caused by the jihad and the inability of the central government to fully protect freeborn Muslims after the Caliphate was established, ransoming became a crucial means of protecting the rights of freeborn Muslims who had been taken captive. While as a matter of policy all the jihad leaders agreed on the

109 Schön, *Magana Hausa: Native Literature in the Hausa Language*, 164–65.

110 Economic History Project interview with Dan Rimin Kano, Kano, December 12 and 30, 1975.

111 Umaru Bakatara, 10th Emir of Gwandu to Sarkin Musulmi Abderrahman, 11th Sarkin Musulmi of Sokoto, n.d., 16.

112 Smith, *Baba of Karo*, 47.

importance of ransoming freeborn Muslims, they differed in their opinions concerning the ransoming of "non-Muslim" prisoners held by their forces. It appears that among the early jihad leaders of the Sokoto Caliphate, while ransoming was a legitimate option for dealing with prisoners, it was practiced with prudence. Yet the Sokoto policy changed throughout the nineteenth century as the state became more established. By the end of the nineteenth century, while ransoming was still viewed primarily as a practical means of protecting freeborn Muslims from enslavement, the ransoming of non-Muslims was also permitted.

The following chapter will examine the jihad of 'Umar Taal in the neighboring region of the western Sudan. Even though Taal was a member of the Tijāniyya ṭarīqa instead of the Qādiriyya ṭarīqa favored in the Sokoto Caliphate, Taal legitimized his jihad in the western Sudan, especially against the Caliphate of Ḥamdallāhi largely on Sokoto intellectual thought. Indeed, indicating how ties between Sokoto and Umarian movements are remembered, in trying to gain support for its movement, ANSARU (which broke away from Boko Haram in 2013), claimed that it was intellectually descendant from both the Fodiye and Taal.[113] Strong parallels can be made between the Sokoto and Umarian movements, including policies concerning ransoming.

---

113 Cook, "Disassociation of the Jamā'āt Anṣār al-Muslimin," 275.

Chapter Four

The Jihad of 'Umar Taal and Its Ransoming Nonpolicies

An Umarian source describes 'Umar Taal's relationship with Muḥammad Bello during his posthajj sojourn in the Sokoto Caliphate as "[Bello] received him with great respect; he lived in the sultan's home for three months, some say even longer, leading military expeditions on behalf of the Sultan until he possessed considerable riches in the form of slaves and other goods."[1] Moreover, according to another Umarian source, it was Taal who was the intellectual superior in the relationship with Bello, that Taal was considered Bello's teacher and that it was Bello who had adopted some of Taal's teachings.[2] Yet, while it makes sense that Taal had an intellectual influence on Bello, evident from the numerous interactions between Bello and Taal and the mutual respect that they had for each other, it is also obvious that the Fodiye had an important impact on Taal's thinking. Taal had lived in Sokoto for six years and only left after he failed to secure its leadership after Bello's death in 1837, which was instead secured by Bello's brother Abūbakar Atikū. When he left for the western Sudan to prepare for his own jihad, his entourage included a number of Sokoto followers (including influential women). Indeed, as B. G. Martin points out, it is from his time in Sokoto that Taal learned how to govern and to command armies while absorbing a lot of Fodiye thinking.[3] Yet the roots and the support for the jihad are complex. Support for Taal's jihad arose out of disillusionment with the Fuuta Jalon and Fuuta Toro jihads, the hope offered by the success of the Sokoto jihad, and the confidence in the righteousness of Tijāniyya Islam. The roots of this jihad show the complexity and entwinedness of the threads of Muslim

1 "The History of al-Hajj Umar," 203.

2 "The Story of Shaykh al-Hajj Umar," 142.

3 Martin, *Muslim Brotherhoods in Nineteenth Century Africa*, 74–75.

West African discourse, how they affected each other, and how intellectual thought was put into practice. Instead of reforming Fuuta Toro and Fuuta Jalon, Taal went out to establish his vision of the ideal Islamic state in the Bambara states of Kaarta and Segu and the Muslim state of Ḥamdallāhi based in the region of Māsina. Taal shared with the Tetravirate the core belief that one of the primary roles of a Muslim state is the protection of the rights of freeborn Muslims including protection from captivity. Ransoming was practiced in territory governed by the Umarians, but unlike the Fodiye, Taal did not articulate his ransoming policies, nor does it appear that Umarian government officials involved themselves in individual ransom negotiations.

This chapter focuses on the social, political, and intellectual factors that gave rise to the Umarian jihad and the formation of the Umarian states. It focuses particularly on the interplay between politics and competing intellectual traditions in the decades leading up to and during the 'Umarian jihad and the transmission, assimilation, integration, and rejection of ideas over the wide geographic space of the western Sudan. This chapter demonstrates that the western Sudan has long been an incubator of new concepts and of transforming beliefs from other parts of Africa and the dār al-islām to suit local purposes. Understanding the complexity of intellectual traditions, the competition between them, and the nineteenth-century states founded on them is especially important when there are twenty-first-century Salafi Jihadist groups in the western Sudan region, and particularly Māsina, who are harkening back to the nineteenth century to justify their actions. Indeed, the Macina Liberation Front claims that it wants to reestablish the Caliphate of Ḥamdallāhi, which had been founded based on Fodiye ideology and which Taal subsequently overthrew using the Fodiye interpretation and use of the concept of takfīr.[4] Understanding nineteenth-century intellectual contestations over Islam and the sociopolitical impacts of these contestations will help in understanding how their memory is evoked in the twenty-first century. This chapter will first examine the impact of the eighteenth-century jihads in Senegambia on Umar Taal, then the formation of Taal's intellectual thought, especially the influence of Sokoto and Kunta thought, the jihad he led based

4 The Macina Liberation Front was founded by Hamadoun Kouffa in 2015 and later merged with other groups to form the al-Qaeda affiliated group Jama'a Nusrat ul-Ilsma wa al-Muslimin (JNIM) in 2017. For more on the Macina Liberation Front and the conflict in central Mali see Leblon, "Pasteurs marginalisés et/ou djihadistes."

on that thought, and the overthrow of the Caliphate of Hamdallāhi, and finally captivity, enslavement, and ransoming in the 'Umarian states.

Roots of the Umarian Jihad–Senegambian Origins

The jihad launched by Taal in the 1850s, which was against the non-Muslim and Muslim states of the western Sudan, had its origins in the politics of Senegambia and the success of the Sokoto jihad. The use of jihad and political revolution as a West African antislavery strategy began with Nāṣir al-Dīn's "Shurr Bubba" 1673–1674 movement in the southwestern Sahara and Senegal River Valley region. Even though, overall, this region was not a major contributor to the transatlantic slave trade, it is not surprising that a Muslim West African antislavery movement began here. In the sixteenth century, the number of enslaved individuals sold through Senegambian ports was 159,026. Between 1600 and 1670, an additional 84,145 people were trafficked.[5] In other areas of West Africa, enslavement of captives was usually the by-product of warfare conducted for political reasons between states. In Senegambia a main cause of warfare was to produce captives to be sold into the transatlantic slave trade. By the seventeenth century, the collection and trade in enslaved people had caused social dislocation and gender imbalance due to the deportation of men.[6] Al-Dīn's aim was to establish governments in the Senegal River Valley (Waalo, Fuuta Toro, Cayor, and Jolof) that supported his interpretation of Islam, especially the protection of freeborn Muslim rights and to establish the dominance of zawāyā (scholarly) lineages over hassānīya (warrior) lineages north of the river.[7] He attracted followers from both sides of the Senegal River, both biḍān (white) and sūdān (black). According to one French observer, the slave trader Louis Moreau de Chambonneau, the substance of al-Dīn's message was that "God in no way

5 *Voyages: The Atlantic Slave Trade Database* http://www.slavevoyages.org. These numbers do not include Sierra Leone ports. They include the ports of Senegambia and the offshore Atlantic. They are categorized in the database as Albreda, Bissagos, Bissau, Cacheu, Casamance, Galam Gambia, Goreé, Joal or Saloum, Portuguese Guinea, Saint-Louis, Cape Verde, Madeira, and Senegambia and offshore Atlantic port unspecified. See also Richardson, "Shipboard Revolts," 69–92.

6 Barry, "The Subordination of Power and the Mercantile Economy," 39–63; Manning, *Slavery and African Life*, 64–65.

7 Barry, "Senegambia from the Sixteenth to the Eighteenth Century," 273–74.

permits kings to pillage, kill, nor enslave their people, but to the contrary, to maintain them and protect them from their enemies."[8] This was very similar to the sentiment that al-Maghīlī had expressed more than a century earlier when he wrote *Taj al-Din yajib 'ala-mulūk*.[9] Even though the movement failed, it established the precedent of using jihad as a means to establish governance based on interpretations of Islam. Moreover, refugees from the movement and their descendants settled throughout the Senegal River Valley and were important in the eighteenth-century jihads that established Fuuta Bundu, Fuuta Jalon, and Fuuta Toro.

Some of the surviving participants of Sharr Bubba settled in the rich agricultural lands of Fuuta Toro and formed the nucleus of one of the many anti–Atlantic slave trade scholarly communities that were established throughout the Senegal River Valley. The settlement of Sharr Bubba participants in Fuuta Toro is especially important since it is from this community that Taal emerged in the nineteenth century. Indeed, as David Robinson argues, Taal drew inspiration from Fuuta Toro's first postjihad Almamy, 'Abd al-Qādir Kan and tried to replicate at Nioro (al-nūr: light), what he renamed the Kaarta capital after he captured it in 1855, what Kan had tried to establish in Fuuta Toro almost a century earlier.[10] The anti–Atlantic slave trade position of Senegambia's scholarly communities was well known. Francis Moore, an employee of the Royal African Company who was posted on the Gambia River for five years between 1730 and 1735 associated the scholarly communities with Fulbe in general. He noted that Senegambian scholarly communities protected each other from enslavement. He wrote in his memoir that "inasomuch that if they know one of them being made a Slave, all the Pholeys [Fulbe] will redeem [ransom] him."[11]

By the 1770s, as the region's and the government's involvement in the slave trade increased, the tōrodḅe community had attracted a large number of followers enticed by the scholars' stance against the slave trade. Scholars such as Sulaymaan Baal, who led the jihad that toppled the Denyanke ruling class and established the Almamate in Fuuta Toro in 1776, emphasized the rights of freeborn Muslims to protection from enslavement. Prior to the jihad Baal was involved in using all sorts of means, including ransoming, to rescue Muslims from enslavement as they were being transported to the coast

8 Moreau de Chambonneau, "L'histoire de Toubenan," 339.

9 al-Maghīlī, *Taj al-Din yajib 'ala-mulūk*, 21.

10 Robinson, "Abdul Qadir and Shaykh Umar," 287.

11 Moore, *Travels into the Inland Part of Africa*, 32–33.

to be sold into the transatlantic slave trade.[12] Baal died in 1776 in a battle against the Banī Ḥasān before he was able to fully establish the Almamate. In his stead, the tōrodḅe community chose Kan, a scholar, teacher, and specialist in Mālikī law (who had not fought against the Denyanke), as their new leader and the first Almamy of their new state. Kan had been educated at Pir, Coki, and throughout southern Mauritania in the tradition of al-Dīn, had kinship ties with most of the important scholarly tōrodḅe families, and was well respected at the Fuuta Bundu court for his expertise in jurisprudence. At the time of Baal's movement in Fuuta Toro, he was teaching in a village in southwestern Fuuta Bundu.[13] Under Kan, the Denyanke were pushed eastward and the Trārza and Brākna confederations, to whom many in Fuuta Toro had been paying tribute, were pushed back to the north bank of the Senegal River. Between 1776 and 1796, Fuuta Toro's influence was extended westward toward Waalo, Jolof, and Cayor and eastward to Bundu, Gajaga, and Khasso, requiring these states to acknowledge their subordinate status and to protect scholars.

The Almamate prioritized protecting freeborn Muslims from the transatlantic slave trade. Antislavery was one of the main issues informing Kan's foreign policy toward both his African and his European neighbors. Kan's anti–Atlantic slave trade focus is further illustrated by his 1785 trade agreement with the French at Ndār (St. Louis). In order to continue non-slave-trading trade in Fuuta Toro, such as in grain and cattle, the French had to cease slave trading within the borders of the Almamate and to neither trade in nor purchase Muslim slaves. Kan consolidated power in a region where regional coalitions of lineage heads usually held more power than the central government. Most importantly, Kan made Mālikī law the focus of the judicial system instead of merely informing judicial decisions. He twinned religious and judicial authority by constructing between thirty and forty mosques, mostly in eastern Fuuta Toro, each with its own imam who, at the village level, served as religious leader, principal teacher, and judge. His judicial infrastructure from local to state level consisted of judges who centered their decisions on Mālikī law.[14] A contemporary of Kan's who had studied with the same Daymāni teacher as Kan, the scholar Mukhtār b.Buna, praised Kan's sense of justice in a poem exclaiming: "For he pleases in deeds,

12 Kamara, *Florilège au jardin de l'histoire des noirs,*" 316–17.

13 Robinson, "The Islamic Revolution of Futa Toro," 195–98.

14 Ware, *The Walking Qu'ran*, 131–45; Robinson, "Abdul Qadir and Umar Tal," 295–96; Robinson, "The Islamic Revolution of Futa Toro," 200.

in intent/ And in his words about sound government./ He raids only when attacked,/ As chastisement after the Holy Month/ He is recognized for his justice in matters/ In which the sons of Shem and Ham apply to him."[15] However, the reformation of the justice system was a major point of contention and caused clashes between Kan and local elites. Kan insisted on the strict application of Mālikī law whereas local elites often wanted to settle criminal and civil cases using preexisting non-Islamic but locally accepted procedures.[16]

Yet after 1796, the authority of both Kan and Fuuta Toro were challenged and in decline. The Wolof state of Cayor successfully rebelled and gained its independence. During the fighting to keep control of Cayor many Fuutanke soldiers were either killed or sold into the transatlantic slave trade. This military defeat was followed by a failed intervention in Fuuta Bundu. The intrusion in Fuuta Bundu also raised the ire of the non-Muslim Bambara state of Kaarta, which also had interests in Fuuta Bundu. Moreover, Kan's 1785 customs treaty with the French where the French agreed to pay duty to trade through the Middle Senegal Valley for non-slave-trade activities also fell apart in this period. More importantly, internally Kan was unable to properly assimilate new lineages into the state leading to a cleavage between "old" and "new" lineages. These failures led to a revolution in Fuuta Toro in 1806, which resulted in the assassination of Kan in 1807. The assassination marked the defeat of the vision of an Islamic state envisioned by Baal and his original followers. As Ware has shown, with the assassination of Kan and the rise of the tōroḍbe as the ruling class, Kan's emphasis on eradicating slavery was replaced by an acceptance of the legality of enslaving individuals considered to be non-Muslim.[17] This is the position that was accepted by all later jihad leaders in West Africa.

The new system for choosing the Almamy reflected the societal division between the new and old lineages. Under the new system, the Almamy was chosen by members of the "new" lineages on the basis of Islamic knowledge from among candidates from the "old" lineages. This system resulted in both a weakened central government and territorial divisions within Fuuta Toro. The central region of the state dominated the political system. The central region produced both the candidates for Almamy and the men who chose the Almamy. The political elite of the central region also maintained control

15 Robinson, "The Islamic Revolution of Futa Toro," 204.

16 See Robinson, "The Islamic Revolution of Futa Toro," 208–10.

17 Ware, *The Walking Qu'ran*, 144.

over national institutions while requiring that the eastern and western regions send a share of their crops and herds to maintain these institutions. For the easterners and westerners, it felt, in the parlance of the American Revolution of a few decades earlier, like a "taxation without representation" system. Moreover, the western region, from which Taal hailed, was faced with security issues that many accused the central Fuuta Toro government of ignoring. To the north, the Brākna Confederation, which coveted gum arabic, land, and enslaved people from Fuuta Toro repeatedly tried to reestablish the tributary relationship that the jihad had broken. To the south, the pastoralist Woodabe and Ururbe frequently raided the villages of the western region. The western region was also more vulnerable to French incursion and raiding from Ndār/St. Louis when French–Fuuta Toro relations were bad.[18] This is the environment in which Taal came of age. He and the men he recruited from Fuuta Toro and Fuuta Jalon in the 1840s became disillusioned with the government of Fuuta Toro but were inspired by Baal on the use of jihad to reform a state, the Islamization of the region by Kan, and the success of the Sokoto jihad.

Intellectual and Political Entanglements—The Influence of the Tijāniyya, the Kunta, and the Fodiye on ʿUmar Taal's Intellectual Thought and Jihad

Like the leaders of the Sokoto jihad and founders of the Sokoto Caliphate, the Fodiawa, Taal was a scholar prior to embarking on jihad in the western Sudan. He was born c. 1796 in the village of Halwar near Podor in Fuuta Toro to a scholarly family. Taal grew up in the aftermath of the Fuuta Toro jihad and, more importantly, in the aftermath of the assassination of Kan. Taal's first teachers, like the Fodiye Tetravirate, were family members, including his father, older brothers, and his brother-in-law, the scholar and Arabic specialist, Lamine Sakho. Sakho was married to Taal's older sister, was a veteran of the Fuuta Toro jihad campaigns in Cayor, and would later provide valuable support to Taal's jihad. Taal spent his teens and twenties traveling, studying, and teaching in the Middle Senegal Valley, including in southern Mauritania and perhaps as far east as Walata. His advanced education included jurisprudence, Arabic grammar, rhetoric, and literature. Even though he disliked law and criticized those who strictly adhered to one school of law, he was well

18 Robinson, *The Holy War of Umar Tal*, 66–69.

read in legal texts, having studied many of the foundational fiqh manuals of a West African legal education. His legal education included ʿAbdullah b. Abī Zayd al-Qayrawānī's *Risāla*, and Khalīl b. Isḥāq al-Jundī's *Mukhtaṣar*, and ʿAbd al-Raḥmān al-Suyūṭī's legal commentaries among others.[19]

It was during his advanced education that Taal was introduced and initiated into the Tijāniyya order. The Tijāniyya order was founded in 1781 by the Fezzan scholar Aḥmad al-Tijānī (d. 1815).[20] Taal had two Tijānī teachers from whom he was spiritually and intellectually descended. His first Tijānī teacher, was the Timbo scholar ʿAbd al-Karīm b. Aḥmad al-Nāqil al-Fūta Jallonī, with whom he studied for just over a year and who conferred on him in 1823 the first part of the Tijānī wird (prayer formula) the ḥizb al-ṣayfi, and also the waẓifa. Through ʿAbd al-Karīm, Taal's Tijāniyya isnād is short. Going backward to al-Tijānī, the isnād is ʿAbd al-Karīm b. Aḥmad Naguel, Sīdī Mawlūd Fāl, Muḥammad al-Hafiz b. Mukhtār (1759/60–1830), then al-Tijānī. It was Muḥammad al-Hafiz, of the Mauritanian clan Idaw u ʿAli, who had been given the mandate to spread the order south of the Senegal River by al-Tijānī.

Taal's second and most influential teacher was Muḥammad al-Ghālī Abū Ṭālib, the Tijānī Khalīfa for the Hijaz with whom he studied between 1828 and 1831 in Mecca during his pilgrimage. Taal devoted more than twenty years to his pilgrimage to Mecca and his return to Fuuta Toro. Al-Ghālī, who was also al-Tijānī's direct student, conferred upon Taal the second part of the Tijānī wird. He also gave him private lessons on the litanies and mystical teachings of the Tijāniyya order. During his time with al-Ghālī, Taal traveled extensively throughout the Hijaz, Syria, and to Jerusalem, thrice performed the hajj rites, assumed important roles in the conduct of Tijānī ceremonies, and accompanied al-Ghālī on official Tijānī business. It was also al-Ghālī

19 See Martin, *Muslim Brotherhoods in 19th Century Africa*, 68–69; Al Habib, "Cheikh el-Hadj Omar Foutiyyu Tall (1794–1864)," 108–17; Robinson, *The Holy War of Umar Tal*, 68–71. David Robinson and Al Habib disagree on whether or not ʿUmar studied at Pir, the prestigious school in Cayor, which many Fulbe scholars attended. See Robinson, *The Holy War of Umar Tal*, 71; and Al Habib, "Cheikh el-Hadj Omar Foutiyyu Tall," 111.

20 For more on Ahmad al-Tijānī and the founding of the Tijaniyya order see El Adnani, "Les origins de la Tijāniyya," 35–68; and Triaud, "La Tijâniyya, une confrérie musulmane pas comme les autres?" 10–17. For more on Tijāniyya belief and practice see Ryan, "The Mystical Theology of Tijānī Sufism and its Social Significance in West Africa," 208–44.

who appointed Taal as the khalīfa for the western Sudan and gave him the mission of spreading Islam and the Tijānī order throughout West Africa.[21]

Even though he was the head of the Tijāniyya in West Africa, Taal did not believe he should be restricted to Tijāniyya doctrine and thinkers nor to the Mālikī madh'hab. This may have been due to his long-time favoring of taṣawwuf (mysticism) over fiqh.[22] Indeed he considered the gates of ijtihad (independent reasoning on legal matters) to be open. In *Rimāḥ al-Raḥīm alā nuḥūr ḥizb al-rajīm* (1845), his most influential work and a foundational text of the Tijāniyya order, Taal reiterated that the Sunni schools of law had developed after the death of the Prophet Muḥammad and that it was not God that required adherence or affiliation to one madh'hab or set of rites and moreover that law should continue to evolve.[23] Indeed he counted Sīdī al-Mukhtār al-Kuntī, Aḥmad Lobbo, ʿUthmān b. Fodiye and Muḥammad Bello among the most important West African scholars, despite their Qādiriyya affiliations, despite the Kunta's opposition to him and the Tijāniyya, and despite the fact that he was going to conquer the state, the Caliphate of Ḥamdallāhi, that Lobbo had established and that the Kunta eventually supported.[24]

Yet, despite his acceptance of Qādiriyya intellectual thought, in his promotion of the Tijāniyya, Taal strained relations with the intellectual and political leaderships of Bornu, Ḥamdallāhi, Timbuktu, and Fuuta Jalon. The only established intellectual/political leader with whom Taal got along was Bello. On his return from Arabia, Taal first stopped in Bornu, then Sokoto and finally Ḥamdallāhi before making his way across Segu and Kaarta to Fuuta Jalon. It was his zeal for promoting the Tijāniyya and for gaining adherents that swore loyalty to him that seemed to most irritate the religious and political establishments of Bornu, Ḥamdallāhi, and Timbuktu. Prior to Taal's arrival in Bornu in 1831 Muḥammad al-Kānimī was already predisposed to distrust him due to his gaining of influential followers in Murzuq at a time of political turmoil in Fazzān and Tripoli, which threatened Bornu's trade interests. In Bornu, Taal threatened the coalition that al-Kānimī had established by snubbing the established mosques; attracting followers,

21 Willis, "The Writings of al-Ḥājj ʿUmar al-Fūtī and Shaykh Mukhtār b. Wadīʿ at Allāh," 177–78.

22 Willis, "The Writings of al-Ḥājj ʿUmar al-Fūtī, and Shaykh Mukhtār b. Wadīʿ at Allāh," 177, 184.

23 Taal, *Rimāḥ al-Raḥīm alā nuḥūr ḥizb al-rajīm*, 65–167.

24 Willis, "The Writings of al-Ḥājj ʿUmar al-Fūtī and Shaykh Mukhtār b. Wadīʿ at Allāh," 181.

including youth from elite and royal families; breaking public conventions by having his followers prominently recite Tijāniyya chants; and challenging local scholars and court clerics.[25] Once Taal left Bornu, in a bid to repair his relationship with him, al-Kānīmī arranged the marriage between Taal and Mariatu who was from an elite Bornu family. Mariatu and Taal had four sons including Muḥammad al-Makkī who became a main contender to succeed his father until his death in 1864.

The Kunta, in particular the brothers Sīdī al-Mukhtār al-Saghīr (d. 1847) and Sīdī Aḥmad al-Bakkay (d. 1865), grandsons of the Kunta Qādiriyya scholar and saint Sīdī al-Mukhtār al-Kabīr, viewed the expansion of the Tijāniyya as a religious threat and, later, the expansion of Umarian political control as an economic threat. In the eighteenth century, the Kunta, based in Timbuktu, through their dominance of Qu'ranic education had established themselves as an important religious and therefore political authority in the region. Indeed, the Kunta were largely responsible for the general rise of Qu'ranic education and specifically of Qādiriyya education in the western and central Sudan, which primed the population for a demand for governments to protect "Muslim rights" and ultimately for jihad from which all of the eighteenth- and nineteenth-century jihad leaders benefited.[26]

The Kunta trace their origins to Sīdī Muḥammad al-Kuntī al-Kabīr who was the son of Ahwa b. Muḥammad Alama b. Kuntī b. Zam, chief of the Sanhaja Ibdukel, and to his teacher Sīdī 'Ali b. al-Najīb, who traced his lineage to the seventh-century Quarawayn cleric 'Uqba al-Mustajab b. Nafi' who led campaigns of conquest in the Draa and Sūs valleys.[27] The Kunta viewed themselves as one of the leading families of the Qādiriyya ṭarīqa in West Africa. Sīdī 'Umar al-Shaykh (d.1552) was the first Kunta member to join the Qādiriyya. He is credited with helping to revive the brotherhood. He traces his silsila back to the twelfth-century Baghdad founder of the order, 'Abd al-Qadīr Jīlānī. The main propagator of the Qādiriyya ṭarīqa in West Africa was Sīdī al-Mukhtār. Due to the number of schools founded by the Kunta that provided both primary and advanced education, post-eighteenth-century West African and western Qādiriyya silsila converge on Sīdī al-Mukhtār. Sīdī al-Mukhtār's school in Timbuktu became a major center

25 Robinson, *The Holy War of Umar Tal*, 100–102.

26 Lofkrantz, "Intellectual Traditions, Education, and Jihad," 75–98.

27 For more on the origins of the Kunta see Batran, *The Qadiryya Brotherhood*, 8–15.

for Qādiriyya learning in the late eighteenth century; hence, Sīdī al-Mukhtār himself became a major influence on West African scholarly thought.[28]

Indeed, the Kunta took pride in the idea that Sīdī al-Mukhtār and his sons spread the brotherhood and gained adherents through peaceful means such as the establishment of schools (zāwiya) dedicated to Qādiriyya teachings and through combining missionary work with their trading activities across the Sahara and western Africa from Bornu to the Senegal River Valley. According to Kunta sources, Sīdī al-Mukhtār's spiritual influence was spread from the northern Sahara throughout Aïr and across West Africa from the Senegal River Valley to Bornu. According to the *Kitāb al-Tarā'if*, the people who sent gifts and swore loyalty to Sīdī al-Mukhtār included "the Fulbe rulers and scholars, in particular Uthman al-Fudi, who summoned people to Allah, his brother, jurist and vizier, Abdalla, and his son and vizier, the learned Muhammad Bello."[29] Through their activities in the seventeenth century, the Kunta laid the groundwork for support for a call to establish governance based on the Mālikī madh'hab and the Qādiriyya ṭarīqa from which both the Fodiye and Aḥmad Lobbo, the founder of Ḥamdallāhi, benefited.

The Kunta used their scholarly prestige to influence the Qādiriyya regimes in Ḥamdallāhi and Sokoto to protect their economic interests and viewed the growth of the Tijāniyya as an economic and not just a religious threat. The Kunta had strong economic interests in the southern Sahara and Niger Bend region. Timbuktu and the Azouad region were dependent on accessing Māsina grain, and the Kunta were major tobacco and salt traders between Timbuktu and Gwandu. They sought to influence the leadership of Ḥamdallāhi, established in 1818 in Māsina, and the Sokoto Caliphate through their scholarly prestige while maintaining their political independence as much as possible. Indeed, as Mauro Nobili demonstrates, while the Kunta were eventually forced to accept Ḥamdallāhi rule, they always maintained their role as the dominant authority in religious and legal matters.[30] As traders, the Kunta wanted access to the Sokoto market. Moreover, as tobacco traders, the Kunta wanted their main trade route between Timbuktu

28 For more on secondary education in precolonial Muslim West Africa see El Hamel, "The Transmission of Knowledge in Moorish," 62–87, Kane, *Beyond Timbuktu*, 75–95, and Batran, *The Qadiryya Brotherhood in West Africa*, 110–16; Ware, *The Walking Qu'ran*, 39–77.

29 Sīdi Muḥammad b. Sīdī al-Mukhtār al-Kunti, *Kitāb al-ṭara'īf wa-'l-talā'id*, 124–25.

30 Nobili, *Sultan, Caliph, and the Renewer of the Faith*, 151–81.

and Gwandu, which passed through Sarayamo, Humburi, Doré, and Say, to remain free from Ḥamdallāhi control as Ḥamdallāhi forbade the transport, sale, and consumption of tobacco. Sīdī Muḥammad, who had succeeded his father, Sīdī Mukhtār, as leader of the Kunta in 1818 was able to maintain the political independence of Timbuktu (and hence the economic independence of the Kunta) until his death in 1826 at which point the city was occupied by Ḥamdallāhi.[31] After the occupation of Timbuktu, the Kunta were able to use their scholarly prestige to influence the Ḥamdallāhi government and protect their economic interests, except their tobacco trade, which Ḥamdallāhi continued to ban.[32]

From both Umarian and Māsina sources, it appears that the Kunta believed that Taal and the Tijāniyya threatened their religious supremacy and therefore their means of influencing Ḥamdallāhi and Sokoto. Oral traditions that David Robinson collected in Māsina tell how local Muslims, upon hearing some of Taal's teaching—perhaps the beginning of the *Rimāḥ* chants in honor of the Prophet Muḥammad—asked to copy the manuscript from which Taal was teaching. When Taal refused, they stole the manuscript.[33] Umarian sources suggest that Sīdī al-Mukhtār and al-Bekkay were angered that some of their students had joined the Tijāniyya.[34] Both sets of sources demonstrate a strong local Ḥamdallāhi interest in the Tijāniyya and in Taal's teaching to the detriment of the Kunta and the Qādiriyya. After Taal had begun his jihad, al-Bakkay distinguished Kunta methods of spreading their beliefs from Taal's. According to al-Bakkay while Taal used force, the Kunta used persuasion. In one letter that al-Bakkay sent to Taal, al-Bakkay states, "We [the Kunta] teach the ignorant, set right those who go astray and meet the needs of whoever asks for our help. We do not dominate anyone, nor are we dominated by anyone."[35] Even so, the prestige of the Kunta was such, that according to Umarian oral tradition, on the eve of war in 1866, Kunta

31 Stewart, "Frontier Disputes and Problems of Legitimization: Sokoto-Masina Relations 1817–1837," 500. See also Stewart, "Southern Saharan Scholarship and the Bilad al-Sudan," 73–93.

32 For a discussion on Ḥamdallāhi laws concerning tobacco see Lydon, *On Trans-Saharan Trails*, 114–16.

33 Robinson, *The Holy War of Umar Tal*, 110–11.

34 Bā and Daget, *Empire Peul de Macina (1818–1853)*, 246–47 and Robinson *The Holy War of Umar Tal*, 110–11.

35 Ahmad al-Bakkay b. Muhmmad al-Khalifa, *Risala ila al-hajj 'Umar*; reprinted in Batran, *The Qadiriyya Brotherhood*, 135.

scholars were close, yet ultimately unsuccessful, to brokering a peace deal between Taal and Aḥmadu b. Aḥmadu of Ḥamdallāhi on the basis that it was unlawful for two Muslim leaders to go to war with each other.[36]

Bello was not as bothered as the other Qādiriyya leaderships by Taal's dedication to promoting the Tijāniyya and recruiting adherents throughout the jurisdictions of his hosts. Taal spent just over six years at Bello's court arriving at the end of 1831 and departing at the beginning of 1837 after Bello's death and the naming of Bello's brother Abūbakar Atikū as the new Sarkin Musulmi. At Bello's court Taal rose to prominence as a judge and helped with supply logistics (particularly in locating water) during the 1835–1836 campaign to secure the northern border and suppress resistance by Gobir, Katsina, and Tuareg forces. As a sign of Bello and Taal's good relationship, at about this time Taal married Bello's daughter Mariam. It would be Mariam's sons, Ḥabīb and Mukhtār who would gain control of the western part of the Umarian territories from Taal's chosen successor, Aḥmad al-Kabīr (also known as Ahmadu Seku), his son, with wife Aisha Dem, who was also from an elite Sokoto family. The fact that Taal's sons from his Sokoto wives played such an important role both before and after Taal's death is a key indication of the importance and influence of the Sokoto background in Umarian affairs. Another sign of the influence of Sokoto on Taal's movement is that Sokoto subjects formed an influential component of the Umarian community established at Diegunko in Fuuta Jalon. It was at Diegunko between 1841 and 1845 that Taal and his community established the intellectual basis for his political movement, opposition to the surrounding governments, and basis for jihad. The Sokoto followers, both men and women, were important in that process. Moreover, when the French conquered Bandiagara, the easternmost Umarian state in 1893, many Umarians committed hijra and sought refuge in the Sokoto Caliphate.[37] Intellectually, Taal shared with the Fodiye the use of al-Maghīlī's definition of a freeborn Muslim to narrow who was considered to be a freeborn Muslim, the Fodiye use of taqlīd, and similar attitudes toward captivity, enslavement, the slave trade, and ransoming.

Similar to the Tetravirate and in the tradition of Kan, prior to launching his jihad, Taal condemned western Sudanese religious and political leaders for not preventing the enslavement and sale of freeborn Muslims and indeed insinuated that they were complicit. Taal shared the Tetravirate's view and policy on enslavement. Like the Tetravirate, he was concerned with

36 Diop, *The Epic of El Hadj Umar Taal of Fuuta*, 31–34.

37 See Robinson, "The Umar Emigration of the Late 19th Century," 245–70.

protecting freeborn Muslims from enslavement and sale into the Atlantic slave trade and outside the dār-al-islām. At the beginning of his scholarly period in Diegunko he wrote *Risālat sahwa al-habīb ilā as'ilat Ibrahīm al-labīb* on the relationship between the Tijāniyya and non-Muslims. In it, he heavily criticized Muslim rulers who did not prevent the enslavement of Muslims and their sale into the transatlantic slave trade. He unequivocally asserted that "to sell Muslim slaves to the Europeans or to others, is totally prohibited," that "worse still we do not see anyone condemning it, nor is there any one from the 'ulama or the amirs, trying to put an end to this illegal practice. They act as if it were no longer obligatory upon them to do so," and that "no one can be more ignorant and arrogant than sinful and criminal people who legalize enslavement of free people by an act of fatwā,"[38] At this time, people were still being sold into the Atlantic slave trade and there was a growing demand in Senegambia after 1833 for enslaved labor in peanut production for the European market. Martin Klein argues that many Senegambians were attracted to nineteenth- century jihad leaders because of their antislavery rhetoric but were ultimately deceived. To fund their military campaigns and to establish stability in conquered territory, many of these reform leaders exchanged enslaved people and slave-produced products for European guns and horses.[39] Yet, Taal's legal position on slavery was the same as the Tetravirate. He was concerned about protecting individuals who he considered to be freeborn Muslims while facilitating what he considered to be legal enslavement and slave trading.

Taal began his jihad in 1852 with an attack on the Mandinka kingdom of Tamba, on the eastern edge of Fuuta Jalon. A few years earlier, he had moved his community from Diegunko to territory on the Tinkisso River, which he called Dinguiraye and that he had leased from King Yimba of Tambo. The move suited everyone involved. From the Almamy's perspective the move would put some distance between Fuuta Jalon proper and Taal's growing military force while possibly expanding trade links to Bure and Kankan and undermining the power of Tamba. He believed that he would still be in the dominant position since the Umarians would need his cooperation and access through Fuuta Jalon to trade at coastal ports such as Freetown. Yimba thought Tambo was gaining a new scholarly community that would

38 Taal, *Risālat shawq al-habīb ilā as'ilat Ibrahīm al-labīb,* 239. See also Jah, "Al-Hajj 'Umar al-Fūtī's Philosophy of Jihad and its Sufi Basis," 29.

39 Klein, "The Impact of the Atlantic Slave Trade," 241–44; Klein, "Social and Economic Factors," 419–41.

pay tribute, provide a protective buffer for Tambo proper and help increase trade along the Tinkisso River. For Taal, under the right conditions it would be easier to declare a jihad against polytheistic Tamba than a Muslim state. Those conditions developed in 1852, when Yimba attacked Dinguiraye out of frustration with Taal's unwillingness to pay tribute; concern for the size of the community, its fortifications, and weaponry; and the breakdown of negotiations with Taal to address his concerns. The attack backfired on Yimba. Not only did the Umarians successfully defend Dinguiraye, but they chased Yimba's force back to the city of Tamba and laid siege. The conquest of Tamba was completed in 1853.[40] The Umarians seized the capital of the Bambara state of Kaarta in 1855 and then Segu in 1862.

Taal viewed the conduct of jihad as an important community responsibility for Muslims. In *Tadhkirat al-Mustarṣidīn* Taal urged Muslims to follow their faith, pray, fast, give alms, make the pilgrimage and perform spiritual jihad and, as a community, to conduct the jihad of war.[41] Taal's intellectual mindset and policies on jihad are most clearly outlined in *Bayān mā waqaʿa*, the book he wrote to justify waging jihad against Ḥamdallāhi and that can be considered to be his equivalent to the exchange of letters between Uthmān b. Fodiye and Bello, and al-Kānimī of Bornu. Even though Taal claimed that Aḥmadu b. Aḥmadu of Ḥamdallāhi's troops attacked him first, just as Sokoto had to justify extending jihad into Muslim Bornu, Taal had to justify extending jihad into Muslim Ḥamdallāhi.[42] In *Bayān mā waqaʿa* Taal responded to five letters sent to him by Aḥmadu b. Aḥmadu, the grandson of Ḥamdallāhi's founder, Aḥmad Lobbo, who became Caliph of Ḥamdallāhi in 1853, challenging Taal's desire to extend jihad into his territories, a recognized Muslim state. *Bayān mā waqaʿa* was that justification based on Taal's interpretation of law and political events. In *Bayān mā waqaʿa* Taal cites numerous authoritative authors in West Africa, including al-Maghīlī, ʿAbd al-Raḥmān al-Suyūṭī, and Abdullah b. Abī Zayd al-Qayrawānī. He also cites Abdullāhi b. Fodiye's *Ḍiyā al-sulṭān* and Uthmān b. Fodiye's *Sirāj al-iḥwān*. In particular, in justifying the use of offensive force, Taal quotes Uthmān b. Fodiye's *Sirāj al-iḥwān* and interprets it as Uthmān arguing that conducting jihad

---

40 "The History of al-Hajj Umar," 205–9; Robinson, *The Holy War of Umar Tal*, 125–32.

41 ʿUmar Taal, *Tadhkirat al-Mustarṣidīn*, BNF MS Arab 5708 f 128–37.

42 For Taal's claims that Aḥmadu b. Aḥmadu troops attacked him first see Al-Hafiz al-Tidjani, *Al-Hadj Omar Tall*, 36.

against "infidels" was an obligation (wājib).[43] Yet, according to Muḥammad al-Hafīz al-Tidjānī, when Taal's forces invaded Ḥamdallāhi, Taal ordered his soldiers not to take captive the wives of the inhabitants nor to loot them.[44] This indicates that although Taal was willing to make intellectual arguments to define Ḥamdallāhi as non-Muslim in order to attack them he was not willing to take captive nor enslave women who he most likely recognized as being Muslim.

Ḥamdallāhi had been established through jihad in 1818. Aḥmad Lobbo (c. 1773–1845) had been one of several scholars in Māsina trying to overthrow Ardo rule who were the Muslim clients of non-Muslim Bambara Segu. While Lobbo's movement was the one that proved ultimately successful, these scholars shared a concern about the growing power of Segu, especially in the Niger Delta region, and a disillusionment with the scholarly elite in Jenne. In addition, they were inspired by the movements that established Fuuta Jalon, Fuuta Toro, and the Sokoto Caliphate.[45] Lobbo was born in Māsina. His first teacher was his maternal grandfather, Alfa Gouro, who raised him after his father died when he was two years old. At age seven, Lobbo was sent to study with Alfa Hambarké Sangaré, and upon that teacher's death with Alfa Samba Hammdi Bamma, and then with the Almamy of Sono. With these three teachers, Lobbo first learned the Qur'ran and its interpretation. At age twenty-two, with students of his own, Lobbo went to Jenne in order to further his education where he became a student of Kabara Farma, who according to Bintou Sanankoua, was Lobbo's most influential teacher. It was from Farma that Lobbo received the Qādiriyya wird. Under the tutelage of Farma, Lobbo immersed himself into the writings of 'Abd al-Qadīr Jīlānī, the founder of the Qādiriyya order. Through his education, Lobbo became an expert on law, theology, and rhetoric. It was also during this time that tension developed between Lobbo and the Jenne intellectual elite. Lobbo refused to recognize the scholarly hierarchy in Jenne and viewed them as corrupt. At the same time, Jenne scholars viewed Lobbo's growing popularity among students and of his teachings as a threat to their influence and to Ardo political control.[46]

---

43 Taal, *Bayān mā waqa'a*, 98.

44 Al-Hafiz al-Tidjani, *Al-Hadj Omar Tall,* 36–38.

45 Ly-Tall, "Massina and the Torodbe (Tukuloor) Empire until 1878," 599–601.

46 Bā and Daget, *Empire Peul de Macina (1818–1853)*, 22–32; Sanankoua, *Un empire peul au XIXe siècle*, 33–42.

Lobbo was also intellectually influenced by both the Fodiye and the Kunta. Indeed, HFC Smith argues that Lobbo owes a large intellectual debt to the Fodiawa and the Sokoto jihad.[47] According to William Brown, the earliest contact between Māsina and Sokoto (but not specifically Lobbo) was when the Sokoto preacher Malam b. Sa'īd came to Fittuga, the northernmost part of the interior Niger delta in 1815–1816. Around this time, Lobbo was also in contact with Abdullāhi b. Fodiye for his feedback on his scholarly criticisms of the Ardo's practice of Islam.[48] Indeed, in 1816, perhaps as a means to increase his political and religious legitimacy (or perhaps out of genuine intellectual and political loyalty) Lobbo pledged allegiance to 'Uthmān b. Fodiye upon which 'Uthmān sent Lobbo a flag, his symbol of support, and several law books—and gave him the title of Shaykh.[49] Lobbo was also directly intellectually connected to the Kunta. One of Lobbo's closest advisors, as well as being the forger of the *Ta'rikh al-fattāsh*, was Alfa Nūḥ b. Tayrū who had been Sīdī al-Mukhtār's student. After the jihad, Nūḥ was responsible for establishing Ḥamdallāhi's education system, hence solidifying a strong Kunta scholarly influence, with a focus on the memorization of the Qu'ran; the study of hadith, tawḥīd (doctrine), uṣūl al-fiqh (principles of jurisprudence), fiqh (law), taṣawwuf (mysticism), naḥw (grammar), and manṭiq (logic), among other disciplines, and the equal but segregated education of girls and boys.[50]

Even though he was intellectually influenced by the Kunta and the Fodiye, Lobbo asserted his independence, and indeed claimed superiority, to the intellectual regimes established in Timbuktu and Sokoto. He did this by manipulating both oral and written traditions. In oral traditions collected by A. H. Bā and J Dajet, the rise of a "Caliph Aḥmad" was foretold during the reign of Askia Muḥammad. According to oral traditions, during Askia Muḥammad's return from his pilgrimage to Mecca, when he was in Cairo, two scholars in his entourage, Alfa Salif Diawara and Alfa Mamadou Toulé, took a nighttime journey to an underground city populated by Muslim jinn, located somewhere between Alexandria and Cairo. There they met a jinn, Chamharouch, who revealed that there were to be twelve Caliphs of which ten had already reigned, the eleventh being Askia Muḥammad, and that the

47 H. F. C. Smith, "A Neglected Theme of West African History," 179.

48 Brown, "The Caliphate of Hamdullahi c. 1818–1864," 20.

49 Stewart, "Frontier Disputes"; Robinson, "Breaking New Ground in 'Pagan' and 'Muslim' West Africa," 308.

50 Stewart, "Frontier Disputes," 500; Loimeier, *Muslim Societies in Africa*, 123.

twelfth would come from the Niger Delta region and be born eleven years before the end of the twelfth century of the Muslim calendar and who would rise to prominence in the thirty-third year of the thirteenth century when he was forty-four years old. According to this oral tradition, upon reporting their journey and the message from Chamharouch, Askia Muḥammad decided to meet with the jinn himself. Among the additional details that Askia Muḥammad got from Chamharouch was that this twelfth Caliph would come from the region of Jenne, that he will restore order all the way to Timbuktu, that he will be respected for his knowledge, spirituality, and sense of justice; that his accomplishments would surpass those of Askia Muḥammad and that his name would be "Aḥmad."[51]

This fit with the oral tradition of Lobbo's family. According to oral tradition, Lobbo's subgroup of Fulbe, the Foyna, had come from Fuuta Toro and had established themselves in the region of Wouro Nguiya between Dogo and Banguita, where their prosperity eventually became viewed as a threat by the ruling Bambara. According to this tradition, one of the court magicians even foretold that a man would be born into one of the sixteen Foyna clans that would overthrow the Bambara kings. Upon hearing this prophecy the King ordered an attack on the Foyna where their herds were seized, the women and girls were enslaved and most of the men were killed. One male survivor, who became known as Hamman Daḍi Foyna, was spared and reestablished himself in Fittouga. His grandson, Alhadji Modi became an important scholar. Alhadji Modi's son, Hammadoun Séghir, also a scholar, left Fittouga for Lake Débo and the border of Diaka. He was the great-great-great grandfather of Aḥmad Lobbo who was born in the village of Malangal, about twenty kilometers from Ténenkou in 1175–76 AH (1789).[52]

The prophecy claiming that Lobbo was the twelfth caliph also appears in the introduction of the *Ta'rikh al-fattāsh*. As demonstrated by Nehemia Levtzion, the prophecy in this written account of political history of the Songhay empire is a forgery by Nūḥ, the Kunta-trained scholar and advisor to Lobbo.[53] In his forgery, similar to the oral tradition collected by Bā and Dajet, the Askia Muḥammad is cast as the eleventh caliph. In this version, it is the famed and influential scholar al-Suyūṭī who prophesizes to the

51 Bā and Daget, *Empire Peul de Macina*, 17–19.

52 Bā and Daget, *Empire Peul de Macina*, 20.

53 See Levtzion, "A Seventeenth Century Chronicle by Ibn Mukhtār," 571–93. See also Nobili, "A Propaganda Document in Support of 19th Century Caliphate of Ḥamdallāhi."

Askia Muḥammad when he is in Cairo that the twelfth caliph will emerge from the Middle Delta and be called "Ahmad." Nūḥ and Lobbo further reinforce the prophecy in the forged *Ta'rikh al-fattāsh* by claiming that upon his return the Askia Muḥammad consulted with al-Maghīlī who confirmed the statements made by al-Suyūṭī.

The oral and written prophecies foretelling the coming of Lobbo and the establishment of his Caliphate established Lobbo's political and religious legitimacy in several ways and addressed slightly different audiences. First, by claiming that al-Suyūṭī and al-Maghīlī prophesied his arrival and establishment of his Caliphate, as in the forged written Arabic account, he appealed to an educated audience familiar with the importance of these two scholars and their impact on West African Muslim intellectual thought. It is a particular appeal to intellectual and religious legitimacy. Second, the assertion that Lobbo was the heir to Askia Muḥammad in both the oral tradition and the written *Ta'rikh al-fattāsh* provided a claim to Timbuktu that directly challenged the political authority of the Kunta while still providing Lobbo the ability to base his religious authority on Kunta intellectual thought. Third, it gave Lobbo a way to renege on his swearing of loyalty to the Sokoto Caliphate. ʿUthmān had died in 1817. While Bello and ʿAbdullāhi were involved in their succession crisis, which was not settled until 1820–21, Lobbo, on his own, had led a coalition of Fulbe against the Ardo dynasty; he had defeated Segu Bambara and his religious rivals in the Middle Niger and had established his capital at Ḥamdallāhi.[54] He no longer needed the support of and therefore no longer needed to be subservient to Sokoto. He wanted to establish the full independence of his Caliphate and to be viewed as the legitimate Caliph and Mālikī and Qādiriyya leader in West Africa.

While Kunta and Sokoto scholarship and precedence influenced Lobbo's interpretation of Islam and implementation of law, he also executed his own thinking as well as his political independence. In asserting his control, Lobbo established the most centralized of West African states founded through jihad. He implemented a strict interpretation of Mālikī law that forbade the consumption of tobacco (which interfered with Kunta economic interests) and also prohibited games, music, and dancing but also made allowances for the Fulbe (Pulaaku) ethical code especially with regard to women.[55] He

54 For more on the relationship between Sokoto and Hamdallāhi see Stewart, "Frontier Disputes."

55 Ly-Tall, "Massina and the Torodbe (Tukuloor) Empire until 1878," 600–603; Loimeier, *Muslim Societies in Africa*, 122–23; Nobili *Sultan, Caliph, and the*

conquered Jenne in 1819, Timbuktu in 1825, and invaded Kaarta in 1843–44. Upon Lobbo's death, he was succeeded by his son Aḥmad Seku, who reigned until 1853, and then by Seku's son Aḥmadu b. Aḥmadu, who was ruling when Māsina was invaded by Taal in 1862.

Just like Sokoto did against Bornu, Taal used the concept of takfīr, declaring a self-professed Muslim to be an infidel to justify his attack on Ḥamdallāhi. It had been Ḥamdallāhi policy since the reign of Lobbo to oppose Taal. Ḥamdallāhi and the Kunta in Timbuktu had opposed Taal's proselytizing the Tijānī message. However, what really increased Taal's ire against Ḥamdallāhi was Aḥmadu's support of Segu. In *Bayān mā waqa'a* Taal declared that Aḥmadu had "abandoned" Islam due to his failure to protect Muslims against non-Muslims and to come to the aid of fellow Muslims, the Umarians, against non-Muslims.[56] This is in reference to Aḥmadu's support of Segu against the Umarian expansion. According to Taal, Ḥamdallāhi's support of non-Muslim Segu made Aḥmadu and Ḥamdallāhi as a whole non-Muslim and therefore a legitimate venue for jihad. He supported this conclusion with Qu'ranic and Sunna verses, and many references to authoritative texts and treatises including those by Uthmān b. Fodiye, 'Abdullāhi b. Fodiye and Bello.[57]

A key to Taal's justification of declaring jihad against states that considered themselves to be Muslim was not only his expansive view of who was an "infidel" but also his narrow view of who was a Muslim. Just like the Tetravirate, Taal based his definition of a Muslim on al-Maghīlī's definition. Al-Maghīlī considered non-Muslims to be people who did not believe in God and the message of the Prophet Muḥammad, people who practiced "unislamic" behaviors, and people who made statements that only non-Muslims would make.[58] For 'Uthmān b. Fodiye non-Muslims were people who rejected Islam or who followed a syncretic form of Islam.[59] As described by Taal, his three categories of unbelievers were first those who were "infidels" by origin such as Christians. "Apostatized" Muslims were considered to

---

Renewer of the Faith, 162–64, 211–18.

56 Taal, *Bayān mā waqa'a*, 107–38.

57 Taal, *Bayān mā waqa'a*, 107–38. For example, texts he quotes heavily include 'Abdullāhi b. Fodiye, *Ḍiyā' al-tāwīl* and *Ḍiyā' al-Sulṭān,* 'Uthmān b. Fodiye *Sirāj al-ikhwān*; Bello *Miftāḥ al-Saḍād, Bulaqi al-Shafi'I al-sirāj al-munīr*, al-Suyūṭī's *Tafsīr al-jalalayn*, various treatises by al-Maghīlī, among many others.

58 Hunwick, *Sharī'a in Songhay*, 74.

59 'Uthmān b. Fodiye, *Nūr-al-albāb*, 300–03.

be the second category. The third category included people who "pretended" to be Muslim but whose actions are those of an "infidel."[60] Similar to the Tetravirate, the Umarians used their narrow definition of a Muslim to classify people who agreed with them as Muslims and people who disagreed with them as non-Muslim regardless of how a particular person self-identified. The Umarian definition of a Muslim also had practical economic overtones. For example, in order to confiscate Maraka goods, land, and labor, Bakary Tako, the Umarian commander of the Sinsani garrison in 1862–63, classified the Maraka as non-Muslim and called them the "the uncircumcised."[61]

More explicitly, Taal's conception of non-Muslims was used to justify attacking specific regions. In the lead-up to his attack on Ḥamdallāhi proper, Taal first invaded Bakunu, which was a frontier region between Kaarta and Ḥamdallāhi, under the control of Ḥamdallāhi but coveted by Taal. Taal had a twofold justification for invading Bakunu. As well as accusing Aḥmadu of failing to protect his agents and alluding that Aḥmadu allowed them to be taken captive and enslaved, Taal argued that the majority of the inhabitants of the region, who at the time were a mixed population of ethnic Soninke, Diawara, Tuareg, and Fulbe, were non-Muslim and that Ḥamdallāhi had failed to spread Islam in the region.[62] According to Taal, the people of Bakunu were composed of three groups. The majority were polytheists who he claimed were Bambara. The second most populous groups were "brigands" and "hypocrites" who mixed polytheistic and Muslim practices and who claimed to be Muslim under the authority of Aḥmadu but who blocked trade routes, imposed illegal taxes, and raided villages. According to Taal, the third group, the smallest of the three, consisted of poor and oppressed Muslims who were frequently taken prisoner by their Bambara neighbors and other polytheists. Taal justified his attack on Bakunu based on his assertions that the majority of the inhabitants were non-Muslim and that the leader pretended to be Muslim but behaved like a non-Muslim and that he was acting in defense of the region's "true" Muslim minority.[63]

Unlike the Tetravirate, Taal's focus was not on reforming his own state, Fuuta Toro, but on establishing a state based on his interpretation of Islam out of the various non-Muslim and Muslim states of the region. Moreover, he recruited his army not from among the population of the region whose

60 Taal, *Bayān mā waqaʿa*, 98.

61 Roberts, *Warriors, Merchants and Slaves,* 97.

62 Taal, *Bayān mā waqaʿa*, 78–80.

63 Taal, *Bayān mā waqaʿa*, 78, 99.

governments he was overthrowing but from Fuuta Jalon, Fuuta Toro, and Fuuta Bundu. Indeed, David Robinson labels Taal's jihad an "imperial jihad" since he recruited his army from the "west" in order to conquer the "east."[64] However, like most of the people who joined the Sokoto jihad, most of the people who joined the Umarian jihad were not primarily motivated by Taal's interpretation of Islam nor his vision of a proper Islamic state. In the 1860s many young men joined with the goal of earning enough money to establish themselves back home. Others, especially households, migrated into territory conquered by the Umarians in search of new land. In the 1880s Wolof soldiers defeated by the French joined the Umarian armies looking for new opportunities. These soldiers were joined by civilians from throughout the Senegal River Valley wanting to escape French governance.[65]

Due to the fact that his was basically an invading army, Taal and his descendants were faced with constant resistance, especially from the Bambara, Maraka, and Masinanke, and later conflict with Samori Turé and the French, in establishing their rule and interpretation of Islam. Taal was killed in an attack by revolting Masinanke in 1864, and his empire was divided due to conflict and infighting between his sons, Aḥmad al-Kabīr (also known as Aḥmadu Seku), Muḥammad al-Makkī, Ḥabīb, and Mukhtār, and his nephew, Aḥmad al-Tijānī: with Aḥmad al-Kabīr taking Segu, al-Makkī taking Nioro, Ḥabīb taking Dinguiray, Mukhtār taking Konyakari, and Tijānī taking Māsina-Bandiagara.[66] These polities operated at various times as independent states, fighting off al-Kabīr's attempts at unification, attacks, and conquest by Samori in the 1880s until finally they were all conquered by the French between 1890 and 1893.

Indeed, from the beginning of the jihad, the Umarians faced two important cleavages in their community. The first cleavage was between the Umarian followers, primarily from Fuuta Jalon, who had joined Taal prior to the jihad and those people, primarily from Fuuta Toro, who were recruited after the declaration of jihad. The second cleavage was within Taal's own family between his wives, concubines, and sons.[67] Upon embarking on the conquest of Ḥamdallāhi, Taal had put al-Kabīr, his son with 'Aisha Dem

64 Robinson, "The Chronicle of the Succession': An Important Document for the Umarian State," 247.

65 Hanson, "Islam, Migration and the Political Economy of Meaning," 39–44.

66 Robinson, *The Holy War of Umar Tal*, 310–11; Loimeier, *Muslim Societies in Africa*, 124.

67 Robinson, "The Chronicle of the Succession," 248.

from Sokoto, in charge of Segu and Kaarta and intended him to be his successor. Taal had installed al-Kabīr as his successor in a ceremony at Markoya in 1859 in the midst of the Segu campaign. Al-Kabīr's main rival for the succession was his younger brother by just a few months, al-Makkī, the son of the elite Bornu woman, Mariatu.[68] In an account of the installation ceremony written by the scholar and Umarian Muḥammad b. Ibrāhīm b.'Umar b. Muḥammad b. Mūsa, most likely soon after the ceremony, it appears that Taal was trying to mitigate the rivalry between al-Kabīr and al-Makkī during the ceremony as well as to garner support for his chosen successor. According to Muḥammad b. Ibrāhīm after Taal named al-Kabīr his successor and gave him his knowledge, including that of the 'awrād (s. wird), to use as he saw fit, he turned to al-Makkī and told him "I give you everything that is in the Rimāḥ and authorize you in regard to it . . . As for you and your rank, follow your brother . . . Keep close ties to your kin. For the two of you [al-Kabīr and al-Makkī] do not let anyone come between you."[69] Al-Makkī died in 1864 thereby resolving that particular rivalry.[70]

Due to its location, Segu—after it was captured—was made the capital of the empire with regional capitals at Nioro and Bandiagara. In 1870 in Kaarta, al-Kabīr was challenged by his brothers, Ḥabīb and Mukḥtār, the sons of Mariam b. Muhammad Bello. They used their mother's prestige and support from Dinguiray to gain control of the western part of the state including Kunjan and Konyakara. Al-Kabīr was able to defeat and capture his brothers and install another brother, Muḥammad al-Muntaga, in Nioro who also later revolted against him.[71] The revolt by Ḥabīb and Mukḥtār encouraged revolts by Bambara and Masinanke forces, which were not suppressed until 1874 by al-Kabīr. In order to assert the legitimacy of his authority and claim to being the rightful heir of Taal, al-Kabīr repeatedly asserted that his father, Taal, had him proclaimed commander of the faithful three times, after the conquests of Kaarta, Segu, and Māsina respectively. He also had himself reproclaimed as commander of the faithful in 1874 in front of West African and North African Tijāniyya leaders.[72] Al-Kabīr was less successful

68 Robinson, "The Chronicle of the Succession," 248–49.

69 Muḥammad b. Ibrāhīm b.'Umar b. Muḥammad b. Mūsa, "The Chronicle of the Succession," 260–61.

70 Hanson, *Migration, Jihad, and Muslim Authority in West Africa,* 95.

71 al-Kabīr was able to retake Kaarta from his brother in 1884.

72 Robinson, *The Holy War of Umar Tal,* 199–201, 314–15; Hanson, "Historical Writing in Nineteenth Century Segu,"105–6. Oloruntimehin questions

in asserting his authority over the eastern part of the former Caliphate of Ḥamdallāhi under the control of his cousins Aḥmad al-Tijānī and Muniru. From his capital at Bandiagara al-Tijānī and his brother Muniru constantly fought off attacks from the Masinanke, the Bobo, and the Kunta who all objected to the conquest. However, al-Tijānī also did not accept the overlordship of al-Kabīr. Al-Tijānī, too, had himself proclaimed the commander of the faithful, and there was very little contact between the two leaders.[73] Indeed, after the death of Taal, as John Hanson argues, there was not one united Umarian Empire but instead a series of Umarian states that shared a common foundation.[74] David Robinson describes the relationship as "a series of towns and hinterlands dominated by the Umarians, separated from one another by dangerous areas dominated by bandits and indigenous people unsympathetic to the invaders."[75] It was in these areas of limited government administration where issues of captive taking and ransoming were negotiated and settled according to local norms and condoned by government. According to Christopher Wise, the Umarian failure to administer effectively was due to a combination of Taal's refusal to assume ultimate political power, in obedience to al-Ghālī's directions to wage jihad in West Africa but not to assume kingly power, and his propensity to appoint his blood relatives (usually his sons)—who had little administrative experience—to rule on his behalf, instead of choosing men with administrative experience.[76]

Enslavement and Ransoming Policy in the Umarian States

Similar to the Sokoto Caliphate, warfare and its subsequent capture of booty in terms of people and goods was an important component of Umarian statecraft. Klein argues that the Umarian forces were dependent on the slave trade in order to purchase European guns from the coast. Moreover, similar to the Sokoto Caliphate, Umarian plantation agriculture was dependent on

the veracity of al-Kabīr's claim that Taal proclaimed him his successor. See Oloruntimehin, *The Segu Tukolor Empire*, 156–57.

73 Robinson, *The Holy War of Umar Tal*, 314–16.

74 Hanson, *Migration, Jihad, and Muslim Authority in West Africa*, 9.

75 Robinson, "Jihad, Hijra, and Hajj in West Africa," 250.

76 Wise, *Archive of the Umarian Tijaniyya*, xxxii–xxxiii.

enslaved labor.[77] However, just like the Tetravirate, Taal was concerned with fostering what he considered to be fair and legal enslavement and preventing what he considered to be illegal enslavement. From the start of the jihad until conquest by the French, the Umarians were in a constant state of war, conquering territory, fighting resisters and themselves, and defending themselves against Samori and the French. The Umarian army was composed of several different groups. At the top of the army hierarchy were the elite cavalry troops who were mostly of Fuutanke origin. Below them were the "new Muslims" who had converted to Islam prior to the beginning of the jihad and local Fulbe. At the bottom of the army hierarchy were the sofa, local polytheists whose leaders were allied to Taal and his successors.[78] Just as with the Sokoto army, booty was an important motivator for the troops, as most soldiers joined in order to gain wealth, and it formed an important source of state revenue. In the Bambara regions, the Umarians used a hybrid of Islamic and Bambara law for the division of booty. In accordance with Mālikī law, the Fuutanke soldiers kept four fifths of the booty they captured and turned over one fifth to the state whereas in accordance with Segu Bambara law the Umarian state claimed half of the booty captured by the sofa. "New" Muslim often failed to turn in any of the booty that they captured.[79] According to Eugene Mage, who was in the region in the early 1860s, corruption in the army was rampant, and all troops were adept at hiding marketable goods such as captives, amber, kola, and horses until after the formal division of booty.[80]

Both the Umarians and the groups revolting against them used similar tactics: raiding was an important one. Richard Roberts argues that for the Umarians, a policy of raids instead of large campaigns was not only a response to resisting Bambara raids but was a deliberate policy choice to help reduce the tension between the Fuutanke solders and sofa in the Umarian army and to use the greater amount of booty achieved through raids than from larger campaigns to reduce Fuutanke discontent with the government.[81] According to Roberts, Bambara resistance to Umarian rule

77 Klein, *Slavery and Colonial Rule*, 58; Hanson, "Islam, Migration and the Political Economy of Meaning," 43.

78 Roberts, *Warriors, Merchants and Slaves*, 90–91.

79 Roberts, *Warriors, Merchants, and Slaves*, 92–94; Robinson, *The Holy War of Umar Tal*, 185–86.

80 Mage, *Voyage (1863–1866) au Soudan Occidental*, 335.

81 Roberts, *Warriors, Merchants, and Slaves*, 94–95.

was characterized by its small-scale, decentralized command, and fluid alliances.[82] All sides were willing to attack and pillage people and villages affiliated and allied to the opposing side. Mage describes how after one battle in February 1865 between Umarian Segu forces and Bambara resisters that he saw soldiers taking captive about thirty-five hundred women and children as well as confiscating calabashes, sacks of millet, lanterns and wicks, doors, guns, lances, tools, ironwork and weaving equipment, cotton, tobacco, and indigo.[83] Joseph Gallieni made similar observations as Mage when he traveled in the area in 1880. While attributing the depopulation of the left bank of the Niger to Umarian raids, he writes that soldiers were constantly conducting raids against Bambara villages and confiscating foodstuffs and animals.[84] Likewise, Bambara resisters to the Umarian regime also used raiding as a strategy to weaken Segu, often raiding Umarian villages for captives, foodstuffs, and other booty.[85] The culture of raiding and captive taking continued into the early years of the French conquest. For example, on January 23, 1893, the village of Kansankousso, near Segu, was raided, and fourteen women and their goods were taken from the market.[86] In another example, in the summer of 1894, thirty-seven men mounted on horseback raided the village of Ouensequellé near Segu, killing two men and taking fourteen people captive.[87] As Marie Rodet has shown, these conflicts in conjunction with Samori's wars of expansion into the region resulted in the formation of diasporic communities across the western Sudan from modern-day Mali to Senegal, as people fled as refugees or were taken captive, enslaved, and sold within the region.[88]

The Umarian economy, like that of the Sokoto Caliphate, was based on plantation agriculture and a constant demand for enslaved labor. The region produced grain for export and cotton for the local textile industry. Prior to

82 Roberts, *Warriors, Merchants, and Slaves*, 95.

83 Mage, *Voyage (1863–1866) au Soudan Occidental*, 437–38.

84 Gallieni, *Voyage au Soudan Français*, 458, 607.

85 Caron, *De Saint-Louis au Port de Tombouktou*, 117; Soleillet, *Voyage à Segou, 1878–1879*, 320.

86 ANM FA 1D 221 Relations de Missions Correspondances Diverse, Cercle de Segou 1891–1898 Mission de Sergent Dechen Nabasso, January 23, 1893.

87 ANM FA 1E 113 Renseignement politiques, Cercle de Segou 1890–1904, 4ieme trimestre 1894.

88 Rodet, "Escaping Slavery and Building Diasporic Communities in French Soudan and Senegal ca 1880–1940," 363–86.

the Umarian conquest of Segu Bambara, Sinsani was the most important commercial and agricultural city. After the conquest, commercial and agricultural hegemony shifted to Banamba. By the 1890s, plantations, worked by enslaved labor, encircled the city for twenty-five to fifty kilometers. Although the number of enslaved people in Banamba is not known, in 1910 it was estimated that twenty thousand enslaved individuals left the region of Banamba and Tuba as part of the 1905–6 slave exodus and that enslaved people had outnumbered free individuals at a ratio of two to one during the height of Banamba's agricultural production.[89] Like in most parts of West Africa, agricultural work in the western Sudan was gendered female. Women captives, valued for their productive and reproductive capacities, were more valued than male captives as slaves. Yet, there was a market for male captives for both ransoming and enslavement even after the end of the "legal" transatlantic slave trade in 1808, which had been the main market for male African prisoners in West Africa. According to Mage's informants in the 1850s, Umarian soldiers were regularly taking male adult prisoners.[90] The market for captive men may have been fueled by the demand for enslaved labor on agricultural plantations, which could not be fulfilled by women captives alone but also to be ransomed. Both men and women taken captive during Umarian warfare and during Samori's wars farther to the south and marked for enslavement were transported to Banamba, which had become the most important slave market in the western Sudan, and sold throughout the region.[91] As Rodet's interviews with the descendants of enslaved individuals have shown, many men were enslaved on agricultural plantations in the last few decades of the nineteenth century.[92] Moreover, as will be discussed in greater detail in chapter 5, many captive men were ransomed.

Ransoming was practiced throughout the region. Even prior to Taal's jihad there was an expectation among freeborn Muslims in the western Sudan that they should be protected from enslavement even in their interactions with

89 Roberts and Klein, "The Banamba Slave Exodus of 1905 and the Decline of Slavery in the Western Sudan, 375–94; Lovejoy, *Transformations*, 191–92. For slave exoduses from other parts of French Soudan and especially the role of women in these exoduses see Rodet, *Les migrants ignores du Haut-Sénégal (1900–1946)* and Rodet, "Migrants in French Sudan: Gender Biases in the Historiography."

90 Mage, *Voyage (1863–1866) au Soudan Occidental*, 153.

91 Klein, *Slavery and Colonial Rule in French West Africa*, 55.

92 See, for example, Rodet, "Mémoires de l'esclavage dans la region de Kayes, histoire d'une disparition," 263–91.

non-Muslims. For example, Mungo Park encountered a woman in Wawra on the border between Kaarta and Segu during his first voyage in 1796. She asked that he enquire after her son "in Bambara or in my own country" who was taken captive in 1793 during a war with Segu. She emphasized that her son, Mamadee was a Muslim, stating that "he was no Heathen, but prayed to God morning and evening."[93] Park's retelling of this conversation with this anonymous woman reveals something important about attitudes toward enslavement and knowledge of the slave trade. By emphasizing that Mamadee was a Muslim, the mother was asserting that his enslavement was unjust and that Mamadee, as a freeborn Muslim, should not have faced the possibility of enslavement. Second, by asking Park to make inquiries at Segu and in his "own country," she demonstrated knowledge of the connections between the regional and transatlantic slave trades. She knew that as a war captive it was possible that her son was enslaved in Segu or that he had been sold into the transatlantic slave trade and she knew that Park was a subject of a major Atlantic slave-trading state, Britain.

As shown by this example, ransoming was practiced in Segu both before and after the Umarian conquests. Park relates that in the early 1800s, when the city was still under Bambara rule, that a captive was ransomed for two enslaved people.[94] About sixty years later, the French explorer Paul Soleillet noted that when he was in Segu in the late 1870s that some men from Beledugu were being held as "hostages" for two to three years.[95] Most likely, these men were captives whose ransoms were being negotiated. In 1896, six years after the French conquest of Segu in 1890 a trader from the village of Keleni near Segu was being held by some of Babemba's soldiers who were demanding ten cattle as ransom. Since the French now governed the region, the Keleni villagers viewed it as the responsibility of the French to either pay the ransom of the trader or to rescue him by other means.[96] Similarly ransoming also took place in Nioro. There, a late 1880s case of failed ransom negotiations made it into the French records.[97]

93 Park, *Travels in the Interior Districts of Africa*, 188–89.

94 Park, *Travels in the Interior Districts of Africa*, 257–58.

95 Soleillet, *Voyage à Segou, 1878–1879,* 436.

96 ANM FA 1E 113 Renseignements politiques-Cercle de Segou 1890 –1904, 4 Trimestre 1896, Keleni, October 14, 1896.

97 ANM FA 2M 22 Justice Indigene Correspondance Cercle de Medine 1887–1905, Medine, le July 28, 1889.

Ransoming also took place in Māsina after the Umarian conquest.[98] For example, under the Umarians, in an incident that took place in either February or March 1889, a caravan was pillaged near Kofoulou by Massinanke. The caravan chief was killed, and ten prisoners were taken. In March 1889, the male captives were returned, most likely upon payment of a ransom; however, the women were not returned.[99] There are a few possible reasons for this. The women may have been viewed as too valuable as potential slaves to be ransomed. Perhaps an agreement could not be reached on the ransom price of the women. Or perhaps the women had not been free but were already enslaved and therefore no one was willing to pay a ransom for them.

In terms of ransoming policy, the Umarian states seemed to follow similar practices as the Sokoto Caliphate. This may be due to a combination of the acceptance of local preexisting ransoming practices, especially of and by Muslims, and the adoption of some Sokoto intellectual thought and policy. One important difference though is that while the Sokoto Caliphate actively supported ransoming by providing mediators and establishing funds to make ransom payments, the Umarian states were less active in actual ransom negotiations. Ransoming was not only practiced in regions conquered by the Umarians such as Segu, Māsina, Nioro and Timbuktu but also in neighboring regions such as Bamako, Kita, and Médine.[100] These preexisting practices jibed with the belief among the Umarians that people they classified as freeborn Muslims ought to be protected from enslavement and that a wide use of methods could be used to achieve that goal. Taal does not specifically address the question of ransoming in his writings. However, from his reliance on Sokoto policy and argumentation, from reading *Bayān mā waqaʿa* where it appears that he indirectly condones the practice of ransoming, and the fact that ransoming was widely practiced in the region throughout the late nineteenth century, it appears that Taal and his successors permitted both the practice of ransoming back their followers and ransoming prisoners that their forces had taken.

98 ANM FA 1E 47 Rapport sur la situation politique du Cercle, Kita, October 15, 1889.

99 ANM FA 1E 47, Rapports politiques et rapports de tournées, Cercle de Kita 1883–1905, Kita October 15, 1889.

100 ANM FA 1E 156 Rapports sur la repression de la traite des esclaves en Haut-Sénégal-Niger, Cercles de Bamako, Bandiagra, Bougouni, Djenne, Kayes, Medine, Nioro, Segou, Sokolo 1894–1904.

Conclusion

The seventeenth-, eighteenth-, and nineteenth-century jihads and leaders were linked through a shared education in the West African Mālikī canon, the transmission of ideas and arguments throughout the region, and through personal relationships including friendships, frictions, and marriage. However, each jihad and the policies that the leadership developed and implemented, based on intellectual thought, was dependent on its own particular socioeconomic-political-religious milieu. This is exemplified by the Umarian jihad. Taal's intellectual thought, just like the jihad that he led, had multiple roots. Fuutanke support for conducting a jihad in the Bambara states of Kaarta and Segu and the Muslim state of Ḥamdallāhi arose out of disillusionment with the outcomes of the Fuuta Jalon and Fuuta Toro jihads, the belief in the righteousness of Tjāniyya Islam and the success of the Sokoto jihad. Intellectually Taal was influenced by his Tijāniyya beliefs, by the Muslim West African canon especially of the Qādiriyya scholars of Timbuktu and Ḥamdallāhi, and more immediately by the intellectual output of the Sokoto Tetravirate. Taal shared with the Tetravirate the core belief that one of the primary roles of a Muslim state was the protection of Muslims, as he defined them, from captivity and enslavement. However, unlike in the Sokoto Caliphate, where ransoming policy was discussed and debated, an Umarian policy was not firmly articulated. However, since ransoms took place openly throughout the territory conquered by the Umarians and in the immediate aftermath of the French conquest there was a general belief that government had a role in facilitating the ransoms of "wrongly" captive individuals, it is logical to assume that ransoming was condoned.

This chapter and the preceding chapter focused on intellectual thought and ransoming policies as articulated (or not) by the state. However, there is often a gulf between what ought to happen according to lawmakers and what actually does happen. The following chapter will focus on actual ransoming practices. It will focus on the motives for ransoming for the individual captor and captive, and the importance of communication links, social status, and the use of mediators in successful ransom negotiations.

Chapter Five

The Negotiation and Practice of Ransoming Prisoners

In an undated letter, written sometime during his reign between 1837 and 1842, Abūbakar Atikū, 'Uthmān b. Fodiye's son, and the third Sarkin Musulmi of the Sokoto Caliphate responded to a query by the scholar Sīdī Mahmūd on the status of a ransom negotiation. The letter does not go into specifics, but Atikū wrote that he too was very concerned about the prisoners, that he also wanted them to be ransomed, and that he was waiting for the return of the mediator in order to conclude the affair.[1] The previous chapters discussed ransoming in its legal and political context in Muslim West Africa and the state-level policy of using ransoming as a way to protect freeborn Muslims from unlawful enslavement according to local interpretations of law. As has been demonstrated, not only was ransoming viewed as a moral and legal obligation (which became especially important during the jihad era) but policies permitting the ransoming of Muslims varied over time. This chapter focuses on ransoming practices. It does so by concentrating on individual cases to illustrate how ransoms were negotiated, the factors that led to successful negotiations, and why they sometimes failed. Historians such as Sandra Greene and Eve Troutt Powell, among others, have demonstrated that an emphasis on individual experiences with enslavement provides a better understanding of how enslaved women and men negotiated the complex legal, social, economic, and cultural milieus in which they found themselves and therefore provides a better understanding of slavery.[2]

1 ANN Boubou Hama, "Journal de 2 mars 1968 à 6 mai 1969," Abūbakar Atikū to Sīdī Mahmūd, n.d., 279.

2 Greene, *Slave Owners of West Africa*; Troutt Powell, *Tell This in My Memory*.

Likewise, by focusing on individual cases, this chapter illustrates how prisoners and their loved ones used ransoming norms to navigate the legal, social, and emotional worlds in which they found themselves in order to regain their freedom before they could be enslaved. A focus on the individual/micro level demonstrates how ransoming actually worked instead of what ought to have happened according to policies and procedures.

The existence of the letter by Atikū to Sīdī Mahmūd hints at key elements in successful ransom negotiations. As will be discussed below, these include the individual motives for participating in ransoming, the importance of communication links between captors and payers of ransom, and the role of mediators in ransom negotiations. It is also important to note that just like in the Mediterranean basin, where both Muslims and Christians were able to ransom back captives, Muslims in West Africa were able to ransom captives from non-Muslim captors because non-Muslim African societies also practiced ransoming. Therefore, the ransoming practices in Muslim societies will be discussed in conjunction with non-Muslim ransoming practices. Understanding how ransoming worked on an individual level gives us a better understanding of captivity and also of enslavement—and hence the slave trade and the formation of culture in the Americas and North Africa. Moreover, an understanding of historical ransoming practices gives us insight into contemporary ransoming practices. This chapter will first discuss the motives of individuals for paying ransoms, followed by factors in successful ransom negotiations, and finally the profit motive for captors and ransom prices.

Motives for Ransoming

Captives were ransomed because people valued their own freedom and the freedom of their family and friends. In West Africa, ransoming was not only a subject of discussion among scholars, but ransoming practices were long-standing, predating the social upheaval of the nineteenth century. For example, according to Songhay oral tradition dating from the sixteenth century, ransoming was a common outcome for prisoners of war.[3] Ransoming was often successful because captors knew that family and friends were willing to go to great lengths to raise ransom fees for captured individuals: these fees were usually set at more than the person would fetch on the slave market.

3 Hama, *Histoire Traditionnelle d'un village Songhay*, 30–31.

Ransoming benefited both the captive and the captor: the captive regained their freedom and previous status, and the captor often garnered at least twice as much as the market price for a slave.

Even if they missed the significance of what it meant in terms of how Africans conceived of captivity and enslavement and remedies for captivity and potential enslavement, Europeans on the coast of West Africa, including governors, soldiers, slave traders, abolitionists, and explorers noted the practice of ransoming. According to John Barnes, governor of Senegal, 1763–1766, in the mid-eighteenth century both non-Muslim Bambara and Muslim Mandinka ransomed prisoners of war.[4] Henry Hew Dalrymple, who was a lieutenant in the British army and was stationed at Gorée between May and September 1779, similarly observed that war prisoners were ransomed in the regions surrounding Gorée and the Gambia.[5] In the 1780s, one of slavery abolitionist Carl Wadström's informants told him that the Mandinka usually went to great efforts to organize ransoms.[6] In referring to the mass capture of Muslims during the Gyaman/Kong revolt against Asante in c. 1797, the British explorer Joseph Dupuis wrote in the 1820s from the recollections of Muslim informants that "among the latter [captives] were upwards of five thousand Moslems who were distributed among the provinces and in the capital. In no instance were these people subject to the penalty of death, as many of the heathens were, neither were they sold into slavery. Some, according to their inclinations or capacity, were suffered to redeem themselves from captivity by paying a ransom; some were ransomed by the pious Moslems of their own country, or by Dagomba."[7] Moreover, just as they participated in African systems of credit and trade, Europeans also participated in African ransoming practices.[8] Richard Miles, who was commander of Cape Coast Castle in the mid to late eighteenth century, noted that on his section of the West African coast, that "there are frequent Wars in this Country,

4 Lambert, *House of Commons Sessional Papers of the Eighteenth Century*, 68:75.

5 Lambert, *House of Commons Sessional Papers of the Eighteenth Century*, 69:26.

6 Wadström, *An Essay on Colonization,* 2:113–14. See 2:17 for an example of a scholar who offered to pay a ransom of two or more slaves for his brother on Gorée island c. 1783.

7 Dupuis, *Journal of a Residence in Ashantee*, 247.

8 For more on Europeans adapting to coastal African credit and trade systems see, for example, Ojo, "The Business of 'Trust'; Newson, "Africans and Luso-Africans in the Portuguese Slave Trade," 1–24; Lovejoy and Richardson "This Horrid Hole," 363–92.

particularly between the Mahometans and the Pagans, and the Prisoners in these Wars are Sold as Slaves; if they have been Freemen originally they are frequently redeemed [ransomed] from us by their Friends who give us other Slaves in return."[9]

As discussed in previous chapters, state law and policy provided the framework under which ransoms could be negotiated. Muslim governments controlled whether or not war captives and non-Muslims held by their forces could be ransomed and whether or not ransoms could take place during times of war. However, the impetus for specific ransom negotiations came from individuals, especially since states tried to offload the cost of ransoming to private families as much as possible. Payers of ransom were motivated to pay a captive's ransom due to a mixture of a sense of religious duty and obligation, honor, and personal attachments. In 1898 Inğīdū b.Fundu's stated reasons for paying the ransom of his niece Na'īma in Timbuktu was "for the sake of Allah the Great and his abundant pardon, and because of the blood ties."[10] Tuareg slave owners often ransomed back their slaves taken from them during a raid: not because of personal attachments to the individual slaves but as a matter of personal honor.[11] Indeed, as discussed in chapter 2, the African American sailor Robert Adams was ransomed along with his owners when they were all held captive in Timbuktu as a matter of honor.[12]

Personal attachments were a strong motivation for ransoming. About 1783 at Gorée Island a Muslim scholar offered to pay any amount of ransom to free his brother from captivity.[13] Indicating personal attachments, Gustav Nachtigal provides an example of the desperation to raise a ransom fee. According to him, about 1862, in Tibesti, an unidentified man stole a well-guarded double-barreled gun, from Nachtigal and his party, to use as part of a ransom payment for his brother who was being held in Kanem by the 'Awlād Sulaymān.[14] In a 1900 example, a Tuareg father followed the

9 Lambert, *House of Commons Sessional Papers of the Eighteenth Century*, 68:120, 124, 126. For more on European-African ransoming negotiations see Diouf, "The Last Resort."

10 IHERIAB, ms 3851/9.

11 Personal communication with Ibrahim Amouren, Director of the Archives d'Agadez, March 2007.

12 Adams, *The Narrative of Robert Adams*, 58.

13 Lambert, *House of Commons Sessional Papers of the Eighteenth Century*, 73:12–13.

14 See Fisher, *Slavery in the History of Muslim Black Africa*, 77.

Second Senegalese regiment in its march to Zinder in order to ransom back his child who was taken by soldiers in the employ of the French.[15]

Families entered into numerous ransom negotiations in the aftermath of Samori Turé's wars and the wars of French expansion. At the end of the nineteenth century and beginning of the twentieth century, much of the ransoming that French officials observed was associated with the warfare and raids related to the establishment and growth of Samori's state. In the 1870s and 1880s Samori, as he is commonly known, had established an expansionist state with his capital of Bissandugu, which controlled the Upper Niger Basin between Bure and Wasulu. Although later claiming religious motivations for his conquests, his primary interest was harnessing control of long-distance trade. He was defeated by the French in 1898 and died in exile in Gabon in 1900.[16] According to French officials, among the non-Muslim Mossi, at the end of the nineteenth century and beginning of the twentieth century, ransoming of an individual by a family member or a friend was also common.[17] The Kankan Cercle Commander wrote in his 1894 report that "we do not consider as slaves those who are reduced momentarily into slavery by the hazards of war but who recover their liberty."[18] Similarly, in the Kenedugu capital of Sikasso, at the end of the nineteenth century, ransoming of prisoners was also widespread.[19] Before both being conquered by the French, the armies of Babemba Traoré of Kenedugu and Samori had often clashed. In the first few years of the twentieth century, survivors of Samori's raids spent years raising funds to ransom back their captive relatives.[20] According to

15 ANN 1E1.3 1900 Rapport de Lieutenant JI Galidon Commandant le 2ème Sénégalais en marche sur Zinder-Tchad.

16 For more on Samori see Osborn, *Our New Husbands Are Here*, 92–115; Person, *Une revolution dyula*, and Kaba, "Islam, Society and Politics in Pre-Colonial Baté, Guinea," 323–44.

17 ANS K19 Enquête sur la captivité, rapports sur la captivité dans les cercles de la Sénégambie-Niger 1904, Résidence du Mossi, Poste de Fenkodogo Rapport sur la captivité, February 25, 1904; ANS K19 Enquête sur la captivité, Rapports sur la captivité dans les cercles de la Sénégambie-Niger 1904, Résidence du Mossi Ouagaoudou, March 4, 1904.

18 ANS K14 Captivité au Soudan, 1894, Cercle de Kankan, rapport sur la captivité dans le Cercle.

19 ANS K19 Enquête sur la captivité, rapports sur la captivité dans les cercles de la Sénégambie-Niger 1904, Cercle de Sikasso, rapport sur la captivité.

20 For more on Babemba Traoré and the Kenedugu state see Konaré, *Sikasso Tata*; Collieaux, "Contribution à l'étude de l'histoire de l'ancien royaume

Jean Delteil, Bougouni Cercle commander, in early 1904 numerous ransoms were made in the aftermath of Samori's raids; but because their families were unable to raise the fee, not all of the people who could have been ransomed were in fact ransomed.[21]

Factors in Successful Ransom Negotiations

Ransom negotiations could fail for a number of reasons. Indeed, even if someone was willing to pay a ransom, negotiations may never have started either due to captor disinterest or a failure to locate the captive and captor. Other reasons for the collapse of ransom negotiations included a failure to agree to a price, failure to deliver payment on time, disputes with the mediator, and government discouragement of the ransoming of certain individuals: for example, when Muḥammad Bello discouraged Bauchi Emirate from ransoming prisoners held by their forces due to political/military uncertainty (as discussed in chapter 3).[22] The real losers in a failed ransom negotiation were the captives and their families. Even if ransom negotiations failed, as long as there was a legal slave trade, a captor could recoup some of their losses. As indicated by oral tradition from Adār, prisoners who were not ransomed by their families could always be sold as slaves.[23] Yet, many ransom negotiations succeeded to such an extent that ransoming was an important strategy to prevent "illegal" enslavement. Ransom negotiations that succeeded with the return of the captive to their home, in return for payment in cash or kind, shared a number of characteristics beyond the prerequisite of a payer of ransom and a captor interested in negotiation. These included communication between the captor and payer of ransom, the use of a mediator, and the social status of the captive.

The first requirement for successful ransom negotiations was communication. Where practices of enslavement and ransoming differed was that while

---

de Kénédougou"; and Holmes, "Tieba Traore, Fama of Kenedougou:Two Decades of Political Development."

21 ANS K19 Enquête sur la captivité, rapports sur la captivité dans les cercles de la Sénégambie-Niger 1904, Cercle de Bougouni, rapport de l'adjoint de A.J Delteil, Commandant le Cercle en réponse de Monsieur le Gouverneur Genéral de l'A.O.F à Kayes, January 18, 1904.

22 For more on failed ransom negotiations see Lofkrantz and Ojo, "Slavery, Freedom and Failed Ransom Negotiations," 25–44.

23 Echard, *L'experience du passé*, 184.

individuals marked for enslavement were quickly moved away from the location of their capture—and communication between the captive and his or her family and friends was suppressed—contact between captor and the friends and families of those being held for ransom was required. An individual's value as a slave increased the farther he or she was taken from the place of capture: this distance made it less likely that they could be located and rescued or reestablish contact with family and friends.[24] The opposite, however, was true for those being held for ransom. Unlike individuals marked for enslavement who underwent processes of "social death," it was the maintenance of a captive's social identity and ability to communicate with people who recognized and valued that social identity that were vital to a successful ransom. Successful ransom negotiations were dependent on the prisoners being located by those willing to pay for their ransoms and on communication between the captive and the payer of ransom. One of Jean-Pierre Olivier de Sardan's Songhay informants, Mounkeila Langey, noted this difference when he stated that kidnapped children who were marked for enslavement were transported a great distance to where no one could find them to offer ransom.[25] Captives being held for ransom were often kept nearby, unless captors feared a counterattack by captives' allies or moved to market towns where payers of ransom could locate their captive kin and friends.[26]

The ransoming of prisoners was possible because of mechanisms that allowed for the exchange of information about captured individuals. Trade routes and the establishment of information networks along those routes were vital to this process. Local trade, regional trade, and long-distance trade

24 Not all enslaved individuals were moved over large distances, as has been shown in Lovejoy, "Biographies of Enslaved Muslims from the Central Sudan in the Nineteenth Century," which demonstrates that many slaves were settled within one hundred kilometers of the place of their enslavement; also see Rodet, "Escaping Slavery and Building Diasporic Communities in French Soudan and Senegal ca 1880–1940."

25 Olivier de Sardan, *Les societés Songhay-Zarma*, 31.

26 As discussed in chapter 2, Europeans taken captive along the Mauritanian coast were often funneled to Guelmīm or Ndār (St. Louis) to arrange their ransoms. Captors in both the Sokoto Caliphate and Yorubaland often brought captives to market towns to be ransomed (see below). For more on ransoming procedures in Yorubaland see Ojo, "'In Search of their Relations," 58–76. For more on African offensive reactions to kin being taken captive, in particular in the aftermath of failed ransom negotiations, see Lofkrantz and Ojo, "Slavery, Freedom and Failed Ransom Negotiations," 35–43.

were all useful as information links.[27] For regional and long-distance trade to take place, communication links had to be maintained even during times of war. As Richard Roberts states, "No matter what the state did or did not do, people produced, traded, and consumed."[28] This was exemplified by traders from the Caliphate of Ḥamdallāhi who insisted on trading with Kaarta despite official injunction in order to purchase grain.[29]

In West Africa, long-distance trade (and therefore communication links) had long been dominated by trading networks based on ethnic and religious identity.[30] Due to the tendency of traders to form trade associations with members of their own ethnic group, they formed unique groups within their host communities based on their status as strangers. Forming a trading diaspora based on ethnicity helped to overcome basic trading issues such as obtaining credit and business information, working within political and religious milieus, and sustaining cultural distinctiveness. The trust and communication links inherent to trading diasporas also helped to facilitate ransoms.

From the seventeenth century to the end of the nineteenth century, Muslim traders dominated long-distance trade in most of West Africa with the exception of the Bight of Biafra. In the western Sudan, long-distance trade was dominated by a trading network known as the Juula among the Malinke of the Upper Niger Valley, Maraka by the Bambara, and as Wangara in Arabic sources, which interacted with both Europeans on the Atlantic coast and with Saharans at the Saharan "ports." The Hausa dominated long-distance trade in the central Sudan. Even in non-Muslim regions of West Africa such as Asante, the Bight of Benin, Dahomey, and Oyo, where political authorities often placed restrictions on their trading activities, Muslim merchants were essential to long-distance trade. Muslim trading networks also operated across the Sahara and into North Africa, and with the development of European posts on the Atlantic Coast linked the Maghrib with Europeans

27 Jan Vansina defines local trade as the exchange of locally produced products using a locally recognized currency. Regional trade is defined as a trade that is conducted over larger distances, in marketplaces close to borders or in capital cities, and under the authority of political authorities of the market where the trade is taking place. Vansina defines long-distance trade as direct trade over large distances of several days' travel. See Vansina, "Long-Distance Trade Routes in Central Africa," 375–90.

28 Roberts, *Warriors, Merchants, and Slaves*, 13.

29 Lydon, *On Trans-Saharan Trails*, 114–16.

30 See Lydon, *On Trans-Saharan Trails*; Lovejoy, *Caravans of Kola*; Lovejoy, *Salt of the Desert Sun*, 405–20; Perinbam, "The Julas in Western Sudanese History."

on the West African coast. While long-distance trade networks intersected and exchanged goods at major port cities such as Timbuktu, where Saharan and West African networks met—and at coastal cities where European and West African networks intersected—there were trade networks, such as the Tikna and the Awlād Bu Ṣbā, that linked such cities as Ndār (St. Louis), Timbuktu, Marrakesh, and al-Ṣawīra.[31] While these trading networks were essential for the conduct of the slave trade, they also allowed for the flow of information, including information on captured individuals who could be potentially ransomed.

Moreover, these expatriate communities were ultimately helpful in identifying captives for ransom and even paying ransoms. Traders and their commercial networks were sources of information for people searching for taken individuals. This was true for both Muslim and non-Muslims. Indeed, in moving goods and people from the interior to the coast, Muslim and non-Muslim networks interconnected.[32] The Yoruba Christian convert William Moore provides an example of using trade networks for information. In 1853, he was able to trace and ransom his mother, who was being held in Ijebu, through Lagos traders who traded with Ijebu. In a letter he wrote to M. A. S Barber, he states that "I sent to a friend at Lagos, to ask him to beg some of the traders at that place, to make enquiry among the Ijebbus for my mother, giving him at the same time her description, name and tribe . . . Then there came one day a man to my sister with a message from my mother."[33]

Ironically, commercial affiliations led to both Ayuba b. Sulayman Ibrahima Diallo of Bundu's (b. c. 1701) captivity and ultimate sale to Maryland and to the attempt to ransom him before his ship sailed. As mentioned in chapter 3, in 1731 Diallo was kidnapped while returning from a trading expedition on the Gambia River. His captors attempted to conceal his kidnapping by trying to disguise him as a war captive and shaving his head and beard.[34] However, Diallo was purchased by his business acquaintance, the English

31 Lydon, *On Trans-Saharan Trails*; Lovejoy, *Caravans of Kola*; Perinbam, "The Julas in Western Sudanese History."

32 For cross-cultural trade between Muslims and non-Muslims in West Africa see Lofkrantz and Lovejoy, "Maintaining Network Boundaries," 211–32. For East Africa see Gooding, "Islam in the Interior of Precolonial East Africa," 191–208.

33 Barber, *Oshielle or Village Life in the Yoruba Country*, 126–27.

34 Bluett, *Some Memoirs of the Life of Job*, 16–18. Diallo was enslaved in 1731 and not in 1730 as Bluett thought. See also Ojo and Lofkrantz, "West African Responses to Illegal Enslavement and Failed Ransom Negotiations," 186–87.

trader, Captain Pike of the slave ship *Arabella*. As Diallo's biographer Thomas Bluett states, "Soon after Job [Diallo] found means to acquaint Captain Pike that he was the same person that came to trade with him a few days before, and after what manner he was taken."[35] Diallo was most likely hoping that due to their previous business relationship, Pike would immediately free him. Instead, it appears that Pike was more concerned with his immediate finances than with future trading relationships. Yet Pike, being profit-motivated, did permit Diallo to contact his family to arrange his ransom. Unfortunately for Diallo, the ship sailed prior to his father being able to send the ransom, and Pike would not accept a promise of a future ransom payment.

People often sought information from travelers. This system worked because of the exchange of information between said travelers. While some of the requests made to European travelers were recorded, it is even more likely that requests for information or help in locating captured individuals were made on a frequent and consistent basis of long-distance traders. For example, as discussed in chapter 4, the eighteenth-century Scottish explorer Park recounted that when he was leaving Wawra for Segu, a group of women asked him to inquire about the fate of their children who had been taken in raids and may have ended up in Segu. He stated that "one woman, in particular, told me that her son's name was Mamadee; that he was no Heathen, but prayed to God morning and evening, and had been taken from her about three years ago, by Mansong's army; since which she had never heard of him. She said, she often dreamed about him; and begged me, if I should see him, either in Bambara, or in my own country, to tell him, that his mother and sister were still alive."[36] As previously noted, Mamadee's mother emphasized that her son was not a "heathen." She was claiming that Mamadee was a Muslim and was therefore asserting that he should have been protected from enslavement. Perhaps by emphasizing this point, the mother was hoping to solicit more aid in finding and freeing Mamadee. While these women had a good idea where their children may have been taken, they also suspected that they might not have been kept within Segu. This was a reasonable assumption. Once an individual entered the slave trade in the western and central Sudan, he or she could be sent north into the Sahara or the Maghrib, kept within the western or central Sudan, or traded closer to the coast and then across the Atlantic. Even if one knew the identity of the slave trader who held one's loved one, it could still be difficult to trace where the individual

35 Bluett, *Some Memoirs of the Life of Job*, 19–20.

36 Park, *Travels in the Interior Districts of Africa*, 188–89.

had gone. For example, the nineteenth-century French explorer Soleillet met a typical trader who sent some of his slaves to Bakel and others to the coast. Soleillet stated that "this chief, named Maka, was born at Ségala, near Kouniakay, lives in Segou had has the support of Sultan Ahmadou. . . . Questioned about the destination of his slaves, he said that some will stay at Bakel and will depart in a few days for Segou while others will go downriver to Podor and even to Saint-Louis where he will bring most of them by the Bondou to Bathurst."[37] It was common to sell enslaved individuals at different markets who had initially been purchased together.

The case of Muḥammad Gardo Baquaqua (b. c. 1824) further demonstrates the importance of trade networks in locating individuals. Baquaqua's family was associated with both the Hausa and Wangara commercial diaspora and trade networks. The family was based in the town of Djougou, to the west of Borgu, with houses in Salaga and Katsina. Djougou was an important trade center located along the main trade route between Asante and the Sokoto Caliphate.[38] While Baquaqua benefited from his connections with a trade network that spanned the region from Katsina to Gonja, he also suffered the risks of long-distance trade. He was taken captive twice. The first time he was taken captive, during the Asante campaign against Gonga (1841–1844), he was ransomed by his brother, who was a well-respected Muslim astrologer associated with the Gonga court; he disguised the ransom as a slave purchase in order to pay a lower price.[39] The second time he was taken captive, c.1844, which resulted in his enslavement, was in Yarakeou, southwest of Djougou. At first, he was hopeful that he would be ransomed. He states that "I was marched forward towards the coast, to a place called Ae-oo-zo [Alejo was about 30 km beyond Yarakeou] there I found some friends, who felt very much about my position, but had no means of helping me. We only stayed there one night, as my master wanted to hurry on, as I had told him I would get away from him and go home. He then took me to a place called Chir-a-chur-ee [Krikri about 15km south of Alejo], there I also had friends, but could not see them."[40] Baquaqua realized that once he reached Abomey, the capital of Dahomey, that he would be outside the region where he could be recognized and helped. Recalling the moment he realized that he was most likely going to end up enslaved and sent across the

37 Soleillet, *Voyage à Segou*, 97.

38 Lofkrantz and Lovejoy, "Maintaining Network Boundaries," 219.

39 Law and Lovejoy, *The Biography of Mahommah Gardo Baquaqua*, 31.

40 Law and Lovejoy, *The Biography of Mahommah Gardo Baquaqua*, 138.

Atlantic and not ransomed or otherwise rescued, Baquaqua stated, "When we arrive here [Abomey] I began to give up all hopes of ever getting back to my home again, but had entertained hopes until this time of being able to make my escape."[41]

Captors interested in ransoming their captives facilitated the search efforts for captives' relatives. In the Sokoto Caliphate it was possible to travel to politically sanctioned market towns to inquire about missing relatives and, at times, to find and ransom them. This was in accordance with Sokoto's policy of condoning ransoming as a preventative measure against the enslavement of freeborn Muslims. Demonstrating similarities between Muslim and non-Muslim ransoming practices, when Sokoto forces attacked Oyo in 1821, some of the Oyo captives were ransomed in Ijaye, an Egba market town.[42] Indeed, during the nineteenth-century Yoruba civil wars it was common for prisoners to be brought to another city in order for them to be ransomed. For example, in 1851, after the Dahomey-Egba war, the Egba brought their Dahomey captives to the Yoruba town of Kétu where they were ransomed.[43] In the Muslim-dominated central Sahel/Adār, the Tuareg Kel Gress usually waited a few weeks in the general area of their raids to see if anyone would send an emissary to conduct ransom negotiations.[44] Similarly during Samori's wars, in the Upper Niger region, villagers taken in combat, after undergoing rituals of submission, were often held to see whether or not their surviving and free relatives and friends might ransom them back.[45]

Once a person had been located and his or her availability to be ransomed was ascertained, it was necessary for the captor and those who wanted to pay the ransom to conduct ransom negotiations. In West Africa, this usually entailed the use of a mediator. This was the second requirement for successful ransom negotiations. When Baquaqua was taken captive for the first time, around 1820 in northern Asante, his brother used a mediator to arrange his ransom.[46] In Muslim regions political or government officials were usually used as mediators, hence indicating official sanction for ransoming. For

41 Law and Lovejoy, *The Biography of Mahommah Gardo Baquaqua*, 144.

42 CMS CA1/079/2 Samuel Crowther to William Jowett, Feb 22, 1837.

43 Ajayi and Smith, *Yoruba Warfare in the Nineteenth Century*, 52. See also Ojo, "'In Search of their Relations," 58–76.

44 Bonte, "Esclavage et relations de dépendance chez les Touaregs Kel Gress," 56.

45 Person, *Samori*, 2:927.

46 Law and Lovejoy, *The Biography of Mahommah Gardo Baquaqua*, 31.

example, Nachtigal witnessed the procedures for negotiations between the Jagada and the Arinda Dirkonma. He states that

> a few days later the surviving members of the expedition returned, and confirmed the melancholy nightmare. On the very same day a near relations of Adama, the chief of the Jagada, who was the most loyal supporter of the Arabs in Borku, was sent to Ennedi, both to get reliable news about the fate of each individual, and also to conduct negotiations for ransoming the prisoners . . . A fortnight later, about the middle of July, there appeared an emissary from the Bidyat Gordoi from the tribe of the Arinda Dirkoma, and therefore a Teda man, many of whom lived in the western valleys of Ennedi to present the conditions for releasing the prisoners, while our envoy remained behind as a hostage.[47]

The choice of mediator is also indicative of the importance placed on ransom negotiations. In this period, while both women and men were payers of ransom, due to gender roles the mediator was usually a man. The necessity of involving a mediator was one of the reasons why ransom negotiations sometimes failed. In involving himself or choosing to continue his involvement in long ransom negotiations, a mediator was not only placing himself in potential physical danger but also forgoing other monetary opportunities as he pursued the negotiation. The cost of ransoming was more than just the ransom payment, and a mediator needed to decide whether these other transactional costs were worth the freedom of the captive. A mediator's status and his continued involvement in a long ransom negotiation indicates the value placed on that particular captive.[48] As shown by Lofkrantz and Ojo, where governments were weak, individuals had more leeway to negotiate ransoms and to take more coercive actions to free a captive if ransom negotiations failed.[49]

The correspondence between the third Sarkin Musulmi of the Sokoto Caliphate, Abūbakar Atikū and the scholar Sīdī Mahmūd, discussed at the beginning of the chapter, suggests that ransoming negotiations

---

47 Nachtigal, *Sahara and Sudan*, 2:377–78.

48 For a discussion of the application of the transactional economics model to ransoming see Ambrus, Chaney and. Salitskiy, "Pirates of the Mediterranean: An Empirical Investigation of Bargaining with Transaction Costs."

49 Lofkrantz and Ojo, 'Slavery, Freedom and Failed Ransom Negotiations," 36–38.

sometimes took a long time and were important to highly placed individuals.[50] According to Baba of Karo, ransom negotiations for the return of her uncle's wife and children involved the governor of Zarewa and the Emir of Katsina as mediators and that the negotiations, raising of the ransom fee, and acceptance of payment took at least six months.[51] The fact that these two men were acting as mediators for an "average" family also reveals the importance the Sokoto Caliphate placed on regaining the freedom of recognized freeborn Muslims even if the government was reticent to use government funds to pay ransoms. As Baba states, after the family had raised the ransom fee, "the Chief of Zarewa was told that it was ready and he summoned young men to carry the loads. Sarken Zarewa and Malam Buhari went with them. Three times they went and on the third journey they completed the ransom and Malam Buhari [Ubangida's older brother] and Ubangida [Baba's uncle] and Sarkin Zarewa went to Bakori to fetch Gambo [Ubangida's wife]; they brought her and the children home."[52]

Unsurprisingly, an emir, the Sarkin Bayaro 'Abdullāhi, was also used to mediate the ransom negotiations for the return of the Sarkin Musulmi 'Abd al-Raḥmān (r. 1891–1902) grandson, Barayi Zaki, who was the son of one of his daughters. Zaki was captured by French troops during a botched raid. Zaki had accompanied his uncle, Mahe, who was a son of 'Abd al- Raḥmān and who held both the honorary title of Sarkin Mafara and the governorship of Dendi on a mission to capture Jan Tullu. While the mission was initially successful, as Jan Tullu was captured, Mahe's party was pursued by the Sarkin Doso Na Mailaya and some French troops. They rescued Jan Tullu and captured Barayi Zaki. In a letter addressed to 'Abd al-Raḥmān, the Sarkin Bayaro Abdullāhi in his capacity as mediator relayed the terms of ransom. He wrote that "your son [grandson Barayi Zaki] is in Dosso, and the Christians have put a heavy ransom on him. They have stipulated for twenty paris of trousers—(Tsamiya)—twenty black Kano cloths (Kore), forty cloths (wawa) and twenty cloths (Kudi da Kudi)—all a hundred also three youths and two girls. This is the ransom which they have imposed, for your information."[53] It is unclear whether the French troops holding Barayi Zaki for ransom in Dosso

50 ANN Boubua Hama "Journal de 2 mars 1968 à 6 mai 1969," Abūbakar Atikū to Sīdī Mahmūd, n.d., 279.

51 Smith, *Baba of Karo*, 69–70.

52 Smith, *Baba of Karo*, 70.

53 Sarkin Bayaro Abdullahi to the Sarkin Musulmi 'Abd al-Raḥmān, *Occupation of Hausaland*, 23–24.

were Africans or Europeans. It is also uncertain if the ransom was ever paid. However, Barayi Zaki eventually regained his freedom, since by 1927 he was living in Denge District in Northern Nigeria.[54]

The choice of mediator is one of the notable differences between ransoming taking place under Muslim and non-Muslim rule in West Africa. While in Muslim territories the mediator was most often a government official of some sort, in non-Muslim societies, the mediator could be anyone who was respected and trusted by both sides to broker an agreement that included both government officials and respected individuals who were not associated with the government. These nongovernmental mediators performed better during peacetime or if they were not associated with any side of the conflict. For example, throughout the eighteenth and nineteenth centuries, Europeans were often used as mediators in coastal ransom negotiations. According to Captain John Marshall, in his testimony at the British inquiry into the slave trade, after one battle between Asante and Fante the slave trader Richard Brew mediated ransom negotiations between the two sides.[55] In another incident in February 1793 in Sierra Leone a man used the governor of Sierra Leone as a mediator in ransom negotiations with the slave-ship captain who was holding his daughter. The governor helped to negotiate the price of ransom from two slaves down to one prime slave but the ship sailed before the father could return with the ransom.[56] In nineteenth-century Yorubaland, European missionaries, who were especially concerned about regaining the freedom of their converts, sometimes fulfilled this role. For example, missionaries from the Church Missionary Society (CMS) helped broker the 1856 ransoming of J. B. Dasala who was held in Dahomey before eventually returning to Abeokuta.[57] In the 1866 case of Doherty, the CMS missionary J. A. Maser thought it was best to offer a ransom through officials in Ouidah. Doherty had been captured in 1862 and brought to Dahomey, where he was held on the Ajagun estate near Abomey. In 1866, a woman named Ibisemi, also from Isaga, escaped from the same estate and made her way back to Isaga, where she relayed Doherty's message about his whereabouts. According to Maser, Doherty told her "to tell the White man who placer [sic] him to

54 Backwell, *Occupation of Hausaland*, 23.

55 Lambert, *House of Commons Sessional Papers of the Eighteenth Century*, 73:384 Testimony of John Marshall.

56 Wadström, *An Essay on Colonization*, 2:80.

57 CMS CA 2/068 J. A. Maser, Abeokuta November 27, 1856. See also CMS CA2/068 Journal of J. A. Maser October 30, 1856.

Isaga that he was still alive as also another man of the Church a Sierra Leone man Jones or Agujobi and he would not forget him."[58] After an Asante military chief took four European missionaries captive in 1868, the British government enlisted a native clerk, Henry Plange, and Prince John Owusa-Ansa, a Western-educated Christian member of the Asante royal family, as mediators in ransom negotiations with the Asante government.[59]

The third important factor affecting whether or not a person would be ransomed was social status. According to the explicit and implicit policies of West African Muslim states, all freeborn Muslims ought to have been ransomed if that was the most convenient method for ensuring their freedom. However, in practice, the social standing of a captive was a key consideration for whether or not they would be ransomed back to their family. This is because only high-status families had the means to make expensive ransom payments without government aid. According to oral traditions, Kado nobles from Anzourou, northwest of present-day Niamey, when captured by Tuareg raiders were always returned upon payment of a ransom.[60] Likewise, according to Zinder oral tradition, important individuals and people of "good birth" taken prisoner were also always offered for ransom.[61] Captors knew that their high-status captives' kin not only had the desire but also the means to pay a ransom for the captives' return.

In the late nineteenth-century Sahara, caravan chiefs, whose families were more likely to have the money to ransom them back, were targeted for kidnapping and ransoming.[62] An example from the western Sudan is that in October 1898, Modi C. from Seguéni near Sikasso reported that his brother's caravan had been pillaged; two free men and two enslaved individuals, along with two loads of kolas, had been taken.[63] While a wealthy merchant

58 CMS CA2/068 J. A. Maser to H. Venn, November 28, 1866, and CMS CA2/068 J. A. Maser to H. Venn December 1, 1866.

59 See Ojo, "White Captives and the Political Economy of Ransoming in Asante, 1869–1864," 119–25.

60 Olivier de Sardan, *Quand nos pères étaient captifs,* 32–34. Anzourou is located near Tillabéry, northwest of present-day Niamey.

61 Salifou, "Colonisation et sociétés indigènes au Niger de la fin du XIXe siècle au debut de la deuxieme guerre mondiale," 249–50.

62 ANM FA 1E 16 Notes sur les rezzous Marocains Tombouctou 1906; 1D 59 10 Notes sur les rezzous Marocains, 1906, Région de Tombouctou; ANM FA 1E 47, rapports politiques et rapports de tournées, Cercle de Kita 1883–1905, rapport sur la situation politique du Cercle, Kita October 15, 1889.

63 ANM FA 1E 113 Renseignement politiques, Cercle de Segou 1890–1904. 4ieme trimestre 1898.

had a good chance of being ransomed, free porters and teamsters were less likely to be. Slaves, unless owned by someone who would ransom them to preserve their own honor, and trade slaves would not have been.[64]

The fact that elite individuals were more likely to be ransomed than people who were less wealthy was not unique to West Africa. In his global study of slavery, in the few pages where he discusses ransoming, Orlando Patterson observes that upper-class captives were usually ransomed and that higher-ranked captives usually commanded greater ransoms.[65] The Sokoto Caliphate tried to mitigate social status as a factor in successful ransoms by having state funds available to pay the ransoms of Muslims who could not afford the payments. Yet, Sokoto officials, as seen in the case of Baba of Karo's family, still put the onus for ransom payments on captives and their families.[66] In the Baba of Karo family case it should also be noted that while the free members of Baba's family were ransomed, the enslaved members of the group who were taken captive at the same time were not. Baba assumed that the enslaved members were quickly sold while her aunt and her aunt's children were held for ransom.[67]

The Profit Motive in Ransoming Prisoners

Elite and wealthy individuals were most likely to be ransomed because captors were motivated to engage in complicated ransom negotiations rather than selling their prisoners on the slave market for greater profit. Profit was also a strong motivator for captors to ransom in West Central Africa as Mariana Candido argues in her discussion of the failed ransom case of Juliana.[68] However, while most captors were primarily motivated by monetary gain, as Ojo argues in his study of ransoming in Yorubaland (and Nathan Carpenter in his study of the Upper Guinea Coast), some captors were also motivated by nonmonetary benefits such as greater strategic interests

64 For more on teamsters see Duffill and Lovejoy, "Merchants, Porters, and Teamsters in Nineteenth-Century Central Sudan," 150.

65 Patterson, *Slavery and Social Death*, 107.

66 NAK A/AR/43/2 'Uthmān b. Fodiye *Irshād al-'ibād ilā ahamm masā'il al-jihād*, 44–45; Abdullāhi b. Fodiye, *Ḍiyā' al-ḥukkām*, 5; Mary F. Smith, *Baba of Karo*, 70.

67 Smith, *Baba of Karo*, 69–70.

68 Candido, *An African Slaving Port and the Atlantic World*, 191–93.

or reciprocity in the treatment of their people.[69] However, captors were most often motivated to ransom because they wanted to gain the slave market price plus the amount that the captive's family and friends were willing to pay for the individual's return. As the CMS missionary, James Frederich Schön reported in his 1885 volume, "On some occasions the children of chiefs are caught. When they capture these[,] they [captors] always rejoice exceedingly, because they know that their relatives will come to ransom them: they charge them heavily."[70]

Captors being motivated by profit is especially apparent in examining ransoming that stemmed from illegal activity rather than the ransoming or selling of prisoners captured through state-sanctioned warfare. Brigandage was technically illegal under Islamic law. Indeed, Abī Zayd al-Qayrawānī, in his *Risāla*, a foundational text widely read across Muslim West Africa, advocated stiff penalties for brigands (muḥāribūn) especially if a person was killed during a raid; yet brigandage, raiding, and ransoming were widespread throughout the western and central Sudan and the Sahara.[71] The French officer, Lieutenant Jean noted in his 1904 reconnaissance report on Aïr, for example, that there had been a series of ransoms throughout the region in the previous year.[72]

In the nineteenth century, brigandage flourished for two reasons. First, the establishment and expansion of the new states in the western and central Sudan, the Sokoto Caliphate, the Umarian states, and Samori's state involved continuous warfare and the gathering of captives on the peripheries. This caused general insecurity and often swept up individuals who should not have been taken captive according to those states' laws. Second, the newly established states were not strong enough to prevent the unofficial, unsanctioned raiding and capture of freeborn Muslims in these regions, especially in rural areas away from centers of state power. Moreover, raiding along the desert edge and in the Sahara was viewed by nomads as an important form of resource redistribution.[73] This view of raiding and ransoming as a form

---

69 Ojo, "I]n Search of their Relations," 66–67; Carpenter, "Ransom as Political Strategy."

70 Schön, *Magana Hausa:Native Literature . . . in the Hausa Language*, 164–65.

71 al-Qayrawānī, *Risālah*, 263.

72 ANN 1E1.32 1904 Poste d'Agadez: rapport en fin de reconnaissance de Lieutenant Jean sur l'escorte de la caravane et la reconnaissance dans l'Aïr.

73 Niang, "Deferred Reciprocity." Niang's argument as applied to the pillaging of caravans by Tuareg in the Sahara is supported by Ibrahim Amouren, director, Archives d'Agadez, personal communication with author, March 14, 2007. In his study of the Arabian Bedouin, Anthony Toth made a similar argument. He

of resource redistribution can be seen in Nachtigal's description of nomad-farmer relations in 1860s Wadai. Nachtigal states, "I knew people there who year in and year out worked and stole, stole and worked, without ever having any immediate enjoyment from even the smallest part of their gains. Everything when to their enemies' country to ransom wives and children, and scarcely was one member of the family restored when another was seized."[74]

Profit motive was a prominent factor in the ransoming of an individual, whether that person was taken through illegal activity for the purpose of ransoming or was taken as a prisoner of war and ransomed as a legitimate option for dealing with a war captive. A captor gained a better price from ransoming a captive rather than selling them as a slave. While slave prices changed over time and had slight variations depending on region, in the western and central Sudan region of West Africa and along the coast, the pattern confirms Lovejoy and David Richardson's findings that "slave prices tended to move in tandem across broad regions."[75]

The price of an enslaved person was dependent on a number of factors such as gender, age, health, and attractiveness. As Paul Staudinger stated during his trip to the Sokoto Caliphate in the 1880s, "The value of a slave is very variable. A vigorous youth costs ten times as much as a weak elderly man."[76] Price was also dependent on slave demand, slave availability, and region.[77] For instance, in times of famine, when there was greater slave availability, slave prices were lower. An example of this is that at the end of the nineteenth century in Koury Cercle, an enslaved person could be sold for as much as 50,000 to 70,000 cowries during harvest time and as little as 10,000 to 15,000 during a famine.[78] Furthermore, during times of intense warfare, such as during the height of the Umarian campaigns of the late 1850s and early 1860s when slave traders were flooding the markets to the north with enslaved individuals, it was commonly believed in the region

---

argues that raiding and pillaging was a means of wealth redistribution in a harsh environment and that there were rules and conventions that regulated pillaging, such as not raiding allied tribes nor those who had paid a *khuwa* (brotherhood) fee. See Toth, "Economic Change in the Bedouin Domain," 2–3.

74 Nachtigal, *Sahara and Sudan*, 2:418.

75 Lovejoy and Richardson, "Competing Markets for Male and Female Slaves," 262.

76 Staudinger, *In the Heart of the Hausa States*, 2:34.

77 For more on factors determining prices of slaves see also Terray, "Reflexions sur la formation du prix des esclaves à l'intérieur de l'Afrique de l'Ouest Précoloniale," 119–44; Lovejoy and Richardson, "Anglo-Rfik Relations."

78 Hubbell, "A View of the Slave Trade from the Margin," 43–44.

that an enslaved person could be bought for as little as a piece of salt the size of their foot.[79] In comparison, in Podor, before the violence associated with the Umarian campaigns led to slave traders inundating the market with enslaved people, an owner was considered wealthy if they owned one or two slaves.[80] Moreover, the price of an enslaved person increased the farther they were taken from the place of capture. According to the 1894 French cercle reports on slavery there was a marked increase in prices from a decade earlier (see table 5.1). Young women and adolescent girls were the most expensive, followed by adult men, with young children being the least expensive. Slave prices from a few years later appear to be similar to the 1894 prices. In January 1895, a biḍān trader bought approximately twenty enslaved people in Banamba with six thousand bars of salt. This works out to an average price of three hundred bars for each person; however, since there was probably a mix of age, gender, and health among these twenty individuals, most likely they all had different prices.[81] In Kayes in 1899 slave prices were slightly higher than the 1894 prices as indicated by the purchase price of one young girl for four hundred francs.[82] In Timbuktu in 1899, a woman of marriageable age was bought for what appears to be ten mithqāls while in 1902 two prepubescent girls were purchased for two hundred francs each.[83] In 1903 and 1904, respectively, in Lobi Cercle in contemporary Burkina Faso, a woman was sold for 230 francs, and a boy was sold by his kidnapper for 150 francs.[84]

79 Webb, "Shifting Sands," 161.

80 ANS K18 Enquête sur la captivité, rapports sur la captivité dans les cercles d'administration directe du Sénégal 1904, rapport sur la captivité dans le Cercle de Podor.

81 ANM FA 1E 156 Rapport sur la repression de la traite des esclaves en Haut-Sénégal-Niger. Cercles de Bamako, Bandiagra, Bougouni, Djenne, Kayes, Medine, Nioro, Segou, Sokolo 1894–1904, Cercle de Bamako, rapport sur la captivité de traite pendant le Mois de Fevrier 1895.

82 ANM FA 2M 16 Justice Indigene Correspondance Cercle de Kayes, 1882–1920, Kayes March 20, 1905.

83 MHT ms 76. The part of the document that states the currency is missing so the price is ten of something. Most likely it was ten mithqāls, considering the number and considering the currencies of the region in this time period. See Hunwick, "Back to West African Zanj Again," 59 ft15.

84 ANM FA 2M 21Justice Indigène Correspondance, Cercle de Koutiala1903–1919, Gaouale November 25, 1903; ANM FA 2M 21 Justice Indigène Correspondance, Cercle de Koutiala 1903–1919, Lobi, July 18, 1904.

Table 5.1. Comparison of Slave, Ransom, and Redemption Prices

Date	Location	Slave Price	Ransom Price	Redemption Price
Early 19th century	Segu		2 slaves	2 slaves
Mid 19th century	Kano	Woman: 30,000–40,000 cowries ($12– $20)	10 bags of cowries (200,000 cowries)	200,000 cowries or more
Late 19th century	Kayes	Girl: 250–300f	2 slaves	Up to 2 slaves
		Youth: 200–250f		
		Man: 200f		
Late 19th century	Bakel	Approx 150–200f	Twice the selling price	Twice the purchase price
Late 19th century	Sumpi		Twice the selling price	Twice the purchase price
Late 19th century	Bamako	Girl: 150–300f	2 slaves	
		Youth: 200–250f		
		Woman: 150–200f		
Late 19th Century	Bougouni	Woman: 200f	3 slaves	
		Girl: 150–175f		
		Boy: 120–150f		
		Man: 80 f		

Source: Park, *Travels in the Interior Districts of Africa*, 257–58, ANM FA 1E 156 Rapport sur la répression de la traite des esclaves en Haut-Sénégal-Niger, Cercles de Bamako, Bandiagra, Bougouni, Djenne, Kayes, Medine, Nioro, Segou, Sokolo 1894–1904; Tambo, "The Sokoto Caliphate Slave Trade in the Nineteenth Century," 211; KSHCB KAN PRO 1/11/7 Rano 1955–59, 19; Economic History Project, Interview with Alhaji Yunusa Mikail. August 2, 1975; ANS K14 Captivité au Soudan 1894 Cercle de Kayes Rapport sur la captivité dans le cercle; ANS K18 Enquête sur la captivité, rapports sur la captivité dans le cercles d'administration directe du Sénégal 1904, Bakel, Questionnaire au sujet de la captivité; ANS K19 Enquête sur la captivité. Rapports sur la captivité dans les cercles de la Sénégambie-Niger 1904, Cercle de Sumpi. Rapport sur l'état de captivité dans le cercle; ANM FA 2M 7 Justice Indigène Correspondance Cercle de Bougouni 1896–1920, Bougouni, May 22, 1900; Klein, "The Slave Trade in the Western Sudan during the Nineteenth Century," 40. Often in the 1890s when slave merchants could not sell their slaves in Médine they sold them in Bakel, Kayes and Futa Toro for a similar price. See ANM FA 1E 74 Cercle de Médine Corrspondances et rapports sure les villages et captifs liberés 1885–1895 and Clark, "Slavery and its Demise in the Upper Senegal Valley," 59.

Ransom prices included the recognition that people valued freedom and were willing to pay to regain it. The net gain for a person on the slave market was the market value of that individual alone. A proportion of an individual's ransom price, however, was based on what his or her family or friends were willing to pay for the return of that person in addition to the market value as a slave. In general, the ransom price was equivalent to at least twice the slave price value (see table 5.1). Ransoms could be paid in cash, kind, slaves, other captives, or a combination depending on the agreement reached between the captor and the payer of ransom. Although as discussed in the introduction, the ransoming of captives and the redemption of slaves are conceptually different, as also seen in table 5.1. The ransom prices of captives were similar to the redemption prices of slaves. This similarity stems from the shared value placed on freedom and a shared context in the ideology of captivity and enslavement and the legal means to escape it.

Ransom prices were connected to slave prices in that the two prices fluctuated in tandem. The price of at least two slaves or more for the return of one individual remained stable throughout the nineteenth century and across the broad region of the western and central Sudan (see table 5.2). Park relates, from a conversation he had with the Damman Jama of Kaarta, prior to Segu and Kaarta being conquered by Taal in the mid-nineteenth century, that the going ransom that the Segu Bambara were willing to accept, in the early 1800s, was two slaves for the return of one captive. Park states, "When a freeman is taken prisoner, his friends will sometimes ransom him by giving two slaves in exchange; but when a slave is taken, he has no hopes of such redemption [ransom]."[85] The ransom price was often more than twice the slave price. This is indicated by the mid-nineteenth-century ransom price of an elite eighteen-year-old Fuuta Jalon woman of ten slaves when in the same period the usual cost of ransom in the Casamance, for both men and women, was six cows—and the usual demand by the 'Awlād Sulaymān was ten camels for the release of one man.[86] According to Captain Binger, in the late nineteenth century, the price of ransom in the western Sudan was often twenty, thirty, or fifty slaves—although this seems abnormally high.[87]

85 Park, *Travels in the Interior Districts of Africa*, 257–58.

86 Conneau, *A Slaver's Log Book*, 144–147; Linares, "Deferring to the Trade in Slaves, 126; Nachtigal, *Sahara and Sudan*, 2:378.

87 Binger, *Du Niger au Golfe de Guinée (1997–1889)*, 1:467. Throughout the nineteenth century in the Zinder region, for example, a horse cost a minimum

Table 5.2. Sample of Nineteenth-Century Western and Central Sudan Ransom Prices

Date	Place	Price	Gender of Captive
Early 1800s	Segu	2 slaves	Male
1810s	Timbuktu	5 camel loads of tobacco for 10 hiṣān men, their 2 male European captives, 1 boy plus the purchase of one adult male slave.	Male
19th Century	Among Songhay	2 or more slaves	Female and Male
19th Century	Aīr	Any price for a "white" Tuareg	Female and Male
1858	Timbuktu	18 1/3 gold bars	Female
Mid-19th Century	Casamance	6 cows	Female and Male
Mid-19th Century	Fuuta Jalon	10 slaves	Female
1860s	Among Awlād Sulaymān	10 camels	Male
1860s	Kano	10 bags of cowries (200,000 cowries)	Female and Male
Late 19th century	Western Sudan	10 camels	Male
Late 19th Century	Kayes	2 slaves	Female and Male
Late 19th Century	Bakel	Twice the selling price	Female and Male
Late 19th Century	Sumpi	Twice the selling price	Female and Male
1890	Médine	5 oxen and 2 gros d'or	Male

—continued

of ten slaves, while in some places a horse could cost twenty slaves and, depending on availability, the value of an individual slave may be low. Salifou, *Le Damagram ou Sultanat de Zinder*, 177; also see Law, *The Horse in West African History* and Webb, *Desert Frontier*, 69–70 for an argument in favor of the "war complex" connection between horses and slaves.

Table 5.2. Sample of Nineteenth-Century Western and Central Sudan Ransom Prices (*concluded*)

Date	Place	Price	Gender of Captive
1890	Médine	14 oxen, 6 cows, 2 pieces of guinea cloth	Male
1890s	Katsina	400,000 cowries	Female
1894	Segu	Load of salt plus 2,000 cowries	Male
Late 1890s	Dosso	100 cloths, 3 youths, two girls	Male
1896	Segu	10 cows	Male
1898	Bamako	1 horse, 1 cow	Male
1899	Bamako	2 slaves	Male
1900	Bougouni	3 slaves and 4 guns	Male

Source: Park, *Travels in the Interior Districts of Africa*, 257–58; Adams, *The Narrative of Robert Adams*, 47–48; Idrissa, "Guerres et societés," 55; personal communication with Ibrahim Amouren, director of the Archives d'Agadez, April 2007; IHERIAB ms 3549; Linares, "Deferring to the Trade in Slaves," 126; Conneau, *A Slaver's Log Book*, 144–47; O'Hear, *Power Relations in Nigeria*, 25; Olivier de Sardan, *Les societés Songhay-Zarma*, 58; Nachtigal, *Sahara and Sudan*, 2:378; KSHCB KANPRO 1/11/7 Rano, 1955–59, 19; Binger, *Du Niger au Golfe de Guinée*, 1:46; ANM FA 2M 7 Justice Indigéne Correspondance Cercle de Bougouni 1896–1920. Bougouni, May 22, 1900; ANS K14 Captivité au Soudan 1894, Bakel; ANS K14 Captivité au Soudan 1894, Sumpi; ANM FA 2M 22 Justice Indigéne Correspondance Cercle de Médine 1887–1905. Médine August 28, 1890; ANM FA 2M22 Justice Indigéne Correspondance Cercle de Médine 1887–1905; Smith, *Baba of Karo*, 69; ANM FA 1E 113 Renseignments politiques, Cercle de Segou 1890–1904. 4ieme trimestre, 1894; Backwell, *The Occupation of Hausaland*, 23–24; ANM FA 1E 113 Renseignments politiques, Cercle de Segou 1890–1904; ANM FA 1E 113 Renseignments politiques, Cercle de Segou 1890–1904; Copi de Registre N2 4 trimestre 1898; Vigné d'Octon, *La gloire du sabre*, 96; ANM FA 2M 7 Justice Indigène Correspondance Cercle de Bougouni 1896–1920, Bougouni, May 22, 1900.

During the 1850s and 1860s Ningi raids on villages in Kano Emirate, the usual ransom price the Ningi demanded was ten bags of cowries, a total of two hundred thousand cowries per person. Oral history describes the Gabo village area of Rano in Kano Emirate as being a "defenceless hamlet the Ningis raided it on one occasion killing some and capturing some women and children. Later some prisoners were freed by relatives who travelled to Ningi and paid a ransom of about ten bags of cauries a hed [sic]. Many however, being Fulani, had already died of chagrin."[88] In the 1890s Baba of Karo reported that her uncle paid ransoms of four hundred thousand cowries for his wife, four hundred thousand for his three children, and four hundred thousand for his unborn child.[89] As previously noted, in the case of Barayi Zaki, the grandson of Sarkin Musulmi ʿAbd al-Raḥmān, the ransom price demanded by the French troops that were holding him was three youths, two girls, twenty pairs of tsamiya, twenty kore cloths, forty wawa cloths, and twenty kudi da kudi cloths.[90]

At the end of the nineteenth century and the beginning of the twentieth, the usual ransom price in Kayes was two slaves, in Bakel and Sumpi it was double the selling price, and in Segu, Sokolo, and Timbuktu it was at the discretion of the owner.[91] Yet prices varied. In an 1890 Médine case, a father had to pay fourteen oxen, six guns, and two pieces of guinea cloth in ransom for his son.[92] In an 1896 instance, a soldier belonging to Babemba Traoré's army demanded ten cows in ransom for the return of a trader that he had kidnapped.[93] At the turn of the twentieth century there were cases in Bamako and Bougouni of ransom prices being set at two slaves, and three slaves plus four guns respectively.[94] The latter case especially demonstrates the connection between emotional ties and ransom prices since this was the ransom price that was being demanded of a wife for the return of her old and sick husband. Since old men, especially old sick men, did not command much on the slave market, the people holding this man captive obviously got a much better price for him from his wife than if they had tried to sell him as a slave.

---

88 KSHCB KAN PRO 1/11/7 Rano, 1955–59, 19.

89 Smith, *Baba of Karo*, 69.

90 Sarkin Bayaro Abdullahi to the Sarkin Musulmi ʿAbd al-Raḥmān, 23–24.

91 See reports on slavery in ANS K14 Captivité au Soudan 1894; ANS K19 Enquête sur la captivité, rapports sur la captivité dans les cercles de la Sénégambie-Niger 1904; and ANM FA 1E 156, rapports sur la répression de la traite des esclaves en Haut-Sénégal-Niger, cercles de Bamako, Bandiagra, Bougouni, Djenne, Kayes, Medine, Nioro, Segou, Sokolo 1894–1904.

92 ANM FA 2M 22 Justice Indigène Correspondance Cercle de Médine 1887–1905. Médine le August 28, 1890.

93 ANM FA 1E 113 Renseignments politiques, Cercle de Segou 1890–1904.

94 Vigné d'Octon, *La gloire du sabre*, 96. ANM FA 2M 7 Justice Indigène Correspondance Cercle de Bougouni 1896–1920. Bougouni, May 22, 1900.

Status was a factor in determining the ransom price and not just in the likelihood of being ransomed. The impact of status on ransom price has been universally observed. For example, as noted by many historians of Mediterranean ransoming, elite Europeans knowing that their ship was about to be boarded and that they were going to be taken captive would often disguise their wealth.[95] They wanted to appear rich enough to be held for ransom in relatively comfortable circumstances but did not want to appear so wealthy that their ransom would be set at an exorbitant amount that would be difficult for their families to pay. According to Kimba Idrissa's informants on nineteenth-century Songhay practices, ransom prices rose according to status. The ransom of a koy-ize, a free man, was much higher than that of a borcin, a manumitted individual, which was yet higher than that of a horso, or house slave, if ransomed at all. While Idrissa's informants did not give a ransom price for a free man, the ransom price of a manumitted individual was generally two slaves, or a horse, or two slaves and ten thousand cowries, whereas the ransom price of a house slave was one slave. Idrissa's informant also stated that the offer of ransom was never refused.[96] If the ransom price of a freed person was at least the equivalent of two slaves, then most likely in this region the ransom price for a free man, who was of higher status, would have been more than two slaves. Yet, one has to question the motivation for exchanging an enslaved person for another captive. While the motivation to ransom on the part of the slave's kin and owner is understandable as a question of honor and emotional ties, one has to wonder what the advantage would have been for the captor of the slave to exchange one captive for another of equal value, unless, as Ojo suggests, captors were also sometimes motivated to ransom a particular captive in order to maintain reciprocal relationships.[97] Similarly among the Tuareg of Aïr, biḍān Tuaregs were always ransomed, and their families were willing to pay any price for their return, while the ransom prices of individuals of bellah identity were lower.[98] The ransom case of Barayi Zaki also exemplifies the importance of status. He was held for ransom instead of being enslaved or executed because he was a grandson of the Sarkin Musulmi. However, because he was a grandson of the

95 See, for example, Davis, *Christian Slaves and Muslim Masters*, 51.

96 Idrissa, "Guerres et societés," 55.

97 Ojo, "In Search of their Relations," 58–76.

98 Personal communication with Ibrahim Amouren, Director of the Archives d'Agadez, March 2007.

Sarkin Musulmi his ransom was set at an exorbitant amount of five people and one hundred cloths of different types.[99]

Lovejoy suggests that the practice of ransoming may have also affected the price of male slaves. Most explanations for the price differential between enslaved women and men in West Africa center on the idea that women were more valued because of their combined productive and reproductive capacities.[100] Klein, however, has noted that the importance of a woman slave's reproductive capability vis-à-vis her work capability was dependent on the slave system she was enslaved in. According to Klein, in a household mode of production where slaves made up a small percentage of the population and lived and worked alongside the free members of the household, an enslaved woman's reproductive capability was more important than her work capability. However, in a slave mode of production system where the slave population was high, slaves lived apart from their owners and their labor sustained the ruling class, the work capability of an enslaved woman was more important than her reproductive capability. To Klein, this became especially apparent toward the end of the nineteenth century, when the price differential between male and female slaves was decreasing as commodity production using slave labor was increasing along with greater workloads more exploitation and lower birth rates.[101]

Lovejoy argues that because of ransoming, the price differential between enslaved men and women was more apparent than real. He suggests that the price for enslaved men was lower because these were the men who could not be ransomed and they were therefore discounted accordingly.[102] While women were ransomed, the vast majority of people who were ransomed were high-status men who were captured during warfare or in economically motivated raids. In comparing the male ransom prices to the male slave prices and the female slave prices of the same region and period, one can see that the ransom prices of men, who constituted the majority of people ransomed, were approximately the same—or one-and-a-half times the slave prices for women who made up the vast majority of the enslaved population of the western and central Sudan. This can be seen by looking at the example of the 1900 case of the woman who had to pay three slaves and four guns in

99 Sarkin Bayaro Abdullahi to the Sarkin Musulmi 'Abd al-Raḥmān, 23–24.

100 See, for example, Baldé, "L'esclavage et la guerre au Fuuta-Jalon," Miers and Kopytoff "Introduction," 3–84, Meillassoux, "Female Slavery," 49–66.

101 Klein, "Women in Slavery in the Western Sudan," 67–72.

102 Lovejoy, "Internal Markets or an Atlantic-Sahara Divide?" 259–79.

ransom for her old and sick husband.[103] In 1894, the last time French officials recorded slave prices, officials noted that the slave price was two hundred francs for a woman, eighty francs for a man, between 120 and 150 francs for a boy, and between 150 and 175 francs for a girl.[104] While we do not know the gender and age of the three enslaved people that formed part of the ransom for the woman's husband, if we assumed (since the captive being held for ransom was male) that the slaves were men, their approximate worth was 240 francs, which is forty francs more than the slave female price. In other words, the ransom for the old and sick husband may have been set at just over the slave price for a woman.

Likewise, using 1894 prices, in the 1899 case of the ransom of a Sikasso notable being held in Bamako, the ransom price of an adult male slave and a young girl slave was approximately 250–500 francs, whereas the slave price of a young woman was between 150 and 300 francs, and an adult woman between 150 and 200 francs.[105] While prices may have changed in six years, it is a safe assumption that the ratios would have remained approximately the same. Similarly in Kayes and Bakel, where the ransom price was the equivalent of two replacement slaves, this would put the male ransom price at approximately one-and-a-half times that of a female slave.[106] If high status and productive male captives were being ransomed at prices equivalent to the slave prices of women, this may, according to Lovejoy, have had a downward effect on the slave prices of the "leftover" male captives.

However, women were also ransomed, and their ransom prices were also at least twice the price they would have fetched on the slave market (see table 5.2). For example, as discussed earlier, the Ningi were demanding two hundred thousand cowries in ransom for women that they took captive during their raids in Kano Emirate in the 1850s and 1860s. In comparison, enslaved women sold for between ten thousand and eighty thousand cowries on the Kano slave market in 1850 and for about ninety thousand cowries on the Zaria slave market in 1862. [107] Likewise, in the 1890s, the ransom

103 ANM FA 2M 7 Justice Indigène Correspondance Cercle de Bougouni 1896–1920. Bougouni, May 22, 1900.

104 ANS K14 Captivité au Soudan, 1894.

105 Vigné d'Octon, *La gloire du sabre*, 96. The man's ransom price was two slaves.

106 See reports on slavery in ANS K14 Captivité au Soudan, 1894, and ANS K16 Enquête sur la captivité en A.O.F 1903–1904.

107 KSHCB KAN PRO 1/11/7 Rano 1955–59, 19; Tambo, "The Sokoto Caliphate Slave Trade in the Nineteenth Century," 212, 216.

price of Baba of Karo's aunt was four hundred thousand cowries; the female slave price in Katsina for a woman was one hundred thousand cowries in 1890 and in Zaria in 1896 for a teenage girl was 233,000 to 333,000 cowries.[108] Women were also being ransomed for about twice or more than they would have been sold for on the slave market. What this reinforces is that people valued their own freedom and the freedom of their loved ones, both women and men. People used ransoming as a means to remove individuals from potential enslavement who they believed ought not to be enslaved and where they had the means to do so. Captors capitalized on emotional attachments by usually demanding at least twice the price, often more, than the individual would fetch on the slave market.

Conclusion

In conclusion, south of the Sahara, as indicated by oral tradition and outside observance, ransoming of freeborn Muslims by other Muslims had long been established. From at least the sixteenth century, ransoming was widely practiced throughout Muslim western Africa on both sides of the Sahara. These practices reflected both the legality of ransoming and the onus upon Muslims to free captive freeborn Muslims. Moreover, the ransoming of Muslims held by non-Muslims could only take place if those non-Muslims were willing to ransom their prisoners. Therefore, it is important to note that non-Muslims in West Africa also practiced ransoming although while Muslim ransoming practices were informed by interpretation of Islamic law, this was obviously not the case for non-Muslims. On the state level, as discussed in the previous two chapters, ransoming was viewed as a useful preventative to the enslavement of freeborn Muslims, which was deemed illegal. On the individual level, however, captors were often motivated to ransom their prisoners for profit, whereas captives' kin engaged in ransoming not only because of religious reasons but also because they valued freedom. In West Africa, according to interpretations of Islamic law established during the jihads of the nineteenth century, all freeborn Muslims ought to have been ransomed or freed from captivity by another method. However, in practice it was high-status individuals who would most likely be held for ransom by their captors and successfully ransomed despite state provision for the ransoming of poor

108 Smith, *Baba of Karo*, 69; Tambo, "The Sokoto Caliphate Slave Trade in the Nineteenth Century," 216–17.

freeborn Muslims. Ransom negotiations required good communication links between captors and those willing to pay ransoms and also a reliance on the use of mediators. Moreover, slave and ransom prices were connected since the ratio of ransom to slave prices remained the same throughout the nineteenth century regardless of the fluctuations in slave prices due to preference and availability. Generally, ransom prices were twice the slave price for both women and men, but they could be higher depending on the status of the prisoner or the value of the slave.

Indeed, the important factors required in historically successful ransom negotiations such as good communication links, use of mediators, and the willingness and ability for someone to pay a high price for the return of a particular individual—all of these remain important factors in contemporary ransoming. In Nigeria, for example, there are reports that in October 2016 the Nigerian government paid a ransom of cash and five Boko Haram fighters in return for twenty-one of the schoolgirls kidnapped from Chibok Government School in 2014.[109] This ransom negotiation was successful for the same reasons that historical ransom negotiations were successful. First, since the beginning of the armed conflict between Nigeria and Boko Haram in 2009, backchannel communications have been maintained between the two sides with periodic bouts of official dialogue. Second, mediators trusted by both the Nigerian government and Boko Haram, in this case provided by the government of Switzerland, were used to negotiate between the two sides. Third, due to the publicity surrounding the Chibok kidnapping, the Nigerian government was highly motivated to secure the release of as many of the kidnapped girls as possible while Boko Haram was motivated to secure a profit and the release of some of their fighters. In the present, just as in the past, people value the freedom of their loved ones and of individuals, such as the Chibok girls, who they believe are being unfairly or illegally held captive. Moreover, in the present, just as in the past, people are willing to pay to secure and reestablish that freedom even when it goes against official government policy not to pay ransom to groups classified as being terrorists. Finally, in the present, just as in the past, negotiations go more smoothly and more safely with better chances of success when the captors and the payers of ransom use a mediator trusted by both sides in order to avoid direct contact with each other and the emotions that might become enflamed.

109 Burke and Akinwotu, "Boko Haram Frees 21 School girls from Group Abducted in Chibok"; Parkinson and Akinbule, "Six Years after #BringBackOurGirls Freed Chibok Girls Faces Fresh Danger."

Conclusion

On February 19, 2018, 110 teenage schoolgirls were kidnapped from the Government Girls' Science and Technical College in Dapchi, Yobe State in northeastern Nigeria by the Islamic State West African Province (ISWAP) faction of Boko Haram led by Abu Muswab al-Barnawi (which had split from the Boko Haram faction led by Abubakar Shekau in 2015). On March 21, 2018, all of the girls except the five who were killed during the kidnapping and the lone Christian girl, Leah Sharibu, were returned in a convoy of trucks, dropped off in front of the school they had been kidnapped from with instructions not to return to school.[1] Why were these Muslim girls unconditionally released, whereas the Boko Haram faction under the leadership of Shekau demanded a ransom or a prisoner exchange in return for the girls, including the self-identified Muslims, he had kidnapped in 2014?

Jacob Zenn argues this was because al-Barnawi follows Islamic State's directions not to take Muslim captives whereas Shekau, contrary to all interpretations of Islamic law, was willing to take Muslims captive.[2] However, what is more likely, is that Shekau did not recognize the Muslim identity of the Chibok girls who self-identified as Muslim whereas al-Barnawi did accept as Muslim the Dapchi girls who self-identified as such. Shekau and al-Barnawi's decisions about who they view as legitimate captives to be enslaved, ransomed, exchanged, killed, or freely released reflect the questions that have been debated throughout Muslim West Africa for centuries: Who is a proper Muslim? What interpretation of Islam should prevail? What is the

---

1 Maclean and Abrak, "Boko Haram Kept One Dapchi Girl Who Refused to Deny Her Christianity." Since 2020, there has been a large increase of mass kidnappings from schools in Nigeria, particularly the north. However, these have been mostly carried out by criminal gangs, known as "bandits," who are motivated by monetary reasons and not ideological ones. Nwaubani, "Nigeria's Chibok Girls: Why Was This Former Captive Treated Differently?"; *Al Jazeera*, "Nigeria Outlaws Ransom Payments, Kidnap Now Punishable by Death."

2 Zenn, "Competing Ideologies at Play in Boko Haram's Return of Dapchi Girls."

role of Islam in the state? Who gets to decide? And who speaks on behalf of a community?

The previous chapters examined the debates and practices of ransoming prisoners in the eighteenth and nineteenth centuries, which was also a time of political and religious strife—of jihad—when these same questions were being intensely debated and fought over. In nineteenth-century West Africa, these questions were framed as debates on who was and was not a Muslim, how could and should Islamic law be implemented, what rights and protections should recognized freeborn Muslims have, and what role should governments play in ensuring those rights. In the nineteenth century, the contestations over these questions led to the overthrow of governments and the formation of new states. Debating who could be taken captive, what could be done with them, who should be ransomed, and who should do the ransoming was a concrete way of defining and addressing this larger set of questions. Just as today, in the past, one's perceived religious identity affected one's possible fate once taken captive. Moreover, these debates on captivity, enslavement, and ransoming—and the practices and norms that emerged from them influenced the strategies of individuals and their families when taken captive. The ransoming of captives, therefore, affected not only who ended up enslaved in West Africa but also who was trafficked across the Atlantic and Sahara, thereby impacting the formation of cultures in both the Americas and the Maghrib.

Nineteenth-century Muslim West African ransoming practices were based on interpretation of law and intellectual perceptions of the purposes and uses for ransoming. The discourse on ransoming, as a remedy for illegal enslavement, was linked to the intellectual discourse on slavery. Indeed, the possibility of ransoming was an important feature of slavery in both Muslim and non-Muslim West African societies. West African Muslim scholars were fully entrenched in the intellectual trends and discourses of the rest of the Islamic world. The Sahara was not a barrier to the exchange or transmission of ideas. In the West African scholars' discourse on enslavement and ransoming, which was firmly rooted in the Mālikī madh'hab, we see a retort to the North African and Saharan discourse on the relationship between racial identity, unbelief, and enslaveability. The West African discourse was also a response to the local sociopolitical economic environment where there was increasing demand for enslaved labor in North Africa, the Americas, and in West Africa—especially in the nineteenth century.

West African scholars and those familiar with the West African sociopolitical-religious environment, consistently reiterated that unbelief was the only legitimate reason for enslavement and that racial categorization was irrelevant. In the West African jihad era, enslaveability was firmly based on perceived personal belief and not racial identity. Moreover, even if they held a narrow view of who they considered to be a freeborn Muslim, scholars also advocated, through both their writings and their actions, a series of remedies for illegal captivity and subsequent enslavement of freeborn Muslims. These included moral suasion of both captors and government to prevent illegal enslavement, political reform, physical rescue of freeborn Muslims, and the ransoming of freeborn Muslims.

Basing their intellectual thought on the West African intellectual canon that had developed over centuries, nineteenth-century scholars argued that ideally individuals suspected to be freeborn Muslims ought to be granted free release, yet they also recognized that ransoming was a practical means for ensuring the freedom of freeborn Muslims. The Sokoto Caliphate proactively encouraged and was involved in the ransoming of their captive subjects whereas the Umarian governments were more tacit in their support of the practice. The debate in the Sokoto Caliphate was on who should pay the ransoming costs and on the prudency of permitting the ransoming of enemy captives. On these questions, pragmatism won out as various emirate and federal Sokoto governments passed the costs of ransoming from government coffers to private families and supported the ransoming of prisoners held by their own forces only when the prisoners did not pose a future threat. This is in contrast to Morocco, where ransoming European captives was viewed as a means to increase government revenue and as political strategy in its dealing with the European powers and in its relationship with the Saharan border regions of al-Sūs and Wād Nūn. Moroccan Sultans though, as Muslim leaders, felt obligated to help free all Muslims held in Europe through either ransoming or captive exchange but were hampered in their efforts by the European preference for enslaved labor rather than the ransom price their captives would fetch.

While enslavement and ransoming were similar in that captives slated for both enslavement and ransoming were taken prisoner mainly through warfare, raiding, and kidnapping, their treatment after capture differed. Unlike an individual marked for enslavement, the value of an individual to be ransomed did not increase the farther away they were taken from the point of capture. Indeed, the maintenance of communication links and the use of mediators were key to successful ransom negotiations. At the state level, the ransoming of freeborn Muslims was viewed as a moral and legal obligation, while at the personal level people were motivated to take part in ransom negotiations because the kin of captive individuals valued the freedom of their relatives; and captors enjoyed the higher rate they could attain by ransoming a person back to family and friends than by selling the individual as a slave. While ransom prices varied, they were generally, for both men and women, about twice what the individual would fetch if sold as a slave, and often more, especially if the captive was of high status. The relationship between ransom and slave prices remained steady throughout the nineteenth century. The high price of ransoming most often limited the practice to elite individuals. Yet, especially in the Sahara and along the desert edge, kidnapped slaves were sometimes ransomed by their owners and returned to their previous slave status as a matter of honor.

In West Africa, ransoming was not exclusive to Muslim societies. The ransoming of freeborn Muslims held by non-Muslims could only take place if non-Muslim societies also practiced ransoming and if their practices shared similarities. For both Muslims and non-Muslims the right to decide to permit the ransoming of captives and the price lay with the captor. Furthermore, both Muslims and non-Muslims were motivated to ransom their captives in order to gain the greater profit from returning a person to a state of freedom than by selling them as a slave, although they could also be inspired by other reasons such as strategic interests. Yet, in one important aspect, ransoming practices differed between Muslims and non-Muslims. In Muslim regions ransoming was governed and justified by interpretation and application of Islamic law. In non-Muslim regions ransoming was regulated through practice. This dissimilarity led to using different types of mediators in ransom negotiations. In Muslim regions, since ransoming was sanctioned by law, often the mediator was an individual who operated within the bureaucracy. In non-Muslim regions, though, the mediator was usually a person who was respected by both sides and was not necessarily attached to the state bureaucracy.

Legal ransoming in the western and central Sudan region of West Africa came to an end with colonial conquest, the imposition of colonial rule, and the outlawing of captive taking and the slave trade. It continued, however, during colonial rule under the guise of third-party slave redemption. Both French and British colonial officials included preexisting redemption practices, with some modifications, in their emancipation policies. Both French and British officials justified the takeover of African territory as a means to end slavery and the slave trade. Redemption was the preferred colonial means for enslaved individuals to gain their freedom as it compensated owners for the loss of their property, sustained economic stability, and maintained the cooperation of many slave-owning elites with the colonial regimes.[3] With the ending of legal captive taking and enslavement, legal ransoming was no longer viable. Yet the practice of illegal ransoming continued under colonial rule and under independence as captive taking continued, just as the practice of slavery has continued.[4]

Indeed, Amy Niang argues that the kidnapping and ransoming taking place in the contemporary Sahara/Sahel is a reaction to a lack of governance and the inability of government institutions to protect local economic interests. For Niang, "Raiding and ransoming strategies have thus been used as acts of defiance, as a form of adaptation to, and a response to various social strains heightened by capitalism, the disruption of traditional trading and economic circuits, and ultimately as a political weapon."[5] She views contemporary kidnapping and ransoming in the region by AQIM and others as a continuation of past practices of raiding, razzia, and ransoming as resource redistribution.

The actions of Boko Haram and its splinter groups can be viewed through a similar lens. Boko Haram is centered on the northeast Nigerian states of Borno, Yobe, and Adamawa, particularly the city of Maiduguri, which was part of the precolonial empire of Bornu. While many followers joined Boko Haram out of religious belief—because they believe its Salafi Jihadist interpretation of Islam—most of the foot soldiers joined for economic reasons.[6]

---

3 Klein, *Slavery and Colonial Rule in French West Africa*; Lovejoy and Hogendorn, *Slow Death for Slavery*. For a discussion of how the French dealt with the question of slavery in Adār see Rossi, *From Slavery to Aid*, 146–201.

4 See, for example, ANM FA 2M 22 Justice Indigène Correspondance Cercle de Médine 1887–1905, Médine August 28, 1890; ANM FA 1E 113 Renseignments politiques, Cercle de Segou 1890–1904, Copi de Registre N2 24 trimestre 1898; ANM FA 1E 113 Renseignments politiques, Cercle de Segou 1890–1904, 4ieme trimestre 1894; ANM FA 2M 7 Justice Indigène Correspondance Cercle de Bougouni 1896–1920. Bougouni, May 22, 1900; Vaughan and Kirk-Greene, *The Diary of Hamman Yaji*. For the continuation of "traditional" forms of slavery see for example, Pelckmans, "Stereotypes of Past-Slavery and 'Stereo-Styles' in Post-Slavery," 281–301 and Rossi, *Reconfiguring Slavery*.

5 Niang, "The Political Economy of Ransoming in the Sahel," 157–84.

6 Botha and Abdile, "Summary—Getting Behind the Profiles of Boko Haram Members and Factors Contributing to Radicalization versus Working towards Peace."

Borno, Yobe, and Adamawa have among the highest rate of unemployment in all of Nigeria, are among the lowest for child school enrollment and are economically and socially highly stratified.[7] Indeed, confirming Niang's argument that raiding and ransoming by Salafi Jihadist groups is viewed by many members as a form of resource redistribution, many local observers of Boko Haram argue that poverty, hopelessness, and a desire for socio-economic change is what attracts many young men to the Boko Haram cause. One observer believes that Boko Haram's message to disenfranchised and alienated youth is: "You don't have anything right now, come join us, we are going to take over towns and claim whatever we find in them and it's all yours."[8]

Just like the leaders of the nineteenth-century jihads, the leaders of Boko Haram believe that the political leadership of its state—in this case, Nigeria—is politically, economically, and religiously corrupt and is failing to properly address the economic, security, and religious needs of its citizenry. However, it is important to note that while the Fodiye and Taal were widely recognized as being properly trained scholars in their madh'hab and ṭarīqa traditions, none of the leaders of Boko Haram have the recognized training in Salafi thought to be viewed as scholars. Moreover, even though Boko Haram claims to be fulfilling the mission set out by 'Uthmān b. Fodiye and draws upon its own novel interpretations of the West African intellectual canon to justify its actions, it thoroughly rejects the Sokoto jihadists' interpretation of Islam based on the Mālikī madh'hab and the Qādiriyya ṭarīqa and seeks to replace the Sokoto intellectual tradition with its own interpretation of Islam based on its unique interpretation of Salafi thought. Yet in taking captives, Boko Haram has the same choices as nineteenth-century captors: to freely release, exchange, kill, enslave, or ransom. What choice they make, just like in the precolonial era, is dependent on the weight that they put on the variables of interpretation of law, their view of past regional ransoming practices, prudency, and cash and labor needs.

---

7 Nigeria National Bureau of Statistics, "National Manpower Stock and Employment Survey" 2010; Humphries et al., "Counted in and Being Out: Fluctuations in Primary School Attendance in Northern Nigeria," 134–43.

8 Interview with Malam Gambo Jika, vice-chair of the Adamawa Peace Initiative and Coordinator of Disaster Relief at Jamatu Nasurul Islam (JNI) Jimeta, April 16, 2018; interview with Bishop Stephen Mamza, Roman Catholic Diocese of Yola and vice-chair of the Adamawa Peace Initiative Jimeta, November 16, 2018; interview with SW, Yola Hunter, Yola, May 6, 2019; interview with YA, Yola Hunter, Yola, May 6, 2019; interview with Abdullahi Bello, founder of Peace through Sports, Yola, April 13, 2018.

Bibliography

Unpublished Primary Sources

Archives nationales du Mali (ANM), Koulouba

FA 1D59 10 Notes sur les rezzous Marocains, 1906.

FA 1D 221 Relations de missions correspondances diverse. Cercle de Segou 1891–1898.

FA 1E 16 Notes sur les rezzous Marocains Tombouctou 1906.

FA 1E 47 Rapport sur la situation politique du Cercle de Kita, 1883–1905.

FA 1E 74 Cercle de Médine Correspondances et rapports sur les villages et captifs liberés 1885–1895.

FA 1E 113 Renseignments politiques. Cercle de Segou 1890–1904.

FA 1E 156 Rapports sur la répression de la traites des esclaves en Haut-Sénégal Niger 1894–1904.

FA 2M 16 Justice Indigene. Correspondances Cercle de Kayes 1882–1920.

FA 2M 21 Justice Indigène Correspondances, Cercle de Koutiala 1903–1919.

FA 2M 22 Justice Indigene. Correspondance Cercle de Medine 1887–1905.

FA 2M 7 Justice Indigène Correspondance Cercle de Bougouni 1896–1920.

Archives nationales du Niger (ANN), Niamey

1E1.16 1902 Rapport Politique sur les sultanats du Tessaoua, du Gober et du Maradi.

1E1.21 1903 Résidence de Tessaoua. Rapports politiques mensual 1903.

1E1.3 1900 Rapport du Lieutenant JI Galidon Commandant le 2ème Sénégalais en marche sur Zinder-Tchad.

1E1.32 1904 Poste d'Agadez.

1E1.34 1904 Cercle de Zinder, Résidence de Tessaoua.

Boubou Hama, Journal novembre 1964 à mars 1965.

Boubou Hama, Journal de 2 mars 1968 au 6 mai 1969.

Bibliothèque nationale du France (BNF)

MS Arabe 5370 Rimāḥ al-Raḥīm alā nuḥūr ḥizb al-rajīm, 'Umar ibn Sa'īd al-Fūtī.
MS Arabe 5708 Tadhkirat al-Mustarṣidīn, 'Umar ibn Sa'īd al-Fūtī.

Church Missionary Society, Yoruba Mission (CMS)—Center for Research Libraries, Chicago

CA 1/O79 Sierra Leone Mission, Original Papers Samuel Ajayi Crowther 1837–1844.
CA 2/O68 Yoruba Mission. JA Maser Letters and Journals 1853–1879.

Civilian Responses to Boko Haram Oral History Project (Jennifer Lofkrantz Collection)

Bishop Stephen Mamza, November 16, 2018, Jimeta.
Malam Gambo Jika, April 16, 2018, Jimeta
SW, May 6, 2019, Yola.
YA, May 6, 2019, Yola.
Abdullahi Bello, April 13, 2018, Yola.

Harriet Tubman Institute for Research on Africa and its Diasporas, York University

Archives nationales du Sénégal (ANS)

K14 Captivité au Soudan, 1894.
K16 Enquête sur la captivité en A.O.F 1903–1904.
K18 Enquête sur la captivité, 1904.
K19 Enquête sur la captivité, 1904.

Bibliothèque commémorative Mamma Haidara (MHT), Timbuktu

MS 76.

Economic History Project

Interview with Dan Rimin Kano, Kano, December 12 and 30, 1975.
Interview with Alhaji Yunusa Mikail, August 2, 1975.

Institut des Hautes Etudes et de Recherche Islamique, Ahmad Baba (IHERIAB), Timbuktu

MS 3549.
MS 3851/9.

Kano State History and Cultural Bureau (KSHCB), Kano

KAN PRO 1/11/7 Rano 1955–59.
Muḥammad Bello. *Miftāh al-Sadād fī aqsām hādhihi 'l-bilād.* Zaria: Shina Commercial Press (undated, uncatalogued).

Nigerian National Archives, Kaduna (NAK)

A/AR/43/2 'Uthmān b. Fodiye, Irshād al-'ibād ilā ahamm masā'il al-jihād.
SNP 7/8 3039/1907 Report on the Nassarawa Province.

Published Primary Sources

Adams, Robert. *The Narrative of Robert Adams, a Sailor, Who Was Wrecked on the Western Coast of Africa in the Year 1810.* London: 1816.

Al Hilli, Ja'far b. al-hasan al-muhaqqiq. *Droit Musulman: Recuil de lois concernant les Musulmans Schyites* translated by Amédée Querry. Paris: Impremerie nationale, 1871.

Al Jawzī, Abū'l Faraj 'Abd al-Raḥman b. *Tanwīr al-ghabash fī faḍl al-sūdān wa-'l-ḥabash* edited by Marzūq 'Alī Ibrāhīm. Riyad: Dār al-sharīf, 1998.

Al Jazeera. "Nigeria outlaws ransom payments, kidnap now punishable by death." April 27, 2022. https://www.aljazeera.com/news/2022/4/27/nigeria-outlaws-ransom-payments-abduction-punishable-by-death.

Al Jundī, Khalīl b. Ishāq. *Abréjé de la loi musulmane selon le rite de l'imām Mālek.* Translated by Georges Bousquet. 4 vols. Paris: A. Maisonneuve, 1962.

Al Maghīlī, Muḥammad. *Taj al-din yajib 'ala-mulūk.* Translated by T. H. Baldwin. Beirut: Impremerie Catholique, 1932.

Al S'adi. Abd al Rahmān, *Tārikh al-Sūdān* translated by O Houdas. Paris: Librairie d'Amerique et d'Orient Adrien-Masonneuve, 1964.

Al Suyūtī,'Abd al-Raḥmān. *Azhār al-'urūsh fī akhbār al-ḥubūsh*, edited by 'Abd Allāh 'Īsā al-Ghazālī. Kuwait: Markaz al-makhṭūṭāt wa-'l-turāth wa-'l-wathā'iq, 1995.

Al Suyūtī, 'Abd al-Raḥmān. *Raf' sha'n al-ḥubshān* edited by Ṣafwān Dāwudī and Ḥassan 'Ubajī Jeddah: Dār al-qiblah li-'l-thaqāfa al-islāmiyya, 1991.

Al Qayrawānī, Abī Zayd b. *Risālah* translated by Leon Bercher, 3rd ed. Algiers: Editions Jules Carbonel, 1949.

Associated Press. "Nigeria: Police Revise Number of Kidnapped Students." May 2, 2014. http://www.nytimes.com/2014/05/03/world/africa/nigeria-police-revise-number-of-kidnapped-students.html

Backwell, H. F., ed. *The Occupation of Hausaland 1900–1904*. London: Frank Cass, 1969.

Barber, M. A. S. *Oshielle or Village Life in the Yoruba Country*. London: James Nisbet & Co, 1857.

Barth, Heinrich. *Travels and Discoveries in North and Central Africa 1849–1855*. London: Frank Cass 1965.

Bello, Muḥammad. *Infāq al-maysūr fi tārīkh bilād at*-takrūr edited by Bahija Chadli. Rabat: Mohammed V University Publications of the Institute of African Studies, 1999.

Bello Muḥammad *Risāla ilā ahl al-ḥaramayn al-sharīfayn wa ilā ahl al-mashriq*. In Umar al Naqar *The Pilgrimage Tradition in West Africa*. Khartoum: Khartoum University Press, 1972. 141–43.

Bewley, Aisha Abdurrahman, trans. *Al-Muwatta of Imam Malik ibn Anas*. London: Kegan Paul International Limited, 1989.

Binger, Louis-Gustave. *Du Niger au Golfe du Guinée (1887–1889)*. Paris: Société d'éditions scientifiques, 1892.

Binger, Louis-Gustave. *Esclavage, Islamisme et Christianisme*. Paris: Societé d'editions scientifiques, 1891.

Bluett, Thomas. *Some Memoirs of the Life of Job, the Son of Solomon the High Priest of Boonda in Africa*. London: Richard Ford, 1754.

Bovill, E. D., ed. *Missions to the Niger*. 4 vols. Cambridge: Cambridge University Press 1966.

Brinner, William M., trans. *The History of al-Tabarī*. Vol. 2. *Prophets and Patriarchs*. Albany: State University of New York Press, 1986.

Burke, Jason, and Emmanuel Akinwotu "Boko Haram Frees 21 School girls from Group Abducted in Chibok," *The Guardian*, October 16, 2016. https://www.theguardian.com/world/2016/oct/13/boko-haram-frees-21-schoolgirls-from-group-abducted-in-chibok.

Caillé, Jacques. *Les accords internationaux du Sultan Sidi Mohammed ben Abdallah (1757–1790)*. Tangiers: Faculté de droit du Maroc, 1960.

Caron, E. *De Saint-Louis au Port de Tombouktou*. Paris: August Challamel Editeur, 1891.

Christelow, Allan, ed. *Thus Ruled Emir Abbas: Selected Cases from the Records of the Emir of Kano's Judicial Council*. East Lansing: Michigan State University Press, 1994.

Cochelet, Charles. *Naufrage du brick français La Sophie*. Whitefish, MT: Kessinger, 2010.

Cochelet, Charles. *Narrative of the Shipwreck of the Sophia*. London: Richard Philip, 1822.

Conneau, Theophilus. *A Slaver's Log Book; or Twenty Years' Residence in West Africa.* Hoboken, NJ: Prentice Hall, 1976.

Cook, David, trans. "Disassociation of the Jamā'āt Anṣār al-Muslimin from Targeting Muslim Innocents." In *The Boko Haram Reader: From Preachers to Islamic State*, edited by Abdulbasit Kassim and Michael Nwankpa. 275–78. Oxford: Oxford University Press, 2018.

Cowdery, Jonathan. *American Captives in Tripoli, or, Dr. Cowdery's Journal in Miniature Kept During his Late Captivity in Tripoli.* 2nd ed. Boston: Belcher & Armstrong, 1806.

De Brisson, Pierre-Raymond. *Account of the Shipwreck and Captivity of Mr. De Brisson with A Description of the Desert of Africa, from Senegal to Morocco and his own Observation, While Harassed from Place to Place by the Wandering Arabs.* London: Robert Barker, 1790.

Denham, Dixon, Hugh Clapperton, and Walter Oudney. *Narrative of Travels and Discoveries in North and Central Africa, 1822, 1823, 1824.* London: Dorf, 1985.

D'Aranda, Emmanuel. *Les captifs d'Alger* edited by Latifa Z'Rari. Paris: Jean-Paul Rocher, 1947.

Diop, Samba, ed. and trans. *The Epic of El Hadj Umar Tal of Fuuta.* Madison: African Studies Program University of Wisconsin-Madison, 2000.

Dodge, Bayard, ed. and trans. *The Fihrist of Al-Nadim; a Tenth-Century Survey of Muslim Culture.* New York: Columbia University Press, 1970.

Dupuis, J. *Journal of a Residence in Ashantee.* London: Cass, 1966.

El Masri, F. H. "A Critical Edition of Dan Fodio's Bayān wujub al-hijra 'ala 'l-'ibad; with introduction, English translation and Commentary." PhD diss., University of Ibadan, 1968.

Es Soudan, Akbar Mulūk. "Histoire de Sokoto." In *Tadhkirat al-Nisyān*, 306–7, 313. Translated by O. Houdas. Paris: Librairie d'Amerique et d'Orient, 1966.

Fodiye b., Abdullāhi. *Tazyīn al-waraqāt* edited and translated by Mervyn Hiskett. Ibadan: Ibadan University Press, 1983.

Fodiye b., Abdullāhi, *Ḍiyā' al-ḥukkām.* In "The Political Ideas of the Jihad Leaders: Being Translation, Edition and Analysis of (1) Usal al-syayasa by Muhammad Bello and (2) Diya' al-Hukkam by Abdullhah B. Fodio." MA thesis, Bayero University Kano, 1975.

Fodiye b., Abdullāhi. *Ḍiyā' al-ḥukkām.* Zārīya: Maktab Nūlā, 1956.

Fodiye b., Asma'u. "Be Sure of God's Truth." In *Collected Works of Nana Asma'u Daughter of Usman dan Fodiyo (1793–1864)*, edited by Jean Boyd and Beverly Mack, 51. East Lansing: Michigan State University Press, 1997.

Fodiye b., Asma'u. "Filitago/Wakar Gewaye." In *Collected Works of Nana Asma'u Daughter of Usman dan Fodiyo (1793–1864)*, edited by Jean Boyd and Beverly Mack, 143, 134–54. East Lansing: Michigan State University Press, 1997.

Fodiye b., Asma'u. "Godaben Gaskiya." In *Collected Works of Nana Asma'u Daughter of Usman dan Fodiyo (1793–1864)*, edited by Jean Boyd and Beverly Mack, 181. East Lansing: Michigan State University Press, 1997.

Fodiye b., Asma'u. "Tabbat Hakika." In *Collected Works of Nana Asma'u Daughter of Usman dan Fodiyo (1793–1864)*, edited by Jean Boyd and Beverly Mack, 52. East Lansing: Michigan State University Press, 1997.

Fodiye b., Asma'u. "Te-Medde Jewgo Fu-nbara." In *Collected Works of Nana Asma'u Daughter of Usman dan Fodiyo (1793–1864)*, edited by Jean Boyd and Beverly Mack, 192. East Lansing: Michigan State University Press, 1997.

Fodiye b., 'Uthmān. *Usulul-Adlilwullatil Umuri wa ahlil-fadli*. Translated by Mohammad Isa Talata. Mafara. Sokoto: 1992.

Fodiye b., 'Uthmān. *Bayān wujūb al-hijra 'ala' l–'ibād*. Edited and translated by F. H. El Masri. Khartoum: Khartoum University Press, 1978.

Fodiye b., 'Uthmān, *Wathīqat ahl al-Sūdān*. In ADH Bivar, "The Wathīqat ahl al-Sūdān: A Manifesto of the Fulani Jihād." *Journal of African History* 11, no. 2 (1961): 235–43.

Fodiye b., 'Uthmān. *Tanbīh al ikhwān alā arḍ al-sūdān*. In "An Early Fulani Conception of Islam (Continued)." *Journal of the Royal African Society* 14, no. 54 (January 1915): 185–92.

Fodiye b., 'Uthmān. *Nūr al-albāb*. Translated by Ismail Hamet. *Revue Africaine* XLI (1897): 300–303.

Follie, Adrien-Jacques. *Voyage dans les deserts du Sahara*. Paris: Imprimerie du Cercle Social, 1792.

Gallieni. Joseph. *Voyage au Soudan Français (Haut Niger et Pays Segou) 1879–1881*. Paris: Librairie Hachet et C, 1885.

Gautier, E. F. *Sahara, The Great Desert*. Translated by Dorothy Ford Mayhew. London: Frank Cass & Co., 1970.

Hama, Boubou, ed. *Histoire Traditionelle d'un Village Songhay: Fonéko*. Paris: Editions Présence Africaine, 1970.

Hiskett, Mervyn. "The 'Song of the Shaihu's Miracles': A Hausa Hagiography from Sokoto." *African Language Studies* 12 (1971): 71–107.

Hiskett, Mervyn. "Kitab al-farq: 'A Work on the Habe Kingdoms Attributed to 'Uthman dan Fodio," *Bulletin of the School of Oriental and African Studies* 23, no. 3 (1960): 558–73.

Hunwick, John. *Timbuktu and the Songhay Empire: Al-S'adī's Ta'rīkh al-sūdān down to 1613 and other Contemporary Documents*. Leiden: Brill, 1999.

Hunwick, John, trans. and ed. *Shari'a in Songhay: The Replies of al-Maghīlī to the Questions of Askia al-hājj Muḥammad*. Oxford: Oxford University Press, 1997.

Hunwick, John. "Back to West African Zanj Again: A Document of Sale from Timbuktu." *Sudanic Africa* 7 (1991): 53–60.

Hunwick, John, and Fatima Harrack, trans. and eds. *Mi'rāj al-Ṣu'ūd, Aḥmad Bābā's Replies on Slavery*. Rabat: Université Mohammed V Souissi Institute of African Studies, 2000.

Juzay, Muḥammad b. Aḥmad b. *Al-Qawānīn al-fiqhiyya*. Edited by Muḥammad Amīn al-Dannāwi. Beirut: Dar al-kutub a-Ilmiyya, 2006.

Kassim, Abdulbasit, trans. "Clearing the Doubts of Scholars." In *The Boko Haram Reader: From Nigerian Preachers to the Islamic State*, edited by Abdulbasit Kassim and Michael Nwankpa, 35–40. London: Hurst & Company, 2018.

Khaldūn, Abd al-Raḥman ibn. *The Muqaddimah: An Introduction to History*. Translated by Franz Rosenthal. Princeton, NJ: Princeton University Press, 1967.

Khaldūn, Abd al-Raḥman ibn. *Kitāb al-ibar wa diwān al-mubtada' wa al-khabar fi ayyam al-'Ajam wa al-barbar*. Beirut: Dar al-kitab al-Lubnani, 1959.

Lambert, Sheila, ed. *House of Commons Sessional Papers of the Eighteenth Century*. London: Parliament House of Commons, 1975.

Law, Robin, and Paul E. Lovejoy. *The Biography of Mahommah Gardo Baquaqua*. Princeton NJ: Markus Weiner, 2001.

Lenz, Oskar. *Timbouctou Voyage au Maroc, au Sahara et au Soudan*. Translated by Pierre Lehautcourt. Paris: Librairie Hachette et C, 1886.

Le Tourneau, Roger. "Histoire de la dynastie sa'idide. Extrait de al-Turguman al-mu'rib 'an duwal al-Masriq wal Maghrib d'Abū al-Qāsim ben Ahmad ben 'Ali ben Ibrahim al-Zayyānī. Texte, traduction et notes presenté par L. Mougin et H. Hamburger." *Revue de l'Occident musulman et de la Méditerranée* 23, no. 1 (1977): 7–109.

Levtzion, Nehemia, and J. F. P Hopkins, eds. *Corpus of Early Arabic Sources for West Africa*. Trenton, NJ: Markus Weiner, 2000.

Levtzion, Nehemia. "A Seventeenth Century Chronicle by Ibn Mukhtār: A Critical Study of 'Ta'rīkh al-fattāsh." *Bulletin of the School of Oriental and African Studies* 34, no. 3 (1971): 571–93.

Maclean, Ruth, and Isaac Abrak, "Boko Haram Kept One Dapchi Girl Who Refused to Deny Her Christianity." *The Guardian*, March 24, 2018. https://www.theguardian.com/world/2018/mar/24/boko-haram-kept-one-dapchi-nigeria-girl-who-refused-to-deny-her-christianity.

Mage, Eugene. *Voyage (1863–1866) au Soudan Occidental*. Paris: Editions Karthala, 1980.

Marty, Paul. "Les tribus de la haute Mauritanie : Les Takna (Oued Noun)," *Bulletin du comité de l'Afrique française* 5 (1915): 136–46.

Matar, Nabil, ed. and trans. *An Arab Ambassador in the Mediterranean World: The Travels of Muḥammad ibn 'Uthmān al-Miknāsī*. New York: Routledge, 2015.

Mercadier, F. J. G. "L'esclave de Timimoun." In *The African Diaspora in the Mediterranean Lands of Islam*, edited by Eve Troutt Powell and John Hunwick, 99–220. Princeton, NJ: Markus Weiner, 2002.

Mockler-Ferryman, A. F. *Up the Niger*. London: George Philip & Son, 1892.

Moore, Francis. *Travels into the Inland Part of Africa*. London: Cave, 1738.

Muhammad, Dalhatu. "The Tabuka Epic (?) in Hausa: An Exercise in Narratology." In *Studies in Hausa Language, Literature and Culture: Proceeding of the Second Hausa International Conference*, edited by Ibrahim Yaro Yahaha, Abba Rufa'I, and Al-Amin Abu-Manga, 397–415. Kano: Centre for the Study of Nigerian Languages, Bayero University, Kano, 1982.

Nachtigal, Gustav. *Sahara and Sudan*. Translated by Allan B. Fisher and Humphrey J Fisher. London: 1980.

Nigeria National Bureau of Statistics. "National Manpower Stock and Employment Survey" Abuja: Nigeria National Bureau of Statistics, 2010.

Nossiter, Adam. "Nigerian Islamist Leader Threatens to Sell Kidnapped Girls." *New York Times*, May 5, 2014. http://www.nytimes.com/2014/05/06/world/africa/nigeria-kidnapped-girls.html.

Nwaubani, Adaobi Tricia. "Nigeria's Chibok Girls: Why Was This Former Captive Treated Differently." *BBC*, April 17, 2022. https://www.bbc.com/news/world-africa-61092882,

Olivier de Sardan, Jean-Pierre. *Les sociétés Songhay-Zarma (Niger-Mali) Chefs, guerriers, esclaves, paysans*. Paris: Editions Karthala, 1984.

Panet, Leopold. "Relations d'un Voyage du Senegal a Souiera (Mogador)." *Revue Colonial* (November 1850), 150–80.

Park, Mungo. *Travels in the Interior Districts of Africa*. Edited by Kate Ferguson Marsters. Chapel Hill: University of North Carolina Press, 2000.

Parkinson, Joe, and Gbenga Akinbule. "Six Years after #BringBackOurGirls Freed Chibok Girls Faces Fresh Danger." *Wall Street Journal*, April 20, 2020. https://www.wsj.com/articles/six-years-after-bringbackourgirls-freed-chibok-captives-face-fresh-danger-11586862002?mod=searchresults_pos6&page=1.

Ray, William. *Horrors of Slavery, or, the American Tars in Tripoli*. Edited by Hester Blum. New Brunswick, NJ: Rutgers University Press, 2008.

Reuters. "Boko Haram Offers to Swap Kidnapped Nigerian Girls for Prisoners." *New York Times*, May 12, 2014. http://www.nytimes.com/video/multimedia/100000002875785/boko-haram-offers-to-swap-kidnapped-nigerian-girls-for-prisoners.html.

Richardson, James. *Narratives of a Mission to Central Africa 1850–1851*. London: Chapman and Hall.

Riley, James. *Loss of the American Brig Commerce, Wrecked on the Western Coast of Africa in the Month of August 1815 with an account of Tombuctoo*. London: John Murray, 1817.

Ritchie, Carson. "Deux Textes sur le Sénégal (1673–1677)." *Bulletin de l'Institut Fondemental de l'Afrique Noire* serie B 30 (1968): 289–353.

Robinson, Charles Henry. *Hausaland or Fifteen Hundred Miles through the Central Soudan*. 3rd ed. London: Sampson, Low and Marston, 1900.

Saugnier, M. "Récit du naufrage du Moghreb." In *Dans les fers du Moghreb*, edited by Albert Savine. Paris: Sociétés des Editions Louis Michaud, 1912.

Schön, J. F. *Magana Hausa: Native Literature in the Hausa Language*. London: SPCK, 1885.

Schwarz, Suzanne, ed. *Slave Captain, The Career of James Irving in the Liverpool Trade*, 2nd ed. Liverpool: Liverpool University Press, 2008.

Scott, Samuel Parsons, trans. *Las Siete Partidas*. Edited by Robert L. Burns. 4 vols. Philadelphia: University of Pennsylvania Press, 2001.

Soleillet, Paul. *Voyage à Segou, 1878–1879.* Edited by Gabriel Gravier. Paris: Challamel ainé Librairie Editeur, 1887.
Smith, Mary F. *Baba of Karo, A Woman of the Muslim Hausa.* New Haven, CT: Yale University Press, 1981.
Staudinger, Paul. *In the Heart of the Hausa States.* Translated by Johanna E. Moody. Athens: Ohio University Center for International Monographs in International Studies, 1997.
Taal, 'Umar. *Bayān mā waqa'a.* Translated and edited by Sidi Mohamed Mahibou and Jean-Louis Triaud. Paris: Editions du centre national de la recherche scientifique, 1983.
Taal, 'Umar. *Risālat shawq al-habīb ilā as'ilat Ibahīm al-labīb.* In Omar Jah, "The Effect of Pilgrimage on the Jihād of Al-Hajj 'Umar al-Futi, 1794–1864." In *The Central Bilād al-Sūdān: Tradition and Adaptation*, edited by Yusuf Fadl Hasan and Paul Doombos, 233–43. Khartoum: University of Khartoum Press.
Tukrur, Muhammad. "Busuraa'u'" In *Chants Musulmans en Peul,* edited by J. Haafkens. Leiden: Brill, 1983.
Vaughan, James, and Anthony Kirk-Greene, eds. *The Diary of Hamman Yaji.* Bloomington: Indiana University Press, 1995.
Verger, Pierre. *Trade Relations between the Bight of Benin and Brazil, 17th–19th Century.* Ibadan: University of Ibadan Press, 1976.
Vigné d'Octon, Paul. *La gloire du sabre.* Paris: Diffusion Ulysse Distribution Distique, 1984.
Voyages: The Atlantic Slave Trade Database. http://www.slavevoyages.org
Wadström, Carl. *An Essay on Colonization Particularly Applied to the Western Coast of Africa with Some Thoughts on Cultivation and Commerce, 1794.* London: August M. Kelly, 1968.
Wise, Christopher, ed. and trans. *Archive of the Umarian Tijaniyya.* Washington DC: Sahel Nomad Books, 2017.

Secondary Sources

Abitbol, M. "Le Maroc et le commerce transsaharien du XVIIe siècle au début du XIXe siècle." *Revue de l'Occident Musulman et de la Méditerranée* 30, no. 2 (1980): 5–19.
Adamu, Mahdi. "The Delivery of Slaves from the Central Sudan to the Bight of Benin in the Eighteenth and Nineteenth Centuries." In *The Uncommon Market, Essays in the Economic History of the Atlantic Slave Trade*, edited by Henry A. Gemery and Jan S. Hogendorn, 163–80. New York: Academic Press, 1979.
Adebayo, A. G. "Of Man and Cattle: A Reconsideration of the Traditions of Origin of Pastoral Fulani of Nigeria." *History in Africa* 18 (1991): 1–21.

Adeleye, Rowland A. "Hausaland and Bornu 1600–1800." In Vol. 1 of *History of West Africa*, edited by J. F. Ade Ajayi and Michael Crowder, 577–623. 3rd ed. New York: Columbia University Press, 1985.

Ajayi, J. F. Ade, and Robert Smith. *Yoruba Warfare in the Nineteenth Century*. Cambridge: Cambridge University Press, 1964.

Akinwumi, Olayemi. "Princes as Highway Men: A Consideration of the Phenomenon of Armed Banditry in Precolonial Borgu." *Cahiers d'Etudes Africaines* 162, no. 2 (2001): 333–50.

Al Bili, Uthman Sayyid Ahmad Ismail, ed. *Some Aspects of Islam in Africa*. Reading, UK: Ithaca Press, 2008.

Al-Hafiz al Tidjani. *Muhammad. Al-Hadj Omar Tall (1794–1864): Sultan de l'état Tidjanite de l'Afrique Occidentale*. Translated by Fernand Dumont. Abidjan: Les Nouvelles Editions Africaines, 1983.

Al Naqar, 'Umar. *The Pilgrimage Tradition in West Africa*. Khartoum: Khartoum University Press, 1972.

Ali, Syed Ameer. *The Personal Law of the Mahommedans, According to All Schools*. London: W. H. Allen, 1880.

Allison, Robert J. *The Crescent Obscured: The United States and the Muslim World, 1776–1815*. New York: Oxford University Press, 1995.

Ambrus, A, E. Chaney, and I. Salitskiy, "Pirates of the Mediterranean: An Empirical Investigation of Bargaining with Transaction Costs." Unpublished working paper. http://www.economics.harvard.edu/faculty/ambrus/files/Barbary.pdf.

Amselle, J. L., and E. Sibeud, "Introduction." In *Maurice Delafosse: Entre orientalisme et ethnographie: l'itinéraire d'un africaniste, 1870–1926*, edited by J. L. Amselle and E. Sibeud, 7–18. Paris: Maisonneuve & Larose, 1998.

André, P. J. *L'islam noir*. Paris: Geuthner, 1924.

Anonymous. "The Popular Discourses of Salafi Radicalism and Salafi Counter-Radicalism in Nigeria: A Case Study of Boko Haram. *Journal of Religion in Africa* 42 (2012): 118–44.

Asad, Muhammad. *The Message of the Qu'ran: The Full Account of the Revealed Arabic Text Accompanied by Parallel Transliteration*. Los Angeles: The Book Foundation, 2005.

Austen, Ralph. *Trans-Saharan Africa in World History*. Oxford: Oxford University Press, 2010.

Austen, Ralph. "The Mediterranean Islamic Slave Trade out Africa: A Tentative Census." In *The Human Commodity: Perspectives on the Trans-Saharan Slave Trade*. Edited by Elizabeth Savage, 214–48. London: Frank Cass & Co. Ltd., 1992.

Austen, Ralph. "The Trans-Saharan Slave Trade: A Tentative Census." In *The Uncommon Market: Essays in the Economic History of the Atlantic Slave Trade* edited by H. A. Gemery and J. S. Hogendorn, 23–76. New York: Academic Press, 1979.

Austen, Ralph, and Jan Jansen. "History, Oral Transmission, and Structure in Ibn Khaldun's Chronology of Mali Rulers." *History in Africa* 23 (1996): 17–28.

Bā, Amadou Hampaté and Jacques Daget. *Empire Peul de Macina (1818–1853).* Paris: Mouton & Co. La Haye, 1968.

Babou, Cheikh Anta. *Fighting the Greater Jihad, Amadu Bamba and the Founding of the Muridiyya of Senegal 1854–1913.* Athens: Ohio University Press, 2007.

Bachrouch, Taoufik. "Rachat et libération des esclaves chrétiens à Tunis au XVIIe siècle." *Revue Tunisienne de Sciences Sociales* 12 (1975): 121–62.

Baldé, M. S. "L'esclavage et la guerre au Fuuta-Jalon." In *L'esclavage en Afrique précoloniale.* Edited by Claude Meillassoux, 183–220. Paris: François Maspero, 1975.

Balogun, S. A. "Succession Tradition in Gwandu History, 1817–1918." *Journal of the Historical Society of Nigeria* 7, no. 1 (1973): 17–33.

Barrio, Gozalo Maximiliano. *Esclavos y cautivos: Conflicto entre la cristiandad y islam en el siglo XVIII.* Valladolid: Servicio de Publicaciones de la Junta de Castilla y León, 2006.

Barry, Boubacar. *La Senégambie du XVe au XIX siècle.* Paris: L'Harmattan, 1998.

Barry, Boubacar. "Senegambia from the Sixteenth to the Eighteenth Century: Evolution of the Wolof, Sereer, and 'Tukuloor'." In Vol. 5 of *UNESCO General History of Africa: Africa from the Sixteenth to Eighteenth Century,* edited by B. A. Ogot, 262–99. Berkeley: University of California Press, 1992.

Barry, Boubacar. "The Subordination of Power and the Mercantile Economy: The Kingdom of Waalo 1600–1831." In *The Political Economy of Underdevelopment: Dependence in Senegal,* edited by Rita Cruise O'Brien, 39–63. Beverly Hills, CA: SAGE, 1979.

Batran, Aziz A. *The Qadiryya Brotherhood in West Africa and the Western Sahara: The Life and Times of Shaykh al-Mukhtar al-Kunti (1729–1811).* Rabat: Publications de l'Institut des Etudes Africaines, 2001.

Batran, Aziz A. "The 'Ulama' of Fas, Mulay Isma'il, and the Issue of the Haratin of Fas." In *Slaves and Slavery in Muslim Africa.* Vol. 2: *The Servile Estate,* edited by John Ralph Willis, 1–15. London: Frank Cass, 1985.

Batran, Aziz A. "A Contribution to the Biography of Shaikh Muḥammad ibn 'Abd al-Karīm ibn Muḥammad 'Umar –A 'mar al-Maghīlī," *Journal of African History* 14, no. 3 (1973): 381–94.

Belhamissi, Moulay. *Les captifs algériens et l'Europe chrétienne* (1518–1830). Algiers: Entreprise nationale du livre, 1988.

Bencheneb. Muhammad. "Khalil b. Ishak." In *The Encyclopedia of Islam.* CD-ROM Edition V.I.I. Leiden, Brill, 2001.

Bennessar, Bartolomé, and Lucile Bennessar. *Les chrétiens d'Allah: l'histoire extraordinaire des rénegats XVIe –XVIIe siècles.* Paris: Perrin 1989.

Bennett, Norman Robert. "Christian and Negro Slavery in Eighteenth Century North Africa." *Journal of African History* 1, no. 1 (1960): 65–82.

Benton, Lauren. *Law and Colonial Cultures: Legal Regimes in World History, 1400–1900*. Cambridge: Cambridge University Press, 2002.

Bivar, A. D. H., and M. Hiskett, "The Arabic Literature of Nigeria to 1804: A Provisional Account." *Bulletin of the School of Oriental and African Studies University of London* 25 (1962): 104–48.

Bivins, Mary Wren. *Telling Stories, Making Histories: Women, Words and Islam in Nineteenth Century Hausaland and Sokoto Caliphate*. Portsmouth, NH: Heinemann, 2007.

Blum, Charlotte, and Humphrey Fisher. "Love for Three Oranges, or, the Akiya's Dilemma: The Askiya, al-Maghīlī and Timbuktu, c. 1500 A.D." *Journal of African History* 34, no. 1 (1993): 65–91.

Blumenthal, Debra. *Enemies and Familiars, Slavery and Master in Fifteenth-Century Valencia*. Ithaca, NY: Cornell University Press, 2009.

Boisard, Marcel A. "On the Probable Influence of Islam on Western Public and International Law." *International Journal of Middle East Studies* 11, no. 4 (1980): 429–50.

Bolster, W. Jeffrey. *Black Jacks: African American Seamen in the Age of Sail*. Cambridge, MA: Harvard University Press, 1997.

Bono, Salvatore. "Slave Histories and Memoirs in the Mediterranean World: A Study of the Sources (Sixteenth-Eighteenth Centuries). In *Trade and Cultural Exchange in the Early Modern Mediterranean, Braudel's Maritime Legacy*, edited by Maria Fusaro et al., 97–115. New York: I. B. Tauris, 2010.

Bonte, Pierre. "Esclavage et relations de dependence chez les Touaregs Kel Gress." In *L'Esclavage en Afrique Précoloniale*, edited by Claude Meillassoux, 49–76. Paris: François Maspero, 1975.

Botha, Anneli, and Mahdi Abdile. "Summary - Getting Behind the Profiles of Boko Haram Members and Factors Contributing to Radicalization Versus Working Towards Peace," 2016 .

Boyd, Jean, and Beverly Mack. *Educating Muslim Women: The West African Legacy of Nana Asma'u, 1793–1864*. Oxford: Interface Publications Ltd, 2013.

Brenner, Louis. *Controlling Knowledge: Religion, Power and Schooling in a West African Muslim Society*. Bloomington: University of Indiana Press, 2001.

Brooks, James F. *Captives and Cousins: Slavery, Kinship and Community in the Southwest Borderlands*. Chapel Hill: University of North Carolina Press, 2002.

Brockopp, Jonathan. *Early Maliki Law: Ibn 'Abd Al-Hakam and His Compendium of Jurisprudence: Studies in Islamic Law and Society*. Leiden: Brill, 2002.

Brown, Christopher Leslie. *Moral Capital: Foundations of British Abolitionism*. Chapel Hill: University of North Carolina Press, 2012.

Brown. Jonathan A. C. *The Canonization of al-Bukhārī and Muslim: The Formation and Function of the Sunnī Ḥadīth Cannon*. Leiden: Brill, 2007.

Brown, William A. "The Caliphate of Hamdullahi c. 1818–1864." PhD diss., University of Wisconsin, 1968.

Burnham, Philip, and Murray Last. "From Pastoralist to Politician: The Problem of a Fulbe Aristocracy." *Cahiers d'Etudes Africaines* 34 no. 134/135 (1994): 313–57.

Burke, Edmund III. *Prelude to Protectorate in Morocco: Patterns of Precolonial Protest and Resistance 1860–1912.* Chicago: University of Chicago Press, 1976.

Burrill, Emily. *States of Marriage: Gender, Justice and Rights in Colonial Mali.* Athens: Ohio University Press, 2015.

Burrill, Emily, Richard Roberts, and Elizabeth Thornberry, eds. *Domestic Violence and the Law in Colonial and Post Colonial Africa.* Athens: Ohio University Press, 2010.

Candido, Mariana, P. *An African Slaving Port and the Atlantic World.* Cambridge: Cambridge University Press, 2013.

Carpenter, Nathan. "Ransom as Political Strategy: Captivity beyond Commercial Transaction on the Upper Guinea Coast in the Late Nineteenth and Early Twentieth Centuries." *Journal of West African History* 4, no. 2 (2018): 1–18.

Christopher, Emma. *Slave Ship Sailors and their Captive Cargoes,1730–1807.* Cambridge: Cambridge University Press, 2006.

Clark, Andrew F. "Slavery and Its Demise in the Upper Senegal Valley, West Africa, 1890–1922." *Slavery and Abolition* 15, no. 1 (1994): 51–71.

Clarence-Smith, William Gervase. *Islam and the Abolition of Slavery.* Oxford: Oxford University Press, 2006.

Cleaveland, Timothy. "Ahmad Baba al-Tinbukti and his Islamic Critique of Racial Slavery in the Maghrib." *Journal of North African Studies* 20, no. 1 (2015): 42–64.

Clissold, Stephen. *The Barbary Slaves.* Totowa, NJ: Rowman and Littlefield, 1977.

Coleman, David. "Of Corsairs, Converts and Renegades: Forms and Functions of Coastal Raiding on Both Sides of the Far Western Mediterranean, 1490–1540." *Medieval Encounters* 19, no. 1–2 (2013): 167–92.

Coleman, David. "Of Corsairs, Converts and Renegades: Forms and Functions of Coastal Raiding on both Sides of the Far Western Mediterranean 1490–1540." In *Spanning the Strait: Studies in the Western Mediterranean*, edited by Yuen-Gen Lian, Abigail Krasner Babale, Andrew Devereux, and Camilo Gomez-Rivas, 167–92. Leiden: Brill, 2013.

Colley, Linda. *Captives, Britain, Empire and the World 1600–1850.* New York: Anchor, 2002.

Collieaux, M. "Contribution à l'étude de l'histoire de l'ancien royaume de Kénédougou (1825–1898)." *Comité d'études historiques et scientifiques de l'Afrique Occidental Française* 9 (1924): 128–81.

Colvin, Lucie. G. "Commerce of Hausaland, 1780–1833." In *Aspects of West African Islam*, edited by Daniel F. McCall and Norman R. Bennett, 101–35. Boston: Boston University Press, 1971.

Cornell, Vincent J. "Ibn Battuta's Opportunism: The Networks and Loyalties of a Medieval Muslim Scholar." In *Muslim Networks from Hajj to Hip Hop*, edited by Miriam Cooke and Bruce B. Lawrence, 31–50. Chapel Hill: University of North Carolina Press, 2005.

Coulon, Christian. "Islam africain ou Islam arabe: Autonomie ou independence." *Année Africaine* (1976): 250–75.

Curtin, Philip. *Economic Change in Precolonial Africa: Senegambia in the Era of the Slave Trade*. Madison: University of Wisconsin Press, 1975.

Daddi Addoun, Yacine, and Paul E. Lovejoy. "The Arabic Manuscript of Muhammad Kaba Sanghanughu of Jamaica, c. 1820." In *Creole Concerns: Essays in Honour of Kamau Brathwaite*, edited by Annie Paul, 313–41. Kingston: University of the West Indies Press, 2004.

Daddi Addoun, Yacine, and Paul E. Lovejoy. "Muḥammad Kabā Saghanughu and the Muslim Community of Jamaica." In *Slavery on the Frontiers of Islam*, edited by Paul E Lovejoy, 201–20. Princeton, NJ: Markus Weiner, 2004.

Davis, Robert C. *Christian Slaves, Muslim Masters: White Slavery in the Mediterranean, the Barbary Coast, and Italy 1500–1800*. London: Palgrave Macmillan, 2003.

Davis, Robert C. "Counting European Slaves on the Barbary Coast." *Past and Present* 172 (2001): 87–124.

Diouf, Sylviane. "The Last Resort, Redeeming Family and Friends." In *Fighting the Slave Trade, West African Strategies*, edited by Sylviane Diouf, 81–100. Athens: Ohio University Press, 2003.

Domingues da Silva, Daniel. *The Atlantic Slave Trade from West Central Africa 1780–1867*. Cambridge: Cambridge University Press, 2017.

Domingues da Silva, Daniel, David Eltis, Nafees Khan, Philip Misevich and Olatunji Ojo. "The Trans-Atlantic Muslim Diaspora to Latin America in the Nineteenth Century." *Colonial Latin American Review* 26, no. 4 (2017): 528–47.

Duffill, M. B., and Paul E. Lovejoy. "Merchants, Porters, and Teamsters in Nineteenth-Century Central Sudan." In *The Workers of African Trade*, edited by Catherine Coquery-Vidrovitch and Paul E Lovejoy, 137–67. Beverly Hills, CA: SAGE, 1985.

Dursteler, Eric R. "On Bazaars & Battlefields: Recent Scholarship on Mediterranean Cultural Contacts." *Journal of Early Modern History* 15 (2011): 413–34.

Echard, Nicole. *L'experience du passé: Histoire de la societé paysanne Hausa de l'Ader*. Niamey: Institut de Recherches en Sciences Humaines, 1975.

El Adnani, Jillali. "Les origines de la Tijāniyya. Quand les premiers disciples se mettent à parler." In *La Tijâniyya. Une confrérie musulmane à la conquête de l'Afrique*, edited by Jean-Louis Triaud and David Robinson, 35–68. Paris: Karthala, 2000.

El Hamel, Chouki. *Black Morocco, A History of Slavery, Race, and Islam*. Cambridge: Cambridge University Press, 2014.

El Hamel, Chouki. The Register of the Slaves of Sultan Mawlay Isma'il of Morocco at the Turn of the Eighteenth Century." *Journal of African History* 51, no. 2 (2010): 89–98.

El Hamel, Chouki. "Race' Slavery and Islam in Maghribi Mediterranean Thought: The Question of the Haratin in Morocco." *Journal of North African Studies* 7, no. 3 (2002): 29–52.

El Hamel, Chouki. "The Transmission of Knowledge in Moorish Society from the Rise of the Almoravids to the 19th Century." *Journal of Religion in Africa* 29, no. 1 (1999): 62–87.

Eltis, David. *Economic Growth and the Ending of the Transatlantic Slave Trade.* Oxford: Oxford University Press, 1987.

Ennaji, Mohammed. *Slavery, the State, and Islam.* Cambridge: Cambridge University Press, 2013.

Ennaji Mohammed. "Sur la repudiation (divorce) qui montre le statut de la femme était lié à l'esclavage" Tubman Seminar, York University, September 25, 2006.

Ennaji, Mohammed. *Soldats, Domestiques et concubines: L'Esclavage au Maroc au XIX siècle.* Paris: Balland 1994.

Ferreira, Roquinaldo. *Cross-Cultural Exchange in the Atlantic World, Angola and Brazil During the Era of the Slave Trade.* Cambridge: Cambridge University Press, 2012.

Fillitz, Thomas. "Uthmân dan Fodio et la question du pouvoir en pays haoussa." *Revue des Mondes Musulmans et de la Médeterranée* 91 (2000): 209–20.

Fisher, Humphrey J. *Slavery in the History of Muslim Black Africa.* New York: New York University Press, 2001.

Fisher, Humphrey J. "A Muslim William Wilberforce? The Sokoto Jihād as Anti-Slavery Crusade: An Enquiry into Historical Causes." *De la traite a l'esclavage du XVIII au XIVieme siècle: Actes du Colloque Internationale sur la traite des Noirs Nantes 1985,* edited by S. Daget, 537–55. Vol. 2. Paris L'Harmattan 1988.

Fodor, Pál. "Introduction." In *Ransom Slavery along the Ottoman Borders,* edited by Géza Dávid and Pál Fodor, XL-1. Leiden: Brill, 2007.

Fodor, Pál. "Maltese Pirates, Ottoman Captives and French Traders in the Early Seventeenth-Century Mediterranean." In *Ransom Slavery along the Ottoman Borders,* edited by Géza Dávid and Pál Fodor, 221–38. Leiden: Brill, 2007.

Fontenay, Michel. "Esclaves et/ou captifs: préciser les concepts." In *Le commerce des captifs: les intermédiares dans l'échange de le rachat des prisonniers en Méditerranée, XVe-XVIII siècle,* edited by Wolfgang Kaiser, 15–24. Rome: Ecole Rome 2008.

Fontenay, Michel. "Le maghreb barbaresque et l'esclavage méditerranéen au XVIè–XVIIè siècles." *Les Cahiers de Tunisie* XLIV (1991): 7–44.

Fontenay, Michel. "La place de la course dans l'économie portuare: l'example de Malte et des ports barbaresques" *Annales. Économies, Sociétés, Civilisations* 43, no. 6 (1988): 1321–347.

Freller, Thomas. "'The Shining of the Moon'—The Mediterranean Tour of Muhammad ibn Uthmān, Envoy of Morocco,in 1782." *Journal of Mediterranean Studies* 12, no. 2 (2002): 307–26.

Friedman, Ellen G. *Spanish Captives in North Africa and the Early Modern Age*. Madison: University of Wisconsin Press, 1983.

Friedman, Ellen G. "Christian Captives at 'Hard Labor' in Algiers, 16th to 18th Centuries." *International Journal of African Historical Studies* 13, no. 6 (1980): 616–32.

Fuglestad, Finn. "A Reconsideration of Hausa History before the Jihad." *Journal of African History* 19, no. 3 (1978): 219–29.

Ghazal, Amal N. "Debating Slavery and Abolition in the Arab Middle East." In *Slavery, Islam and Diaspora*, edited by Behnaz Mirzai, Ismael Montana, and Paul Lovejoy, 139–54. Trenton, NJ: Africa World Press, 2009.

Gershovich, Moshe. *French Military Rule in Morocco: Colonialism and its Consequences*. London: Frank Cass, 2000.

Gooding, Philip. "Islam in the Interior of Precolonial East Africa: Evidence from Lake Tanganyika." *Journal of African History* 60, no. 2 (2019): 191–208.

Gomez, Michael A. *African Dominion: A New History of Empire in Early and Medieval Africa*. Princeton, NJ: Princeton University Press, 2018.

Gomez, Michael A. *Pragmatism in the Age of Jihad.* Cambridge: Cambridge University Press, 1992.

Gómez-Rivas, Camilo. "Qāḍī 'Iyāḍ (d. 544/1149)." In *Islamic Legal Thought, A Compendium of Muslims Jurists*, edited by Oussama Arabi et al., 323–38. Leiden: Brill 2013.

Gordon, David M. "Slavery and Redemption in the Catholic Missions of the Upper Congo, 1878–1909." *Slavery & Abolition* 38, no. 3 (2017): 577–600.

Gozalo, Maximiliano Barrio. *Esclavos y cautivos: Conflicto entre la cristiandad y islam en el siglo XVIII*. Valladolid: Servicio de Publicaciones de la Junta de Castilla y León, 2006.

Greene, Molly. "Beyond the Northern Invasion: The Mediterranean in the Seventeenth Century." *Past & Present* 174 (2002): 42–71.

Greene, Sandra E. *Slave Owners of West Africa: Decision Making in the Age of Abolition*. Bloomington: Indiana University Press, 2017.

Greene, Sandra E. "Minority Voices: Abolitionism in West Africa." *Slavery & Abolition* 36, no. 4 (2015): 642–61.

Gwandu, Abdullahi A. "A Pragmatic Administrator's Approach to Fiqh—The Case of Amir al-Mu'minin Muhammad Bello." Seminar on the Life and Ideas of Amir-al-Mu'minun Muhammad Bello, Centre for Islamic Studies, University of Sokoto April 15–18 1985, Conference Proceedings.

Haefeli, Evan. "A Note on the Use of North American Borderlands." *American Historical Review* 104, no. 4 (1999): 1222–25.

Haïdara, Ismael Diadié. *Jawdar Pasha et la conquête Saâdienne du Songhay (1591–1599)*. Rabat: Institut des Etudes Africaines, 1996.

Hall, Bruce S. *A History of Race in Muslim West Africa, 1600–1960*. Cambridge: Cambridge University Press, 2011.

Hall, Bruce S. "The Question of 'Race' in Pre-colonial Southern Sahara." *Journal of North African Studies* 10, no. 3–4 (2005): 339–67.

Hall, Bruce S., and Charles C. Stewart, "The Historic 'Core Curriculum' and the Book Market in Islamic West Africa." In *The Trans-Saharan Book Trade: Manuscript Culture, Arabic Literacy and Intellectual History in Muslim Africa*, edited by Graziano Krätli and Ghislaine Lydon, 109–74. Leiden: Brill, 2011.

Hallaq, Wael B. *The Origins and Evolution of Islamic Law*. Cambridge: Cambridge University Press, 2005.

Hamani, Djibo. *L'Islam au Soudan Central: Histoire de l'Islam au Niger de VIIe au XIXe siècle*. Paris: L'Harmattan, 2007.

Hamman, Mahmoud. *The Middle Benue Region and the Sokoto Jihad, 1812–1869*. Kaduna: Ahmadu Bello University Press, 2007.

Hanson, John. *Migration, Jihad, and Muslim Authority in West Africa*. Bloomington: University of Indiana Press, 1996.

Hanson, John. "Islam, Migration and the Political Economy of Meaning: Fergo Nioro from the Senegal River Valley, 1862–1890." *Journal of African History* 35, no. 1 (1994): 37–60.

Hanson, John. "Historical Writing in Nineteenth Century Segu: A Critical Analysis of an Anonymous Arabic Chronicle." *History in Africa* 12 (1985): 101–15.

Hasad, Talal. *The Idea of an Anthropology of Islam*. Washington DC: Center for Contemporary Arab Studies Georgetown University, 1986.

Hershenzon, Daniel. "'[P]ara que me saque cabesea por cabasa . . .': Exchanging Muslim and Christian Slaves across the western Mediterranean." *African Economic History* 42 (2014): 11–36.

Hiribarren, Vincent. *A History of Borno: Trans-Saharan African Empire to Failing Nigerian State*. London: Hurst & Company, 2017.

Hiskett, Mervyn. *The Sword of Truth: The Life and Times of the Shehu Usuman dan Fodio*. New York: Oxford University Press, 1973.

Hiskett, Mervyn. "An Islamic Tradition of Reform in the Western Sudan from the Sixteenth to the Eighteenth Century" *Bulletin of the School of Oriental and African Studies* 25, no. 1/3 (1962): 577–96.

Hodges, Anthony. *Historical Dictionary of the Western Sahara*. London: Scarecrow, 1982.

Hopkins, A. G. *An Economic History of West Africa*. New York: Longman, 1973.

Hoexter, Miriam. *Endowments, Rulers and Community, Waaqf al Haramayn in Ottoman Algiers*. Leiden: Brill, 1998.

Holmes, L. "Tieba Traore, Fama of Kenedougou: Two Decades of Political Development," PhD diss., University of California, Berkeley, 1977.

Horden, Peregrine. "Situations Both Alike? Connectivity, the Mediterranean, the Sahara." In *Saharan Frontiers: Space and Mobility in Northwest Africa*, edited by James McDougall and Judith Scheele, 25–38. Bloomington: Indiana University Press, 2012.

Hubbell, Andrew. "A View of the Slave Trade from the Margin: Souroudougou in the late Nineteenth-Century Slave Trade of the Niger Bend." *Journal of African History* 42, no. 1 (2001): 25–47.

Humphreys, Sara and Dauda Moses, Jiddere Kaibo and Máiréad Dunne "Counted In and Being Out: Fluctuations in Primary School Attendance in northern Nigeria," *International Journal of Educational Development* 44 (2015): 134–43.

Hunt, Nancy Rose. "The Affective, the Intellectual and Gender History." *Journal of African History* 55, no. 3 (2014): 331–45.

Hunwick, John. "Islamic Law and Polemics over Race and Slavery in North and West Africa (16th -19th Century)." In *Slavery in the Middle East* edited by Shaun E. Marmon, 43–68. Princeton NJ: Markus Weiner, 1999.

Hunwick, John. "Secular Power and Religious Authority in Muslim Society: The Case of Songhay." *Journal of African History* 37 no 2 (1996): 175–94.

Hunwick, John, ed. *Arabic Literature of Africa*. Vol. 2: *The Writings of Central Sudanic Africa*. Leiden: Brill, 1995.

Hunwick, John. "Al- Maghīlī and the Jews of Tuwāt: The Demise of a Community." *Studia Islamaica* 61 (1985): 155–83.

Idrissa. Kimba. "Guerres et societés: Les populations du "Niger" Occidental au XIX siècle et leurs reactions face à la colonizations 1896–1906." PhD diss., Université de Paris VII, 1979.

Ismail, U. S. A., and A. Y. Aliyu. "Muhammad Bello and the Tradition of Manuals of Islamic Government and Advice to Rulers." *Nigerian Administration Research Project: Second Interim Report* (Zaria: 1975). Reprinted in Uthman Sayyid Ahmad Ismail al-Bili, eds., *Some Aspects of Islam in Africa*, 65–102. Reading UK: Ithaca, 2008.

Jah, Omar. "The Effect of Pilgrimage on the Jihād of Al-Hajj 'Umar al-Futi, 1794–1864." In *The Central Bilād al-Sūdān: Tradition and Adaptation,* edited by Yusuf Fadl Hasan and Paul Doornbos, 233–43. Khartoum: University of Khartoum Press, 1979.

Jah, Omar. "Al-Hajj 'Umar al-Fūtī's Philosophy of Jihad and its Sufi Basis" PhD diss., McGill University, 1973.

Jean-Baptiste, Rachel. *Conjugal Rights: Marriage, Sexuality and Urban Life in Libreville Colonial Gabon*. Athens: Ohio University Press, 2014.

Jennings, Lawrence. *French Anti-Slavery: The Movement for the Abolition of Slavery in France 1802–1848*. Cambridge: Cambridge University Press, 2000.

Johnston, H. A. S. *The Fulani Empire of Sokoto*. London: Oxford University Press, 1967.

Ka al Habib, Thierno. "Cheikh el-Hadj Omar Foutiyyu Tall (1794–1864) Ses etudes et sa formation." In *Bicentenaire de la naissance du Cheikh el hadj Oumar al-Futi Tall 1797–1998*, 103–125. Rabat: Publications de l'Institut des Etudes Africaines, 2001.

Kaba, Lansiné. "Islam, Society and Politics in Pre-Colonial Baté, Guinea," *Bulletin de l'IFAN*, series B, 35, no. 2 (1973): 323–44.

Kaiser, Wolfgang. "Zones de transit. Lieux, temps, modalités du rachat de captifs en Méditeranneé." In *Les Musulmans dans l'histoire de l'Europe*. Vol. 2: *Passages et contacts en Méditerranée*, edited by Jocelyne Dakhlia and Wolfgang Kaiser, 251–72. Paris: Albin Michel, 2013.

Kaiser Wolfgang, ed. *Le commerce des captifs: les intermédiares dan l'échange et le rachat des prisonniers en Méditerranée, XVe-XVIIIe siècle*. Rome: Ecole Rome, 2008.

Kaiser, Wolfgang. "L'économie de la rançon en Méditerranée occidentale (XVIe-XVIIe siècle)." In *Ricchezza dal mare, secc XIII-XVIII*, edited by Simonetta Cavaciocchi. 689–701. Vol. 2. Florence: Le Monnier 2006.

Kaiser, Wolfgang, and Guillaume Calafat. "The Economy of Ransoming in the Early Modern Mediterranean: A Form of Cross-Cultural Trade between Southern Europe and the Maghreb (Sixteenth to Eighteenth Centuries)." In *Religion and Trade: Cross-Cultural Exchanges in World History, 1000–1900*, edited by Francesca Trivellato, et al., 108–31. Oxford: Oxford University Press, 2014.

Kamara, Muusa. *Florilège au jardin de l'histoire des noirs, Zuhūr al-Basātīn: l'aristocraties peule et la revolution des clercs musulmans, vallée du Sénégal*, edited by Jean Schmitz and translated by Saïd Bousbina. Paris: Centre National de Recherche Scientifique, 1998.

Kane, Ousmane Oumar. *Beyond Timbuktu: An Intellectual History of Muslim West Africa* Cambridge, MA: Harvard University Press, 2016.

Kariya, Kota. "Free Choice Theory and the Justification of Enslavement in the Early Sokoto Caliphate," *Islamic Africa* (2020): 1–41.

Kassim, Abdulbasit. "Defining and Understanding the Religious Philosophy of Jihādī-Salafism and the Ideology of Boko Haram." *Politics, Religion and Ideology* 16, no. 2/3 (2015): 173–200.

Khani, Muhammad Ahmad. *The Intellectual Origin of Sokoto Jihad*. Ibadan: Iman, 1984.

Khoury, Raif Georges. "Wahb b. Munabbih." In *The Encyclopedia of Islam*. CD-ROM Edition V.I.I. Leiden: Brill, 2001.

Konaré, Alpha O. *Sikasso Tata*. Bamako: Editions Imprimerie du Mali, 1983.

Klein, Martin. *Slavery and Colonial Rule in French West Africa*. Cambridge: Cambridge University Press, 1998.

Klein, Martin. "The Slave Trade in the Western Sudan during the Nineteenth Century." In *The Human Commodity*, edited by Elizabeth Savage, 39–60. Philadelphia: Routledge: 1992.

Klein, Martin. "The Impact of the Atlantic Slave Trade on the Societies of the Western Sudan. " *Social Science History* 14, no. 2 (1990): 241–44.

Klein, Martin. "Women in Slavery in the Western Sudan." In *Women and Slavery in Africa*, edited by Claire Robertson and Martin A. Klein, 67–88. Madison: University of Wisconsin Press, 1983.

Klein, Martin. "Social and Economic Factors in the Muslim Revolution in Senegambia." *Journal of African History* 13, no. 2 (1972): 419–41.

Krätli, Graziano, and Ghislaine Lydon, eds. *The Trans-Saharan Book Trade: Manuscript Culture, Arabic Literacy and Intellectual History in Muslim Africa*. Leiden: Brill 2011.

Kumar, Dharma. "Colonialism, Bondage and Caste in British India." In *Breaking the Chains: Slavery, Bondage and Emancipation in Modern Africa and Asia*, edited by Martin Klein, 112–30. Madison: University of Wisconsin Press 1993.

Lambert, Frank. *The Barbary Wars: American Independence in the Atlantic World.* New York: Hill and Wang, 2005.

Landers, Jane. *Atlantic Creoles in the Age of Revolutions*. Cambridge, MA: Harvard University Press, 2011.

Larquie, Claude. "La Méditerrannée, l'Espagne et le Maghreb au XVIIe siècle: le rachat des chrétiens et le commerce des hommes." *Les Cahiers de Tunisie* (1991): 75–90.

Last, Murray. "The Book and the Nature of Knowledge in Muslim Northern Nigeria 1457–2007." In *The Trans-Saharan Book Trade: Manuscript Culture, Arabic Literacy and Intellectual History in Muslim Africa*, edited by Graziano Krätli and Ghislaine Lydon, 175–210. Leiden: Brill, 2011.

Last, Murray. "The Book in the Sokoto Caliphate." In *The Meaning of Timbuktu*, edited by Shamil Jeppie and Souleymane Bachir Diagne, 135–63. Cape Town: HSRC, 2008.

Last, Murray. "1903 Revisited" In *Northern Nigeria: A Century of Transformation, 1903–2003*, edited by A. M. Yakubu, I. M. Jumare, and A. G. Saeed, 61–94. Kaduna: Arewa House Ahmadu Bello University, 2005.

Last, Murray. "Towards a Political History of Youth in Muslim Northern Nigeria `1750–2000" Conference Paper, ASC Leiden April 24, 2003.

Last, Murray. "Reform in West Africa: The Jihad Movements of the Nineteenth Century." *History of West Africa*, edited by Jacob Ajayi and Michael Crowder, 1–29. Vol. 2. New York: Longman, 1985.

Last, Murray. *The Sokoto Caliphate*. London: Longmans, Green, 1967.

Launay, Robert. "An Invisible Religion? Anthropology's Avoidance of Islam in Africa" In *African Anthropologies: History, Critique, and Practice*, edited by Mwenda Ntarangwi et al., 188–203. London: Zed, 2006.

Law, Robin. "Legal and Illegal Enslavement in West Africa in the Context of the Trans-Atlantic Slave Trade." In *Ghana in Africa and the World: Essays in Honor of Adu Boahen*, edited by Toyin Falola, 513–33. Trenton NJ: Africa World Press, 2003.

Law, Robin. *The Horse in West African History*. Oxford, Oxford University Press, 1980.

Leblon, Anaïs. "Pasteurs marginalisés et/ou djihadistes: représentations des Fulbe dans le traitement médiatique de la crise au centre de Mali (2015-juin 2017)." In *Identités sahéliennes en temps de crise. Histoire, enjeux et perspectives*, edited by Baz Lecocq and Amy Niang, 93–133. Munster: Lit Verlag, 2019.

Levtzion, Nehemia. "The Eighteenth Century Background to the Islamic Revolutions in West Africa." In *Eighteenth Century Renewal and Reform in Islam*, edited by Nehemia Levitzion and John O Voll, 21–38. Syracuse NY: Syracuse University Press, 1987.

Lewis, Bernard. *Race and Slavery in the Middle East*. Oxford: Oxford University Press, 1992.

Linares, Olga F. "Deferring to Trade in Slaves: The Jola of Casamance, Senegal in Historical Perspective." *History in Africa* 14 (1987): 113–39.

Lofkrantz, Jennifer. "Intellectual Traditions, Education and Jihad: The (Non) Parallels between the Sokoto and Boko Haram Jihads." *Journal of West African History* 4, no. 1 (2018): 75–98.

Lofkrantz, Jennifer. "Intellectual Discourse in the Sokoto Caliphate: The Triumvirate's Opinions on the Issue of Ransoming, ca 1810." *International Journal of African Historical Studies* 45, no. 3 (2012): 385–401.

Lofkrantz, Jennifer. "Protecting Freeborn Muslims: The Sokoto Caliphate's Attempts to Prevent Illegal Enslavement and its Acceptance of the Strategy of Ransoming." *Slavery & Abolition* 32, no. 1 (2011): 109–27.

Lofkrantz, Jennifer. "Ransoming Captives in the Sokoto Caliphate." In *Slavery, Islam, and Diaspora*, edited by Behnaz Mirzai, Ismael Montana, and Paul Lovejoy, 115–27. Trenton, NJ: Africa World Press, 2009.

Lofkrantz, Jennifer. "Ransoming Policies and Practices in the Western and Central Bilād al-Sūdān c 1800–1910." PhD diss., York University, 2008.

Lofkrantz, Jennifer, and Paul Lovejoy. "Maintaining Network Boundaries: Islamic Law and Commerce from Sahara to Guinea Shores." *Slavery & Abolition* 36, no. 2 (2015): 211–32.

Lofkrantz, Jennifer, and Olatunji Ojo. "Slavery, Freedom and Failed Ransom Negotiations in West Africa, 1730–1900." *Journal of African History* 53, no. 1 (2012): 25–44.

Loimeier, Roman. *Muslim Societies in Africa: A Historical Anthropology*. Bloomington: Indiana University Press, 2013.

Loimeier, Roman. "Boko Haram: The Development of a Militant Religious Movement in Nigeria." *Africa Spectrum* 47, no. 2/3 (2012): 137–55.

Loimeier, Roman. *Between Social Skills and Marketable Skills: The Politics of Islamic Education in 20th Century Zanzibar*. Leiden: Brill, 2009.

Loimeier, Roman. *Islamic Reform and Political Change in Northern Nigeria*. Evanston IL: Northwestern University Press, 1997.

Lovejoy, Paul. *Jihād in West Africa during the Age of Revolutions*. Athens: Ohio University Press, 2016.

Lovejoy, Paul. *Transformations in Slavery, A History of Slavery in Africa*. 3rd ed. Cambridge: Cambridge University Press, 2012.

Lovejoy, Paul. "Internal Markets or an Atlantic-Sahara Divide? How Women Fit into the Slave Trade of West Africa." In *Women and Slavery*. Vol 1: *Africa, the Indian Ocean World, and the Medieval North Atlantic*, edited by Gwyn Campbell, Suzanne Miers, and Joseph C. Miller, 259–79. Athens: Ohio University Press, 2007.

Lovejoy, Paul. "The Context of Enslavement in West Africa: Aḥmad Bābā and the Ethics of Slavery" In *Slaves, Subjects and Subversives: Blacks in Colonial Latin America* edited by Jane Landers and Barry M. Robinson, 9–38. Albuquerque: University of New Mexico Press, 2006.

Lovejoy, Paul. "Biographies of Enslaved Muslims from the Central Sudan in the Nineteenth Century." In *The Sokoto Caliphate: History and Legacies, 1804–2004*, edited by M Yakubu, 187–216. Vol. 1. Kaduna: Arewa House, 2006.

Lovejoy, Paul. *Slavery Commerce and Production: Essays in the Social and Economic History of the Central Sudan*. Trenton, NJ: Africa World Press, 2005.

Lovejoy, Paul. "The Bello-Clapperton Exchange: The Sokoto Jihad and the Transatlantic Slave Trade." In *The Desert Shore: Literatures of the Sahel*, edited by Christopher Wise, 201–29. Boulder, CO: Lynne Reinner, 2001.

Lovejoy, Paul. "Murgu: The Wages of Slavery in the Sokoto Caliphate." *Slavery & Abolition* 14 (1993): 168–85.

Lovejoy, Paul. *Salt of the Desert Sun*. Cambridge: Cambridge University Press, 1986.

Lovejoy, Paul. "Slavery in the Sokoto Caliphate." In *The Ideology of Slavery in Africa*, edited by Paul Lovejoy, 11–38. Beverly Hills: SAGE, 1981.

Lovejoy, Paul. *Caravans of Kola: The Hausa Kola Trade 1700*–1900. Zaria: Ahmadu Bello University Press, 1980.

Lovejoy, Paul. "The Characteristics of Plantations in Nineteenth-Century Sokoto Caliphate." *American Historical Review* 84 (1979): 1267–292.

Lovejoy, Paul, and Stephen Baier. "The Desert-Side Economy of the Central Sudan." *International Journal of African Historical Studies* 8, no. 4 (1975): 551–81.

Lovejoy, Paul, and Jan Hogendorn. *Slow Death for Slavery, The Course of Abolition in Northern Nigeria, 1897–1936*. Cambridge: Cambridge University Press, 1993.

Lovejoy, Paul, and David Richardson. "Anglo-Efik Relations and Protection against Illegal Enslavement at Old Calabar, 1740–1807." In *Fighting the Slave Trade, West African Strategies*, edited by Sylviane Diouf, 101–20. Athens: Ohio University Press, 2003.

Lovejoy, Paul, and David Richardson. "'This Horrid Hole': Royal Authority, Commerce and Credit at Bonny, 1690–1840." *The Journal of African History* 43, no. 2 (2002): 363–92.

Lovejoy, Paul, and David Richardson. "Competing Markets for Male and Female Slaves: Prices in the Interior of West Africa 1780–1850." *The International Journal of African Historical Studies* 28, no. 2 (1995): 261–93.

Ly-Tall, M. "Massina and the Torodbe (Tukuloor) Empire until 1878." In *Africa in the Nineteenth Century until the 1880s*. Vol. 6 of *General History of Africa*, edited by J. F. Ade Ajayi, 600–635. New York: UNESCO, 1989.

Lydon, Ghislaine. *On-Trans-Saharan Trails: Islamic Law, Trade Networks, and Cross-Cultural Exchange in Nineteenth-Century Western Africa*. Cambridge: Cambridge University Press, 2009.

Lydon, Ghislaine, "Slavery, Exchange and Islamic Law; A Glimpse from the Archives of Mali and Mauritania." *African Economic History* 33 (2005): 117–48.

Mack, Beverly, and Jean Boyd. *One Woman's Jihad: Nana Asma'u, Scholar and Scribe*. Bloomington: Indiana University Press, 2000.

Maïga, Haroun Almahadi. "Letter Writing between West and North Africa." In *Saharan Crossroads: Exploring Historical, Cultural, and Artistic Linkages*, edited by Tara F. Deubel et al., 333–52. Newcastle: Cambridge Scholars, 2014.

Mahadi, Abdullahi. "State and the Economy: The Sarauta System and its Roles in Shaping the Society and Economy of Kano with Particular Reference to the 18th and 19th Centuries." PhD diss., Ahmadu Bello University, 1982.

Mann, Kristin. *Slavery and the Birth of an African City: Lagos, 1760–1900*. Bloomington: University of Indiana Press, 2007.

Manning, Patrick. *Slavery and African Life: Occidental, Oriental, and African Slave Trades*. Cambridge: Cambridge University Press, 1990.

Mansour, Mansour H. *The Maliki School of Law: Spread and Domination in North and West Africa 8th to 14th Centuries C.E.* London: Austin & Winfield, 1995.

Martin, B. G. *Muslim Brotherhoods in 19th Century Africa*. New York: Cambridge University Press, 1976.

Martínez Torres, José Antonio. *Prisioneros de los infieles: vida y rescate de lost cautivos cristianos en el Mediterráneo musulmán (siglos XVI-XVII)*. Barcelona, 2004.

Masquelier, Adeline. *Women and Islamic Revival in a West African Town*. Bloomington: Indiana University Press, 2009.

Matar, Nabil. *British Captives from the Mediterranean to the Atlantic, 1563–1760*. Leiden: Brill, 2014.

Matar, Nabil. "Piracy and Captivity in the Early Modern Mediterranean: The Perspective from Barbary." In *Pirates? The Politics of Plunder, 1550–1650*, edited by Claire Jowitt. 56–73. New York: Palgrave Macmillan, 2007.

Matar, Nabil. *Britain and Barbary, 1589–1689*. Gainesville: University of Florida Press, 2005.

Matar, Nabil. "Introduction: England and Mediterranean Captivity, 1577–1704." In *Piracy, Slavery and Redemption, Barbary Captivity Narratives from Early Modern England*, edited by Daniel J. Vitkus, 1–54. New York: Columbia University Press, 2001.

Mazur, Peter. "Combatting 'Mohammedan Indecency': The Baptism of Muslim Slaves in Spanish Naples, 1563–1667." *Journal of Early Modern History*, 13 (2009): 25–48.

McDougall, E. Ann. "On Being Saharan." In *Saharan Frontiers: Space and Mobility in Northwest Africa*, edited by James McDougall and Judith Scheele, 25–58. Bloomington: Indiana University Press, 2012.

McDougall, E. Ann. "Conceptualizing the Sahara: The World of Nineteenth-Century Beyrouk Commerce." *The Journal of North African Studies* 10, no. 3/4 (2005): 369–86.

McDougall, E. Ann. "Discourse and Distortion: Critical Reflections on the Historiography of the Saharan Slave Trade." *Outre-Mers: Revue d'Histoire* 336/337 (2002): 87–101.

McDougall, James. "Frontiers, Borderlands, and Saharan/World History." In *Saharan Frontiers: Space and Mobility in Northwest Africa*, edited by James McDougall and Judith Scheele, 73–93. Bloomington: Indiana University Press, 2012.

McMahon, Elisabeth. *Slavery and Emancipation in Islamic East Africa: From Honor to Respectability*. Cambridge: Cambridge University Press, 2013.

Meillassoux, Claude. *The Anthropology of Slavery: The Womb of Iron and Gold*. Translated by Alide Dasnois. Chicago: University of Chicago Press, 1991.

Meillassoux, Claude. "Female Slavery." In *Women and Slavery in Africa* edited by Claire Robertson and Martin A Klein, 49–66. Madison: University of Wisconsin Press, 1983.

Messick, Brinkley. *The Calligraphic State, Textual Domination and History in a Muslim Society*. Berkeley: University of California Press, 1993.

Miege, Jean-Louis. "Le commerce trans-saharien au XIXe siècle: Essai de quantification," *Revue de l'Occident Musulman et de la Méditerranée* 32, no. 2 (1981): 93–119.

Miers, Suzanne, and Igor Kopytoff. "Introduction." In *Slavery in Africa*, edited by Suzanne Miers and Igor Kopytoff, 3–84. Madison: University of Wisconsin Press, 1977.

Minna, M. T. M. "Succession and Legitimacy: The Leadership Crisis and Intellectual Dispute between Abdullahi b. Fodio and Muhammad Bello." Seminar on the Life and Ideas of Amir-al-Mu'minun Muhammad Bello, Center for Islamic Studies, University of Sokoto, Conference proceedings, April 15–18, 1985.

Mohamed, Mohamed Hassan. *Between Caravan and Sultan: The Bayruk of Southern Morocco: A Study in History and Identity*. Leiden: Brill, 2012.

Montana, Ismael. "The Trans-Saharan Slave Trade in the Context of Tunisian foreign trade in the western Mediterranean." *The Journal of North African Studies* 20, no. 1 (2015): 27–41.

Montana, Ismael. *The Abolition of Slavery in Ottoman Tunisia.* Gainesville: University of Florida Press, 2013.

Monteil, Vincent. *L'Islam noir.* Paris: Le Seuil, 1980.

Naylor, Paul. *From Rebels to Rulers: Writing Legitimacy in the Early Sokoto State.* Suffolk, UK: James Currey, 2021.

Naylor, Paul, and Marion Wallace "Author of this own Fate?" The Eighteenth-Century Writings of Ayuba Sulayman Diallo." *Journal of African History* 60, no. 3 (2019): 343–77.

Newson, Linda. "Africans and Luso-Africans in the Portuguese Slave Trade on the Upper Guinea Coast in the Early Seventeenth Century." *Journal of African History* 53, no. 1 (2012): 1–24.

Niang, Amy. "Deferred Reciprocity: Historical and Theoretical Perspectives on Ransoming and the Ethics of Compensatory Justice." In *Ransoming, Captivity, and Piracy in Africa and the Mediterranean*, edited by Jennifer Lofkrantz and Olatunji Ojo, 229–57. Trenton, NJ: Africa World Press, 2016.

Niang, Amy. "The Political Economy of Ransoming in the Sahel: The History, the Ethics and the Practice." *African Economic History* 42 (2014): 157–82.

Nicolas, Guy. "Détours d'une conversion collective. Ouverture à l'Islam d'un bastion soudanais de résistance à une guerre sainte." *Archives de sciences sociales des religions* 48, no. 1 (1979): 83–105.

Nobili, Mauro. *Sultan, Caliph, and the Renewer of the Faith: Aḥmad Lobbo, the Tarīkh al-fattāsh, and the Making of an Islamic State in West Africa.* Cambridge: Cambridge University Press, 2020.

Nobili, Mauro. "A Propaganda Document in Support of the 19th Century Caliphate of Ḥamdallāhi: Nuḥ b. al-Ṭahir al-Fulānī's 'Letter on the Appearance of the Twelfth Caliph' (Risāla fī ẓuhūr al-khalīfa al-thānī 'ahar) *Institut des Mondes Africains* 7, no. 7 (2016). https://journals.openedition.org/afriques/1922

Norris, H. T. *The Arab Conquest of the Western Sahara: Studies of the Historical Events, Religious Beliefs and Social Customs which Made the Remotest Sahara a Part of the Arab World.* London: Longman, 1986.

Nwokeji, G. Ugo. *The Slave Trade and Culture in the Bight of Biafra: An African Society in the Atlantic World.* Cambridge: Cambridge University Press, 2010.

O'Brien, Donal B. Cruise. "La filière musulmane: confréries soufies et politique en Afrique noire." *Politique africaine* 1, no. 4 (1981): 7–30.

O'Hear, Ann. *Power Relations in Nigeria: Ilorin Slaves and their Successors.* Rochester: University of Rochester Press, 1997.

Ochonu, Moses. "Caliphate Expansion and Sociopolitical Change in Nineteenth-Century Lower Benue Hinterlands." *Journal of West African History* 1, no. 1 (2015): 133–76.

Ojo, Olatunji. "White Captives and the Political Economy of Ransoming in Asante, 1869–1864." *African Economic History* 42 (2014): 109–36.

Ojo, Olatunji. "The Atlantic Slave Trade and Local Ethics of Slavery in Yorubaland." *African Economic History* 41 (2013): 73–100.

Ojo, Olatunji. "The Business of 'Trust' and the Enslavement of Yoruba Women and Children for Debt." In *Debt and Slavery in the Mediterranean and Atlantic Worlds*, edited by Gwyn Campbell and Alessando Stanziana, 77–92. London: Pickering & Chatto, 2013.

Ojo, Olatunji. "'[I]n Search of their Relations: To Set at Liberty as Many as they Had the Means': Ransoming Captives in Nineteenth Century Yorubaland." *Nordic Journal of African Studies* 19, no. 1 (2010): 58–76.

Ojo, Olatunji, and Jennifer Lofkrantz. "West African Responses to Illegal Enslavement and Failed Ransom Negotiations." In *Ransoming, Captivity, and Piracy in Africa and the Mediterranean*, edited by Jennifer Lofkrantz and Olatunji Ojo, 81–96. Trenton, NJ: Africa World Press, 2016.

Oloruntimehin, B. O. *The Segu Tukolor Empire*. London: Longman, 1972.

Osborn, Emily. *Our New Husbands Are Here: Households, Gender, and Politics in a West African State from the Slave Trade to Colonial Rule*. Athens: Ohio University Press, 2011.

Palais, James. *Confucian Statecraft and Korean Institutions*. Seattle: University of Washington Press, 1996.

Panzac, Daniel. *Les corsaires barbaresques, la fin d'une épopée 1800–1820*. Paris: CNRS Éditions, 1999.

Parker, Richard B. *Uncle Sam in Barbary: A Diplomatic History*. Gainesville: University Press of Florida, 2004.

Patterson, Orlando. *Slavery and Social Death, A Comparative Study*. Cambridge, MA: Harvard University Press, 1982.

Patton, A. Jr. "An Islamic Frontier Polity: The Ningi Mountains of Northern Nigeria, 1846–1902." In *The African Frontier*, edited by Igor Kopytoff, 193–213. Bloomington: Indiana University Press, 1987.

Pelckmans, Lotte. "Stereotypes of Past-Slavery and 'Stereo-styles' in Post-Slavery: A Multidimensional Interactionist Perspective on Contemporary Hierarchies." *The International Journal of African Studies* 48, no. 2 (2015): 281–301.

Pennell, C. R. *Morocco since 1830: A History*. New York: New York University Press, 2000.

Perinbam, Marie. "The Julas in Western Sudanese History: Long-Distance Traders and Developers of Resources." In *West African Cultural Dynamics: Archaeological and Historical Perspectives*, edited by B. K. Swartz and R. Dumet, 455–76. The Hague: Mouton, 1980.

Person, Yves. *Samori: Une Revolution Dyula*. Dakar: IFAN, 1968–1975.

Reese, Scott S. "Islam in Africa/Africans and Islam." *The Journal of African History* 55, no. 1 (2014): 17–26.

Reese, Scott S. "Introduction: Islam in Africa: Challenging the Perceived Wisdom," In *The Transmission of Learning in Islamic Africa*, edited by Scott S. Reese, 1–14. Leiden: Brill, 2004.

Reichmuth, Stefan. "Murtadā al-Zabīdī (1732–91) and the Africans: Islamic Discourse and Scholarly Networks in the Late Eighteenth Century." In *The Transmission of Learning in Islamic Africa*, edited by Scott S. Reese, 121–54. Leiden: Brill, 2004.

Reid, Richard. *War in Pre-Colonial Eastern Africa*. Athens: Ohio University Press, 2007.

Reynolds, Jonathan. "Good and Bad Muslims: Islam and Indirect Rule in Northern Nigeria." *International Journal of African Historical Studies* 34, no. 3 (2001): 601–18.

Richardson, David. "Shipboard Revolts, African Authority and the Atlantic Slave Trade." *William & Mary Quarterly* 58, no. 1 (2001): 69–92.

Roberts, Priscilla H., and James N. Tull. "Moroccan Sultan Muhammad Ibn Abdallah's Diplomatic Initiatives toward the United States, 1777–786." *Proceedings of the American Philosophical Society* 143, no. 2 (1999): 233–65.

Roberts, Richard. *Warriors, Merchants, and Slaves: The State of the Economy of the Middle Niger Valley 1700–1914*. Stanford: Stanford University Press, 1987.

Roberts, Richard, and Martin Klein. "The Banamba Slave Exodus of 1905 and the Decline of Slavery in the Western Sudan." *The Journal of African History* 21, no. 3 (1980): 375–94.

Roberts, Richard, and Benjamin Lawrence, eds. *Trafficking in Slavery's Wake: Law and the Experience of Women & Children in Africa*. Athens: Ohio University Press, 2012.

Robinson, David. "Breaking New Ground in 'Pagan' and 'Muslim' West Africa." *Canadian Journal of African Studies* 42, no. 2–3 (2013): 300–313.

Robinson, David. "Jihad, *Hijra*, and Hajj in West Africa." In *Just Wars, Holy Wars, and Jihads: Christian, Jewish, and Muslim Encounters and Exchanges*, edited by Sohail H. Hashmi, 246–62. Oxford: Oxford University Press, 2012.

Robinson, David. "The Chronicle of the Succession': An Important Document for the Umarian State." *The Journal of African History* 31, no. 2 (1990): 245–62.

Robinson, David. "The Umar Emigration of the Late 19th Century." *International Journal of African Historical Studies* 20, no. 2 (1987): 245–70.

Robinson, David. *The Holy War of Umar Tal: The Western Sudan in the Mid-Nineteenth Century*. Oxford: Clarendon, 1985.

Robinson, David. "The Islamic Revolution of Futa Toro." *The International Journal of African Historical Studies* 8, no. 2 (1975): 185–221.

Robinson, David. "Abdul Qadir and Shaykh Umar: A Continuing Tradition of Islamic Leadership in Futa Toro." *International Journal of African Historical Studies* 6, no. 2 (1973): 286–303.

Rodet, Marie. "Escaping Slavery and Building Diasporic Communities in French Soudan and Senegal ca 1880–1940." *International Journal of African Historical Studies* 48, no. 2 (2015): 363–86.

Rodet, Marie. "Islam, pluralisme juridique et relations de genre dans les "tribunaux indigènes du Soudan Français 1900–1925." *Outre-Mers. Revue d'histoire* 99, no. 370/371 (2011): 173–83.

Rodet, Marie. "Mémoires de l'esclavage dans la region de Kayes, histoire d'une disparition." *Cahiers d'Ètudes Africains* 50, no. 197 (2010): 263–91.

Rodet, Marie. *Les migrants ignorés du Haut-Sénégal (1900–1946)*. Paris: Karthala, 2009.

Rodet, Marie. "Migrants in French Sudan: Gender Biases in the Historiography." In *Trans-Atlantic Migration: The Paradoxes of Exile* edited by Toyin Falola and Niyi Afolabi, 165–82. New York: Routledge, 2007.

Rossi, Benedetta. *From Slavery to Aid: Politics, Labour and Ecology in the Nigerien Sahel.* Cambridge: Cambridge University Press, 2015.

Rossi, Benedetta, ed. *Reconfiguring Slavery: West African Trajectories*. Liverpool: Liverpool University Press, 2009.

Rothman, E. Natalie. "Becoming Venetian: Conversion and Transformation in the Seventeenth-Century Mediterranean." *Mediterranean Historical Review* 21, no. 1 (2006): 39–75.

Rudt de Collenberg, Wipertus H. *Esclavage et rançons des chrétiens en Méditerranée (1570–1600)*. Paris: Éditions le léopard d'or, 1997.

Ryan, Patrick J. "The Mystical Theology of Tijānī Sufism and its Social Significance in West Africa." *Journal of Religion in Africa* 30, no. 2 (2000): 208–44.

Saad, Elias N. *Social History of Timbuktu: The Role of Muslim Scholars and Notables 1400–1900.* Cambridge: Cambridge University Press, 1983.

Saidu, Garba. "The Significance of the Shehu's Sermons and Poems in Ajami." In *Studies in the History of the Sokoto Caliphate: The Sokoto Seminar Papers*. Edited by Y.B Usman., 195–216. Zaria: Ahmadu Bello University, 1979.

Salau, Mohammed Bashir. *The West African Slave Plantation: A Case Study.* New York: Palgrave Macmillan, 2011.

Salau, Mohammed Bashir. "Ribats and the Development of Plantations in the Sokoto Caliphate: A Case Study of Fanisau." *African Economic History* 34 (2006): 23–43.

Salifou, André. "Colonisation et sociétés indigènes au Niger de la fin du XIXe siècle au debut de la deuxieme guerre mondiale." PhD diss., Université de Toulouse-Le Mirail, 1977.

Salifou. André. *Le Damagram ou Sultanat de Zinder au XIXe siècle*. Niamey: Centre Nigérien de Recherches en Sciences Humaines, 1971.

Sankoua, Bintou. *Un Empire Peul au XIXe siècle*. Paris: Karthala, 1990.

Sanneh, Lamin. *The Jakhanke Muslim Clerics: A Religious and Historical Study of Islam in Senegambia*. Lanham, MD: University Press of America, 1989.

Sartain, E. M. *Jalāl al-dīn al-Suyūṭī: Biography and Background*. Cambridge: Cambridge University Press, 1975.

Sartain, E. M. "Jalal ad-Din As-Suyuti's Relations with the people of Takrur." *Journal of Semitic Studies* 16, no. 2 (1971): 193–98.

Schacht, Joseph. "Malik b. Anas." *The Encyclopedia of Islam*. CD-ROM Edition V.I.I. Leiden: Brill, 2001.

Schacht, Joseph. *Introduction to Islamic Law*. Oxford: Clarendon, 1964.

Schwarz, Suzanne. "Ransoming Practices and "Barbary Coast" Slavery: Negotiations Related to Liverpool Slave Traders in the Late 18th Century." *African Economic History* 42 (2014): 59–86.

Sears, Christine E. "'In Algiers, the City of Bondage': Urban Slavery in Comparative Context." In *New Directions in Slavery Studies: Commodification, Community, and Comparison*, edited by Jeff Forret and Christine E. Sears, 201–18. Baton Rouge: Louisiana State University Press, 2015.

Sears, Christine E. *American Slaves and African Masters: Algiers and the Western Sahara, 1776–1830*. New York: Palgrave Macmillan, 2012.

Seck, Abdourahmane. *La question musulmane au Sénégal. Essai d'anthropologie d'une nouvelle modernité*. Paris: Kathala, 2010.

Shumway, Rebecca. *The Fante and the Transatlantic Slave Trade*. Rochester: University of Rochester Press, 2011.

South Africa Broadcasting Corporation. *The Manuscripts of Timbuktu*. 2009.

Smaldone, Joseph. *Warfare in the Sokoto Caliphate: Historical and Sociological Perspectives*. Cambridge: Cambridge University Press, 1977.

Smith, HFC. "A Neglected Theme of West African History." *Journal of the Historical Society of Nigeria* 11, no. 2 (1961): 169–85.

Smith, M. G. *Government in Kano 1350–1950*. Boulder, CO: Westview, 1997.

Stella, Alessandro. *Histoires d'esclaves dans la Péninsule Ibérique*. Paris: École des Hautes Études en Sciences Sociales, 2000.

Stewart, C. C. "Frontier Disputes and Problems of Legitimization: Sokoto-Masina Relations 1817–1837." *The Journal of African History* 17, no. 4 (1976): 497–514.

Stewart, C. C. "Southern Saharan Scholarship and the Bilad al-Sudan." *The Journal of African History* 17, no. 1 (1976): 73–93.

Stilwell, Sean. *Paradoxes of Power: The Kano "Mamluks" and Male Royal Slavery in the Sokoto Caliphate 1804–1903*. Portsmouth, NH: Heinemann, 2004.

Sunseri, Thaddeus. "Slave Ransoming in German East Africa, 1885–1922." *The International Journal of African Historical Studies* 26, no. 3 (1993): 481–511.

Sweet, James H. *Domingos Álvares, African Healing, and Intellectual History of the Atlantic World*. Chapel Hill: University of North Carolina Press, 2011.

Talbi, Muhammad. "Sahnun." In *The Encyclopedia of Islam*. CD-ROM Edition V.I.I. Leiden: Brill, 2001.

Tambo, David C. "The Sokoto Caliphate Slave Trade in the Nineteenth Century." *The International Journal of Historical Studies* 9, no. 2 (1976): 187–217.

Taylor, Raymond. "Of Disciples and Sultans: Power, Authority and Society in the Nineteenth-Century Mauritania Gebla." PhD diss., University of Illinois at Urbana-Champaign, 1996.

Tayob, Abdulkader. *Islam in South Africa: Mosques, Imams and Sermons.* Gainesville: University of Florida Press, 1999.

Terray, Emmanuel. "Reflexions sur la formation du prix des esclaves à l'intérieur de l'Afrique de l'Ouest Précoloniale." *Journal des Africanistes* 52 (1982): 119–44.

Thornton, John. "African Political Ethics and the Slave Trade." In *Abolitionism and Imperialism in Britain, Africa, and the Atlantic*, edited by D. L. Peterson, 38–62. Athens: Ohio University Press, 2010.

Torres, José Antonio Martínez. Prisioneros de los infieles: vida y rescate de los cautivos cristianos en el Mediterráneo musulmán (siglos XVI-XVII). Barcelona: Editions Bellatora, 2004.

Toth, Anthony. "Economic Change in the Bedouin Domain: Case Studies in the Era Before Oil, 1830–1950." PhD diss., Oxford University, 2000.

Triaud, Jean-Louis. "Giving a Name to Islam South of the Sahara: An Adventure in Taxonomy." *The Journal of African History* 55, no. 1 (2014): 3–15.

Triaud, Jean-Louis. "La Tijâniyya, une confrérie musulmane pas comme les autres?" In *La Tijâniyya. Une confrérie musulmane à la conquête de l'Afrique*, edited by Jean-Louis Triaud and David Robinson, 9–17. Paris: Karthala, 2000.

Trimingham, J. Spencer. *A History of Islam in West* Africa. London: Oxford University Press, 1964.

Troutt Powell, Eve. *Tell this in my Memory: Stories of Enslavement from Egypt, Sudan, and the Ottoman Empire.* Stanford: Stanford University Press, 2012.

Usman, Y. B., ed. *Studies in the History of the Sokoto Caliphate: The Sokoto Seminar Papers*. Zaria: Ahmadu Bello University, 1979.

Vansina, Jan. "Long-Distance Trade Routes in Central Africa" *Journal of African History* 3, no. 3 (1962): 375–90.

Vergniot, Olivier. "De la distance en histoire: Maroc—Sahara occidental: Les captifs du hasard (XVIIe–XXe siècles)." *Revue du Monde Musulman et de la Mediterranée* 48, no. 1 (1988): 96–125.

Ware, Rudolph T. III. *The Walking Qu'ran, Islamic Education, Embodied Knowledge and History in West Africa.* Chapel Hill: University of North Carolina Press, 2014.

Waterbury, John. *The Commander of the Faithful: The Moroccan Political Elite—A Study in Segmented Politics.* New York: Columbia University Press, 1970.

Waterman, Peter. "The Jihad in Hausaland as an Episode in African History—Some Concepts, Theories, and Hypotheses." *Kroniek in Africa* 2, no. 5 (1975): 141–52.

Webb, James, Jr. *Desert Frontier: Ecological and Economic Change along the Western Sahel 1600–1850.* Madison: University of Wisconsin Press, 1995.

Webb, James Jr. "Shifting Sands: An Economic History of the Mauritanian Sahara 1500–1850." PhD diss., Johns Hopkins University, 1983.

Weiss, Gillian. "Ransoming 'Turks' from France's Royal Galleys." *African Economic History* 42 (2014): 37–57.

Weiss, Gillian. *Captives and Corsairs, France and Slavery in the Early Modern Mediterranean.* Stanford: Stanford University Press, 2011.

Wilks, Ivor. "The Juula and the Expansion of Islam into the Forest." In *The History of Islam in Africa*, edited by Nehemia Levtzion and Randall Pouwels, 93–115. Cambridge: Cambridge University Press, 2000.

Wilks, Ivor. "The Transmission of Islamic Learning in the Western Sudan." In *Literacy in Traditional Societies*, edited by Jack Good, 162–97. Cambridge: Cambridge University Press, 1968.

Willis, John Ralph. "Jihad and the Ideology of Enslavement." In *Slaves and Slavery in Muslim Africa.* Vol. 1: *Islam and the Ideology of Slavery* edited by John Ralph Willis, 16–26. London: Frank Cass, 1985.

Willis, John Ralph. "The Writings of al-Ḥājj 'Umar al-Fūtī and Shaykh Mukhtār b. Wadī' at Allāh: Literary Themes, Sources, and Influences." In *Studies in West African Islamic History*. Vol. 1: *The Cultivators of Islam*, edited by John Ralph Willis, 177–210. London: Frank Cass, 1979.

Wills, Mary. *Envoys of Abolition: British Naval Officers and the Campaign against the Slave Trade in West Africa.* Oxford: Liverpool University Press, 2019.

Wise, Christopher, ed. *The Desert Shore: Literatures of the Sahel.* Boulder, CO: Lynne Rienner, 2001.

Wright, John. "Morocco: The Last Great Slave Market?" *The Journal of North African Studies* 7, no. 3 (2002): 53–66.

Wright, Zachary. "Introduction: The Sufi Scholarship of Islamic West Africa." In *The Jihad of the Pen: The Sufi Literature of West Africa*, edited by Amir Syed, Rudolph Ware, and Zachary Valentine Wright, 1–24. Cairo: American University of Cairo Press, 2018.

Yamusa, Shehu. "The Political Ideas of the Jihad Leaders: Being Translation, Edition, and Analysis of (1) Usual a-syayasa by Muhammad Bello and (2) Diya' al-Hukka, by Abdullhah b. Fodio." MA thesis, Bayero University Kano, 1975.

Zehnle, Stephanie. *A Geography of Jihad: Sokoto Jihadism and the Islamic Frontier in West Africa.* Berlin: Walter de Gruyer GmbH, 2020.

Zehnle, Stephanie. "War and Wilderness—The Sokoto Jihad and its Animal Discourse." *Critical African Studies* 8, no. 2 (2016): 216–37.

Zemon Davis, Natalie. *Trickster Travels: A Sixteenth Century Muslim between Worlds.* New York: Hill & Wang, 2006.

Zenn, Jacob. "Competing Ideologies at Play in Boko Haram's Return of Dapchi Girls," *Council of Foreign Relations.* April 4, 2018. https://www.cfr.org/blog/competing-ideologies-play-boko-harams-return-dapchi-girls.

Index

Page numbers in italics refer to figures and tables.

'Abaydallah b. Sālam, 70–72
Abdallah, 'Ali ben, 37n43
Abdūl Qādir Kan, 34
abolition, 7–8, 11, 20, 37–38, 40–41, 78, 145
Adams, Robert, 72, 74–75, 146
Agadez, 100
agriculture, 42, 60, 82, 84, 91, 97–98, 116, 136, 138–39
Ahl Barikallah, 71
Aḥmadu, Aḥmadu b., 125, 132
Algeria, 14, 24, 45–46, 60, 63, 67
Algiers, 24, 57, 60–62, 62n29, 63–65, 67, 76
Ali, Syed Ameer, 37
American Southwest, 9n22
Amselle, J. L., 16
ANSARU, 112
al-'Āqil, Khadīja b. Muḥammad, 34
Aqīt, Maḥmūd b. 'Umar b. Muḥammad, 46, 49
Arabization, 43
Asad, Talal, 15
Asante, 82, 84–85, 145, 150, 153–54, 157–58
Askia al-hāj Muḥammad, 45, 129–31
Atikū, Abūbakar, 19, 113, 125, 143, 155–56
Atlantic slave trade, 6, 10, 18, 23–25, *26*, 59, 72, 84, 87, 88n23, 100, 115–18, 126, 139–40
Awlād Bū al-Sibā', 76–77
al-'Azīz, Mawlāy 'Abd, 55

Bā, A. H., 129
Baal, Sulaymaan, 116–17
Bābāal-Tinbuktī, Aḥmad, 27–28, 36, 45–52, 80
Babemba Traoré, 147
Babou, Cheihk Anta, 17
Bakatara, Umaru, 111
al-Bakkay, Sīdī Aḥmad, 122
al-Balbālī, Makhlūfi b.'Alī b Sāliḥ, 46
Bambara, 25, 114, 118, 127–28, 130–31, 133–35, 137–40, 142, 145, 150, 152, 164
Baquaqua, Muḥammad Gardo, 153–54
Barber, M. A. S., 151
al-Barnawi, Abu Muswab, 173
Barnes, John, 145
Bayān mā waqa'a (Taal), 127
Bayān wujūb al-hijra 'alā 'l— 'ibād (Fodiye), 104
Bayrūk family, 70–72
Bello, Ahmadu, 2
Bello, Muḥammad, 36n39, 48, 80–81, 86n15, 89–91, 93–97, 99–100, 102, 104, 107–9, 113, 121, 123, 125, 127, 131–32, 135, 148
Bencheneb, Muhammad, 33
Bentahar, Mohamed/David, 72
Berbers, 42–43

Binduri, ʻUthmān, 34–35
Blackness, 41, 43–44, 46–47, 55
Bluett, Thomas, 152
Boisard, Marcel A., 57n9
Boko Haram, 1–2, 4n9, 112, 172–74, 177–78
Bono, Salvatore, 58
Brākna Confederation, 119
Brockopp, Jonathan, 38
Brooks, James F., 9n22
Brown, Wililam, 129
al-Bukhārī, Muhammad, 31
Buna, Mukhtār b., 117
Burdulla, Abu- ʻAbdallāh Sidi Muḥammad al-ʻArabī b. Aḥmad, 54–55
Burkina Faso, 92, 162

Candido, Mariana, 159
Carpenter, Nathan, 159
Casablanca, 69
Castilian law, 56–57
Cayor, 115, 117–19, 120n19
Central African Republic, 92
children, 33, 38, 41–42, 56, 58, 82, 88, 97, 105, 138, 149, 152, 156, 159–62, 166–67
Church Missionary Society (CMS), 157
Cochelet, Charles, 71–72, 75
color prejudice, 41–44. *See also* race
Constantinople, 57, 61–62, 62n29
creditor, master as, 13
Crowdery, Jonathan, 64–65
Cruise O'Brien, Donal, 17

Dabo, Ibrahim, 95
Dadi, Muḥammad Sharefa dan, 83
Dādi, Yaʻqūb b., 107
Dajet, J., 129
Damergou, 100
Dasala, J. B., 157
Davis, Robert C., 59
Davison, James, 74
al-Daymāni, Muḥammad al-Yadāli b. al-Mukhtār b. Maḥam Sa'id, 29–30
De Brisson, Pierre-Raymond, 69n58
debtor, slave as, 13
Denyanke, 87, 116–17
al-Dhahab al-ibrīz fi tafsīr al-kitāb al-ʻazīz (al-Daymāni), 29–30
Diallo, Ayuba b. Sulayman Ibrahima, 84, 151–52
Diawara, Alfa Salif, 129
al-Dimashqī, Shams al-Dīn al-Anṣārī, 41
al-Dīnawarī, ʻAbd Allāh b. Qutayba, 41
al-Dīn's, Nāṣir, 3, 115–16
Diouf, Sylviane, 10
discursive tradition, Islam as, 16
Diy'ā al-hukkām (Fodiye), 105, 107–8
Diy'ā al-sulṭān wa-ghayrihi min al-ikhwān fi ahamm mā yuṭlabu ʻilmuhu fi umūr al-zamān (Fodiye), 94, 127
Djenne, 35–36
Dolbie, Stephen, 74
Dupuis, Joseph, 145

East Africa, German, 10–11
education, 31–36, 80–83, 117, 122, 129, 142
Egypt, 35
El Hamel, Chouki, 41
enfranchisement, 14–15, 178
Ennaji, Mohammed, 14
European slavery, 59–63
exchange value, 11–12

al-Fāsi, Muḥammad b. al-Ḥasan al-Bannāni, 32–33
Fatḥ al-rabbānī fi mā dhalala ʻan-hu al-Zurqānī (al-Fāsi), 32–33

fiqh, 32, 36, 38n48, 44, 80, 121, 129. *See also* law
Fodiye, ʿAbdullāhi b., 34–36, 80–81, 91, 93–95, 104–12, 127, 129, 132
Fodiye, Asmaʾu b., 81, 87, 96n55
Fodiye, ʿUthmān b., 27–29, 34–36, 48–49, 80–81, 86–91, 93–97, 96n55, 99–100, 104–5, 112, 127–29, 132, 143, 178
Follie, Adrien-Jacques, 72–73, 75–76
Fontenay, Michel, 11–12
Foyna, 130
Foyna, Hamman Daḍi, 130
freedom, 7, 172; bias toward, in Islam, 50; children and, 56; conversion to Islam and, 62; enfranchisement and, 14–15; ransoming and, 144–45, 155, 175; redemption and, 176–77
Fulbe, 83–84, 90, 92, 99–100, 116, 130
Fundu, Inğīdū b., 146
Fuuta Bundu, 84, 116–18, 134
Fuuta Jalon, 3, 25n6, 31, 113–14, 116, 119, 121, 125–26, 128, 134, 142, 164
Fuuta Toro, 3, 34, 87, 88n23, 114–17, 119–20, 128, 130, 134

gender, 8, 78, 115, 139, 155, 161–62, *165–66*, 170
German East Africa, 10–11
Ghadames, 24
al-Ghālī Abū Ṭālib, Muḥammad, 120–21
al-Gharnāṭi, Muḥammad b. Muḥammad b. ʿĀṣim, 32
al-Ghazāl, Aḥmad b. Mahdī, 67
Gobir, 51, 82, 90, 97, 102, 125
Goldie, George, 20
Gordon, David, 11
Gouro, Alfa, 128
Greene, Sandra, 6, 143
Gress, Kel, 102
Guelmīm, 71–73, 76–77, 149n26

Haefeli, Evan, 29
al-Ḥafīẓ, Mawlāy ʿAbd, 55
Haïdara, Ismael Diadié, 60
Hall, Bruce, 5, 42–43, 48
Ḥamdallāhi, 3, 112, 114, 121, 123–25, 127–29, 131–34, 136, 142, 150
Hamitic thesis, 41–42, 44
Hānafi law, 30, 106
Ḥanbalī law, 30
Hausa city-states, 82–92
Hausaland, 24–25, 31, 36, 44, 82, 85, 98
Hershenzon, Daniel, 11–12
Hunt, Nancy Rose, 5
Hutchinson, John, 73

Idea of an Anthropology of Islam, The (Asad), 15
illegality, 37–51
intellectuals, 26–27, 82–92. *See also* scholars
Irving, James, 72–73, 75
Islam. *See also* Qur'an: as discursive tradition, 15; "Islam noir," 16–17; scholarship, 27–36; sub-Saharan, 16–17; West African, thought in, 15–18
Islamic State West African Province (ISWAP), 173
isnād affiliations, 17–18
ISWAP. *See* Islamic State West African Province (ISWAP)
ʿIyaḍ b. Mūsā, 31

Jagha, 31
Jakhanke, 31–32
Jallonī, ʿAbd al-Karīm b. Aḥmad al-Nāqil al-Fūta, 120

Jam' al-jawāmi' fi'l-uṣūl (al-Subkī), 44
Jama'a Nusrat ul-Ilsma wa al-Muslimin (JNIM), 114n4
Jamaica, 32n26, 34, 84
al-Jawzī, Abū'l Faraj 'Abd al-Raḥman b., 45
jihad: issues grappled with, 4–5; kufr and, 13; in Lovejoy, 3; ransoming and, 80–112; slavery and, 37; Sokoto, 3, 30, 80–112; of 'Umar Taal, 113–42; Umarian, 30
Jīlānī, 'Abd al-Qadīr, 128
al-Jirārī, Sa'īd b. Ibrāhīm, 51
jizya, 14, 37, 108
Jolof, 115, 117
judges, 31, 54, 101, 117, 125
jurists, 27–28, 30, 38, 40, 46, 49, 62, 89, 97, 123
Juzay, Muḥammad b. Aḥmad b., 39, 52, 105

Kaarta, 25, 79n82, 114, 116, 118, 121, 127, 132–33, 135, 140, 142, 150, 164
Kabā Sagnanughu, Muḥammad, 31–32, 34, 84
al-Kabīr, Aḥmad, 134–36
al-Kabīr, Sīdī Mukhtār al-Kunti, 34, 122
Kan, 'Abd al-Qādir, 116–18
Kane, Ousmane, 5
al-Kānimī, Muḥammad, 121–22
Kano, 82, 97–98, 102–3, 109–10, 170
Kano, Aminu, 2
Kano, Dan Rimin, 111
al-Kanūsi, 'Abdallah Muḥammad b. Aḥmad, 67
Kariya, Kota, 89
Katsina, 24, 35, 51, 82, 90, 97, 100, 105, 125, 153, 156
al-Kawkab al-sāti (al-Suyūṭī), 44
Kel Gress, 102, 154
Khaldūn, 'Abd al-Raḥman b., 30, 43–44
Khalīl b. Isḥāq al-Jundī, 32, 37n43, 39–40, 50, 52, 105, 120
Kitāb al-farq (Fodiye), 96
Kitāb al-'ibar (Khaldūn), 43
Kitāb al-shifā' bi-ta'rif ḥuqūq al-muṭṭafā ('Iyaḍ b. Mūsā), 31–32, 36
Kitāb al-Tarā'if, 123
Klein, Martin, 19n53, 126, 169
Kouffa, Hamadoun, 114n4
Krätli, Graziano, 17
Kunta, 83, 114, 119–36

Lagos, 25, *26*, 151
law: abolition and, 40–41; British, 1; Castilian, 56–57; colonial, 7; government and, 2, 4; Hānafi, 30, 106; Ḥanbalī, 30; Mālikī, 2, 5, 30–32, 37, 38n49, 40, 44–45, 52, 55, 62, 66, 80, 92–99, 117–18, 123, 137, 174; ransoming and, 174; ransoming *vs.* redemption in, 13–14; scholars and, 20; Shāfi'ī, 30; slave trade and, 24; Sunni, 30, 38
legality, 37–51, 65–66
Levtzion, Nehemia, 130
Lobbo, Aḥmad, 34, 128–30, 132
Loimeier, Roman, 3
Lovejoy, Paul, 3, 161, 169
Lugard, Frederick, 20
Lydon, Ghislaine, 17

Macina Liberation Front, 114, 114n4
Mage, Eugene, 137–38
al-Maghīlī, Muḥammad, 23, 28, 30, 35–36, 39, 43, 45, 50–52, 80, 83, 88, 116, 127, 131–32
al-Makkī, Muḥammad, 134–35
Mali, 51
Mālik b. Anas, 30–32, 36

Mālikī madh'hab, 2, 5, 30–32, 37, 38n49, 40, 44–45, 52, 55, 62, 66, 80, 92–99, 117–18, 123, 137, 174
Mansour, Mansour H., 30
al-Mansūr, Sultan Ahmad, 61
manumission, 14–15, 37, 99–103
Maradi, 97, 102, 111
Marshall, John, 157
Martin, B. G., 113
Masā'il muhimma (Fodiye), 99–100
Maser, J. A., 157
Māsina, 114, 123–24, 128–29, 132, 134–36
Masquelier, Adeline, 16
al-Mas'ūdī, Abū al-Ḥasan 'Alī b. al-Ḥusayn, 42
Mawlāy Ismā'īl, 55, 65
Mawlāy Sūlayman, 70, 78–79
Mazur, Peter, 68n55
McDougall, James, 29
mediator, in ransoming, 148, 154–57, 172, 176
Meillassoux, Claude, 14, 57n10
Messick, Brinkley, 19
Miftāh al-Sadād fī aqsām hādhihi 'l-bilād (Fodiye), 100
al-Miknāsī, Muḥammad b. 'Uthmān, 67–68
Miles, Richard, 145
Mi'rāj al-Ṣu'ūd (Bābāal-Tinbuktī), 36, 46–47, 49
modernists, 2
"modernization shock," 1–2
Modi, Allhadji, 130
Montana, Ismael, 61
Moore, Francis, 116
Moore, William, 151
Moreau de Chambonneau, 115–16
Morocco, 10, 24, 37n43, 46, 47n74, 54, 57, 60–61, 66–70, 72, 78
Muḥammad Rumfa of Kano, 50
al-Mukhtār, Sīdī, 122–24, 129
Mukhtaṣar al-shaykh Khalīl (al-Jundī), 32, 36, 39, 50, 120
Muqaddima (Khaldūn), 43–44
al-Muwaṭṭā' (Mālik b. Anas), 30–32, 36

Nachtigal, Gustav, 146, 155, 161
Naguel, 'Abd al-Karīm b. Aḥmad, 120
Nagwamase, Ibrahim, 102
al-Najīb, Sīdī 'Ali b., 34
Najm al-ikhwān yahtadūna bihi bi-idhn Allāh fī umūr al-zamān (Fodiye), 81, 94
Napoleon, 78
Niang, Amy, 160n73, 177
Nigeria, 1–2, 92, 157, 172–73, 178
Nobili, Mauro, 123
Norris, H. T., 29
Northern Elements Progressive Union, 2

Ochonu, Moses, 96
Ojo, Olatunji, 12n30, 155, 159, 168
Ottoman Empire, 11, 35, 57, 59, 61, 63–64, 99
Owusa-Ansa, John, 158
Oyo, 82, 85, 100, 154

Panet, Leopold, 79, 79n82
Park, Mungo, 140, 152, 164
Patterson, Orlando, 12–13
Phildelphia (American frigate), 64–65
Pike, Stephen, 84, 152
Plange, Henry, 158
Portugal, 59, 66
prices: ransom, 144, 161–71, *163*, 164, *165–66*, 168–70, 172, 176; slave, 22, 76, 161–62, *163*
profit motive, in ransoming, 159–71, *163*, *165–66*

al-Qaḍī 'Iyāḍ, 36
Qādiriyya, 2, 35–36, 36n39

Qādiriyya ṭarīqa, 34, 80, 92, 112, 121–23
al-Qaeda, 114n4
Qawānīn al-aḥkām al-shar'iya wa-masā'il al-furū' al-fiqhiya (Juzay), 39
al-Qayrawānī, 'Abdullah b. Abī Zayd, 30, 32, 120, 127, 160
Qur'an. *See also* Islam: slavery in, 37–38, 101

race, 40–45, 47–49, 55, 61, 78
al-Raḥmān, Mawlāy 'Abd, 70, 111
al-Raḥmān, Musulmi 'Abd, 156, 167
Rāji, Muḥammad b., 35
ransoming: Atlantic Sahara and, 68–78; compensation of individuals paying for, 40; condoning, 103–11; defined, 12; as gendered, 7; information exchange and, 149–50; jihad and, 80–112; law and, 174; legality of, 65–66; mediator in, 148, 154–57, 172, 176; in Mediterranean basin, 8–9; in Mediterranean world, 57–68; motives for, 144–48; negotiation and practice of, 143–72; policy and practice of, 53–79; prices in, 144, *163*, 164, *165–66*, 168–70, 172, 176; profit motive in, 159–71, *163*, *165–66*; redemption *vs.*, 10–11, 13–14, 164; shifts in policies with, 103–11; slavery and, 5–7; slavery *vs.*, 175–76; Sokoto Caliphate and, 80–112; successful, factors in, 148–59; 'Umar Taal and, 113–42; in Umarian states, 136–41
Ray, William, 64–65
redemption: Catholic Church and, 62; defined, 10; freedom and, 176–77; manumission and, 15; prices, *163*; ransoming *vs.*, 10–11, 13–14, 164; third-party, 176
Reichmuth, Stefan, 18
renegades, 12, 62
Rgaybāt, 71
Richardson, David, 161
Riley, James, 72, 75–77
Rimāḥ al-Raḥīm alā nuḥūr ḥizb al-rajīm (Taal), 121
Risāla (al-Qayrawānī), 32, 120, 160
Risālat sahwa al-habīb ilā as'ilat Ibrahīm al-labīb (Taal), 126
Roberts, Richard, 137–38
Robinson, David, 116, 134
Rodet, Marie, 138
Rothman, E. Natalie, 9
Roume, Ernest, 20
Royal Niger Company, 20
Rudt de Collenberg, Wipertus H., 62n29

al-Sa'dī, 'Abd al-Raḥman b. 'Abd Allāh, 32
al-Saghīr, Sīdī al-Mukhtār, 122
Sahel, 28–29, 42–43, 49, 52–53, 55, 74, 83, 98, 110, 154, 177
sa'ibah, 14–15
Salafī, 2, 4n9, 114, 177–78
al-Salām, 'Abd, 94
al-Salām, Mawlāy 'Abd, 73
Sambo, Muḥammad, 34–35
Samori Turé, 147
Sanankoua, Bintou, 128
Sangaré, Alfa Hambarké, 128
al-Sanūsī, Muḥammad b. Yusuf, 36
Sarki Muḥammad Rumfa, 45
Saugnier, M., 72, 75
al-Ṣawīra, 69, 79
Schacht, Joseph, 30
scholars, 26–27, 37–51, 54–57. *See also* intellectuals

scholarship, 27–36
Schön, James Frederich, 160
Seck, Abdourahmane, 17
Segu, 25, 114, 121, 127–28, 131–32, 134–35, 137–42, 152, 158, 164, 167
Seku, Aḥmad, 132
Senegambia, 24–25, *26*, 114–19, 126
Sharḥ 'Abd al-Bāqī li-mukhtaṣar Khalīl (al-Zurqāni), 32–33
Sharibu, Leah, 173
Sīdī Hamit, 76–77
Sīdī Mahmūd, 143, 155
Sīdī Muḥammad, 53, 65–70, 72–73
Sierra Leone, 25n6, 115n5, 157–58
Siete Partidas, Las, 56–57
Sinsani, 133, 138–39
Sirāj al-iḥwān (Fodiye), 127
Sīse, al-Ḥājj Salīm Suwarī, 31
slavery: abolition and, 7–8, 11, 20, 37–38, 40–41, 78, 145; arguments against, 37–38; European, 59–63; jihad and, 37; legality and illegality of, 37–51; population in, 23–25, *26*; prices in, 161–63, *163*; in Qur'an, 37–38, 101; ransoming and, 5–7; ransoming *vs.*, 175–76; scholars and question of, 54–57; Sokoto Caliphate and, 99–103; transatlantic slave trade, 6, 10, 18, 23–25, *26*, 59, 72, 84, 87, 88n23, 100, 115–18, 126, 139–40; in Umarian states, 136–41
Smith, HFC, 129
Smith, M. G., 95
"social death," 12–13, 149
social status, 13–14, 22, 43, 142, 148, 158
Sokoto Caliphate, 2–3; enslavement and, 99–103; establishment of, 92–99; manumission and, 99–103; in sources, 19
Sokoto jihad, 3, 30
Soleillet, Paul, 140
Songhay, 37n43, 44, 46, 51, 55, 60–61, 168
sources, 18–20
Spain, 56, 59, 66–67
Staudinger, Paul, 161
Stella, Alessandro, 58
al-Subkī, Abd al-Wahhāb b. 'Ali b. 'Abd al-Kāfī Tāj al-Dīn, 44
Sudan, 3, 24–25, 27–36, 42–43, 53, 84–85, 88, 114, 119, 139, 160
Sufi brotherhoods, 2
Sunni law, 30
Sunni madhāhib, 38, 38n48
Sunseri, Thaddeus, 10–11
al-Suyūṭī, 'Abd al-Raḥmān, 43–45, 45n68, 120, 130–31
Sweet, James, 5

Taal, 'Umar, 30–31, 36n39, 49, 112–42, 178
al-Ṭabarī, Abū Ja'far Muḥammad b. Jarīr, 42
Tadhkirat al-Mustarṣidīn (Taal), 127
Tafsīr al-Jalālayn, 31–32, 44
Taj al-Din yajib 'ala-mulūk, (al-Maghīlī), 23, 36, 50–51, 116
Tajakānit, 71
takfīr, 4, 4n9, 48, 90, 114, 132
Tanbīh al ikhwān alā arḍ al-sūdān (Fodiye), 97
al-Tanūkhī, Saḥnūn b. Sa'id, 30
Ta'rikh al-fattāsh (Tayrū), 129–31
Tārīkh al-Sūdān (al-Sa'dī), 32
Tassaoua, 100
tawḥid, 36, 80, 129
taxation, 5, 14, 37, 54, 56, 65, 83, 91, 96, 108, 119, 133

Tayrū, Alfa Nūḥ b., 129
teachers, 17, 31–36, 80–83, 86, 119
textual domination, 19
al-Tidjānī, Muḥammad al-Hafīz, 128
al-Tijānī, Aḥmad, 120, 134, 136
Tijāniyya ṭurūq, 2, 36, 36n39, 113, 119–36
Timbuktu, 28, 32, 32n26, 33, 35–36, 37n43, 74, 84, 123, 132, 141–42, 146, 162, *165*
Toulé, Alfa Mamadou, 129
transatlantic slave trade, 6, 10, 18, 23–25, *26*, 59, 72, 84, 87, 88n23, 100, 115–18, 126, 139–40
Troutt Powell, Eve, 8, 143
Tuareg, 33, 36, 43, 74, 83–84, 86, 102, 125, 133, 146–47, 154, 158, 160, *165*, 168
Tuḥfat al-ḥukkām fi nakt wa-'l-aḥkām (al-Gharnāṭi), 32
Tukur, Muḥammad, 86
Tullu, Jan, 156
Turkur, Muḥammad, 106

'Umar, Jibrīl b., 35–36
Umarian campaign, 161
Umarian jihad, 30
Umarian movement, 3, 112
Umarian states, 136–41
Umarians, 114
unemployment, 178
use-value, 11–12
Usulul-adliliwullatil umuri wa ahlil-fadli (Fodiye), 96

value, in ransoming and redemption, 11–12
Vansina, Jan, 150n27

Waalo, 115, 117
Wād Nūn, 66, 68–75, 77, 79
Wahb b. Munabbih, Abū 'Abd Allāh, 41
Wahhābi, 2
Walata, 35, 119
Waldström, Carl, 145
Ware, Rudolph, 5, 88n23, 118
Webb, James, 42
Weiss, Gillian, 9, 58
Willis, John, 13
women, 81–82, 131, 162, 169–71
Wouro Nguiya, 130
Wright, Zachary, 18

al-Yazīd, Mawlāy, 70
Yorubaland, 84, 92, 149n26, 159
Yusuf, Muhammad, 4n9

al-Zabīdī, Murtadā, 18
Zaki, Barayi, 156–57, 168
Zakzak, 48, 51
Zamfara, 82, 90
Zaria, 48, 98–99, 102, 109, 170–71
Zehnle, Stephanie, 95
Zenn, Jacob, 173
Zurb, Abū'l—Asbagh b.Sahl Muḥammad b. Yaḥyā b., 49
al-Zurqāni, 32–33

www.ingramcontent.com/pod-product-compliance
Lightning Source LLC
Chambersburg PA
CBHW070802230426
43665CB00017B/2463